TEJANO SOUTH TEXAS

NUMBER FIVE *Jack and Doris Smothers Series in Texas History, Life, and Culture*

Daniel D. Arreola

Tejano South Texas

A MEXICAN AMERICAN CULTURAL PROVINCE

AUSTIN UNIVERSITY OF TEXAS PRESS

Requests for permission to reproduce material from this work should be sent to Permissions, University of Texas Press, P.O. Box 7819, Austin, TX 78713-7819.

(∞) The paper used in this book meets the minimum requirements of ANSI/NISO Z39.48-1992 (R1997) (Permanence of Paper).

Library of Congress Cataloging-in-Publication Data
Arreola, Daniel D. (Daniel David), 1950–
    Tejano south Texas : a Mexican American cultural province / Daniel D. Arreola.—1st ed.
        p.   cm.—(Jack and Doris Smothers series in Texas history, life, and culture ; no. 5)
    Includes bibliographical references and index.
    ISBN 0-292-70510-7 (cloth : alk. paper)—ISBN 0-292-70511-5 (pbk. : alk. paper)
    1. Mexican American—Texas, South—History. 2. Mexican Americans—Texas South—social life and customs.   3. Mexican American—Texas, South—Ethnic identity.   4. Landscape—Social aspects—Texas, South.   5. Texas, South—Social life and customs.   6. Texas, South—Ethnic relations.   7. Human geography—Texas, South.   8. Human geography—Mexican-American Border Region.   9. Mexican-American Border Region—Social life and customs.   10. Mexican-American Border Region—Ethnic relations. I. Title. II. Series.

F395.M5 A77 2002
976.4'40046872—dc21   2001044294

Dedicado a mis abuelos,

hijos de Jalisco e inmigrantes a California.

León Díaz, 1888–1974

Juan Santana Arreola, 1899–1962

Contents

LIST OF FIGURES

LIST OF TABLES

Acknowledgments

Tejano South Texas was initiated in 1987 when I was on the faculty at Texas A&M University, College Station. My appointment in the Department of Geography required me to regularly teach a semester course on the geography of Texas. Through considerable reading and field explorations, I became convinced that South Texas was a unique subregion of the Mexican American borderland. I continued with the project upon my appointment to Arizona State University, Tempe, in 1990, although interruptions and new duties delayed completion of the research and writing until 2000.

Dozens of individuals and institutions have supported this project, although no major funding sources sponsored the research. Campbell W. Pennington, Head, Department of Geography at Texas

A&M University, first invited me to Texas for a visiting appointment in 1980, and I returned there to a permanent post in 1983. I am thankful to those who supported my travels to South Texas to engage in archival and field research. Over the years, assistance was provided by Brian W. Blouet, Head, Department of Geography, Texas A&M University; Patricia Gober, Anthony Brazel, and Breandán Ó hUallacháin, Chairs, Department of Geography, Arizona State University; and Raymond Padilla and Felipe Castro, Directors, Hispanic Research Center, Arizona State University.

Many archives and museums provided essential materials for the project: Institute of Texan Cultures, University of Texas at San Antonio; Center for American Studies and Benson Latin American Collection, University of Texas at Austin; Lower Rio Grande Historical Collection, University of Texas, Pan American, Edinburg; Luciano Guajardo Historical Collection, Laredo Public Library, Laredo, Texas; Hidalgo County Historical Museum, Edinburg, Texas; La Paz Museum, San Ygnacio, Texas; South Texas Museum, Alice, Texas; Colonel José Antonio Zapata Museum, Zapata, Texas; and Ramon Hernandez Archives, San Antonio, Texas.

Research specialists who gave generously of their time and expertise included George R. Gause, Jr., Special Collections Librarian, University of Texas, Pan American; David J. Mycue, Curator of Archives and Collections, Hidalgo County Historical Museum; Luciano Guajardo, Director, Special Collections, Laredo Public Library; Joe Moreno, Jr., Special Collections Librarian, Luciano Guajardo Historical Collection, Laredo Public Library; Adán Benavides, Research Programs, Benson Latin American Collection, University of Texas at Austin; and Ramon Hernandez, Musical Archivist, San Antonio.

Individuals who agreed to be interviewed and who kindly permitted me to ask questions about their knowledge of South Texas include Alfredo E. Cardenas, Publisher, *Duval County Picture*, San Diego, Texas; Higinio Martínez Jr., City Administrator, City of Cotulla; Adrián Martínez, San Ygnacio; Poncho Hernandez Jr., Benavides; Roque Salas, Concepción; Joel Uribe and Marcos Martínez, Laredo; Joe Bernal, San Antonio; and Abelardo H. Cantú, Mary Louise T. Cantú, Oliver Pérez, and Rose Marie de la Peña, Los Angeles.

Professional colleagues who answered questions and provided materials include Joe S. Graham, Texas A&M University, Kingsville; Norma Cantú, and Jerry Thompson, Texas A&M International University, Laredo; Mark Glazer, Head, Rio Grande Folklore Archive, University of Texas, Pan American; Jorge González, Director, Nuevo Santander Museum,

Laredo; Mario L. Sánchez, Texas Department of Transportation, Austin; Nina Nixon Mendez, Historic Preservation Officer, City of Laredo; Arnoldo De León, San Angelo State University; and Robert C. Spillman, Bishop, Texas.

I thank the American Geographical Society publishers of *Geographical Review*, the Popular Press publishers of the *Journal of Cultural Geography*, and the National Council for Geographic Education publishers of Pathways in Geography Series for permission to reproduce portions of my previously published papers. The Institute of Texan Cultures, American Geographical Society, Benson Latin American Collection, Laredo Public Library, South Texas Museum, and the Texas Historical Commission, each permitted the reproduction of illustrations from their respective works and archives.

I am grateful to colleagues who read and responded kindly to draft chapters of the manuscript, especially James R. Curtis, William E. Doolittle, Richard L. Nostrand, Oscar J. Martínez, F. Arturo Rosales, Malcolm L. Comeaux, and Carolyn M. Daugherty. I owe a great debt to Barbara Trapido-Lurie, Research Associate in the Department of Geography at Arizona State University, for her unwavering commitment to drafting and supervising the cartography for the many maps and graphics that appear here from my sketches. I also acknowledge the Arizona Geographic Alliance, which generously supported a portion of the cartographic production costs. At the University of Texas Press, I thank William V. Bishel, sponsoring editor, Leslie Doyle Tingle, assistant managing editor, and Letitia Blalock, who edited the manuscript. In Texas, Bill Doolittle, Michael Yoder, and Terry Haverluk occasionally provided shelter and companionship during my visits, and for that hospitality and friendship I am especially thankful.

I express my appreciation to three extraordinary musical talents, Ry Cooder, John Hiatt, and Lowell George, whose inimitable lyrics and sounds livened *mi único camino* when the airwaves dissolved across the expanse that is South Texas. I applaud the utter dependability of one 1983 Toyota Mojave pickup truck that transported me for the thousands of miles I crisscrossed South Texas.

Finally, I thank all South Texans for permitting me, an outsider, to engage their place and to share in their experience. I hope that through this work they might come to appreciate the value of the geographer's point of view.

TEJANO SOUTH TEXAS

The United States–Mexico border is the most extensive geographical area in which two of the principal cultures of this hemisphere actually meet. More than half of that border, approximately one thousand miles, is also the southern boundary of Texas.   —PAULINE R. KIBBE, *LATIN AMERICANS IN TEXAS*, 1946.

There can be no doubt that the Spanish-speaking constitute a clearly delineated ethnic group. But one must also recognize that there is no more heterogeneous ethnic group in the United States than the Spanish-speaking.

—CAREY MCWILLIAMS, *NORTH FROM MEXICO*, 1948.

Borderland Culture Region

No one can quite remember how long the Mexican flag has hung alongside the United States flag in the city council chambers in Brownsville, Texas, but during the Texas sesquicentennial in 1986, a non-Hispanic resident of this Rio Grande Valley town contested the propriety of that display. "We are Americans," he said, "the Mexicans are people who live on the other side of the river."[1] In Brownsville, as in dozens of communities across South Texas, resident Mexican Americans contend, however, that ancestral, cultural, and even economic ties are far stronger across the Rio Grande to places like Matamoros, Mexico, than to most northern American cities.

That the eagle and serpent banner stands next to the stars and stripes in this border town is not an isolated example of bicultural expression in the region. In San Antonio, some four hours by auto north of Brownsville, the city's leading daily is the only major American newspaper with a weather map that shows all of Mexico as well as the United States. Along the Rio Grande between Brownsville and Laredo upriver, some 140 *parteras* or midwives service Mexican women who flock to South Texas to give birth on American soil and thereby confer U.S. citizenship upon their newborn. If raised in Mexico until the completion of elementary school, then such children must be bused to secondary school in the United States, because the Mexican government prohibits the registration in public schools of children born in the United States.[2]

In this southernmost periphery of the mainland United States rests what may be America's largest ethnic subregion, Mexican South Texas. South Texas is the southeastern edge of what has been identified as the Hispanic American borderland. To the Spanish-speaking population of this region, the borderland includes parts of California, Arizona, New Mexico, and Colorado as well as Texas, the states where some 83 percent of Americans of Mexican ancestry reside. One historian called the area a lost homeland, the conquered northern half of the Mexican nation. Mexican Americans, along with Hispanos (Spanish Americans) and Native Americans, are unique among southwestern ethnic groups in that each is a territorial minority, having occupied land before the arrival of Anglo American colonists.[3]

At the close of the nineteenth century, a writer observed that South Texas is "*terra incognita* to the rest of the United States" where the Rio Grande, which figures as the southeastern boundary of the United States on most maps, "can in no sense be regarded as fulfilling any of the conditions of a line of delimitation" between Mexico and Texas.[4] Regional ambiguity and confused political and cultural demarcation have long been associated with South Texas, and still, today, the region remains an enigma in the popular imagination. Typically, South Texas is lumped together with other parts of the borderland, sometimes called "MexAmerica." A feature story in a national news-magazine labeled the entire region "Selena Country," after the celebrated slain pop singer from Texas.[5]

But Mexican South Texas is a distinctive borderland, unlike any other Mexican American subregion.[6] That assertion is the underlying thesis of this book. The reasons for this distinctiveness are many and complex, and they have roots in a distant past. In the chapters that follow, I make the case for geographical distinctiveness, and from several perspectives. First, however, I need to set the context for a cultural geographic view of this region. Because this work is a cultural geography, I begin with that idea and that point of view.

CULTURAL GEOGRAPHIC VIEW

Cultural geography is a subfield of geography with a scholarly tradition that is some seven decades old in the United States. Its conventions and standards of analysis have been declared and interpreted by geographers and researchers in cognate fields.[7] Plural research themes characterize cultural geography, yet there is ambiguity still about the nature of culture and its application in this widely defined subfield.[8] Despite a lack of definitional consensus, culture is part of everyday lives, and it gives meaning to those lives. It is the search for meaning, as Clifford Geertz suggested, that makes the study of culture an interpretive exercise, not an experimental science.[9] Cultures can be seen to change, and they can be contested. Ultimately, cultures are produced and reproduced through a range of forms and practices that are embedded in spaces.[10] Cultural geography, like the discipline of which it is a part, is less easily defined by its subject of study than by a point of view. If geographers are concerned with the study of phenomena and ideas from a spatial perspective, then cultural geographers are interested in studying aspects of culture, spatially represented. Three spatial abstractions have chiefly concerned how cultural geographers assess cultures, and each of these is significant to the present study; they are region, place, and landscape.

Region is the highest resolution of abstraction that concerns cultural geographers. The modern culture region idea stems from the Annales School in early twentieth-century France and especially the writings of Paul Vidal de la Blache, who argued that *genre de vie* or way of life is represented best through the study and exploration of regional personality. In the United States, Carl Ortwin Sauer and his students at the University of California at Berkeley carried out regional studies of culture areas, what Sauer termed "the oldest tradition of geography" and "a form of geographic curiosity that is never contained by systems."[11] Other cultural geographers have argued for a perspective that emphasizes how regions act as forms of communication and how regions are shaped in the geographic past.[12] In North America, there has been a resurgence of interest in assessing cultural regions from both scholarly and popular points of view.[13]

The concern for regional understanding is not unique to geography. In the study of Mexican Americans, borderland historians especially have examined the varied regional experiences of this large ethnic population in Southern California, southern Arizona, West Texas, and South Texas.[14] While regional history informs substantially about the relationships among ethnic subcultures, its goal is not geographic explanation. The intent of regional cultural understanding is to analyze the meanings behind the region. These can include knowing the ancestral geographic roots of the residents, how the region came to be formed politically and demographically, how identity is vested through cultural representations, and how the region is emblematic of a particular identity and, therefore, different from other cultural regions. Cultural geographers study these varied meanings through the process of place making and the symbolic attachments that cultures create in landscape.

Place making is the process of settling, and eventually bonding, to place. It is a universal human quality but with variations that are specific to people and their place. Yet, cultural geographers have demonstrated that traditions established through long residence in one place can be transferred and to some extent replicated in another setting.[15] Cultures, then, have particular ways to make a place, and understanding that process is part of the contribution geographers bring to cultural and regional studies. Place making is typically understood as a synthesis of various components, and charting the arrangement and significance of those elements is a complex exercise. Cultural geographers adhere to diachronic analysis in their study of place and believe that understanding of the human-place bond requires reconstruction of critical pieces of a past, whether institutional, material, or popular. The ground level analysis of place typically involves an assessment of a culture's landscape, the physical manifestation of ideas in space. Landscape analysis has figured as one of the distinguishing hallmarks of cultural geography.[16]

The idea of landscape as a political visual concept and scholarly subject has been assessed and reviewed by geographers.[17] That landscape can have multiple meanings to different groups as well as individuals has been explored, and several geographers have articulated systematically how landscapes can be read, providing insight into place and social situation.[18] Most cultural geographers accept the fact that landscapes are socially constructed. For example, the notion, cited above, that regions can be considered communicative devices studied by cultural geographers has been applied to the study of landscape as a representation of social identity.[19] Landscape can act as a signifying framework through which a social system is communicated, reproduced, experienced, and explored.[20] Signification typically implies more than the practical and thus is grounded in symbolic representation. Dwellings, for example, are primarily for shelter, but in some—perhaps many—cultures, dwellings can become so elaborate, like palaces, that the signifying factor of the structures exceeds the primary factor. Understanding a culture's landscape, then, becomes more than recognition of signatures: it is a reading of the meaning behind the signatures, an unraveling of a social code.

Social codes are most elaborately presented in written texts that become allegorically reproduced in a landscape. However, many vernacular cultures and subcultures lack elegantly written texts that might reveal a landscape code. In such instances, landscape meaning must be sifted through deep reading of people and place, an examination of folk cultures long resident in particular habitats.[21] Nevertheless, cultural geographers have begun to study industrial and postindustrial landscapes, especially urban and suburban environments, a departure from more traditional cultural geographic studies of folk cultures.[22]

The practice of cultural geography, then, has evolved to mean the prioritizing of culture in scholarship through emphasis on the study of cultural systems and their signification, and especially how culture is represented in space, place, and landscape.[23]

MEXICAN SOUTH TEXAS

Cultural geographic study of ethnic variation at the scale of subregions in the United States found early direction by Wilbur Zelinsky, who outlined the rudiments of twelve major groups during the 1960s and created a structure for classifying regional units by culture area.[24] Hispanic American culture region study was pioneered by Richard Nostrand, whose 1970 paper "The Hispanic American Borderland: Delimitation of an American Culture Region" created the foundation for further inquiry of this regionalization.[25] Nostrand's historical and cultural geographic study of the Hispanos or Spanish Americans of north-central New Mexico suggests that this subgroup is culturally distinctive among Spanish-speaking populations in the United States, and that their four-century occupancy of this region has created a homeland that is stamped with attributes of that distinctiveness.[26] While cultural geographers like Nostrand and others have continued to elaborate the geographical personality of

Hispanos, little effort has been made to distinguish geographically other Hispanic subgroups of the borderland.[27]

As described in the opening of this chapter, Mexican South Texas regionally and culturally is a distinctive part of the Hispanic American borderland, and this book assesses the nature of that geographical condition. My methods include areal analysis to delimit Mexican South Texas and place-landscape interpretations to analyze ethnic identity of the region. Regional bounding is a time-honored tradition of geographical study, but it is neither absolute nor constructed without inherent bias. Geographers classify regions at many scales, and I am principally concerned with meso-scale analysis to study phenomena between local and national resolutions. Geographers continue to debate the adequacy of the regional concept, yet the concept and methods of regionalizing persist.[28] Why region continues as a useful concept may suggest that it is not simply an end in itself, but rather a descriptive and analytical tool that facilitates the spatial organization of ideas.

In Chapter 2, I lay the basis for considering South Texas as a distinctive cultural region. I demonstrate that this area was not seen as a differentiated region until quite recently, and that its earliest historical identity lacked clarity. The association of the region as a Hispanic area is even more recent, despite early evidence of Spanish colonial settlements. This delayed perception of the region as a human-settled environment may have been influenced by its early identification as a wild land that was without potential human use. In Chapter 3 I construct the historical geography of South Texas as a Hispanic cultural framework, first through political claim and boundary alignment, then via colonization and transformation to Mexican American territory. Culture regions are not always coincident with political borders, but political process can be significant in setting an areal perimeter and in exercising control and authority over space. Finally, Chapter 4 charts the geographic evolution of South Texas as a Mexican American homeland. Demographic and cultural data are structured into four temporal cross sections to reveal the changing dominance of this ancestry group in the region, from early-twentieth-century expansion and immigration to a veritable stronghold condition by the end of the century.

Beyond culture region, I assess cultural representations of place and landscape to investigate aspects of Mexican American identity in South Texas. Cultural representation, like region, is an abstract concept, yet it too is complex and never absolute or neutral. Representation is a symbolization of the material and ideological, and place and landscape are vehicles for its interpretation. While nongeographers typically accept place and landscape as unambiguous and self-evident, geographers realize that these concepts allow cultures to shape space into place through various experiences and from varied points of view.[29] In the second part of the book, I examine this active place-making process as it involves Mexican Americans in the region. The goal is to understand how South Texas Mexican society became a specific regional subculture, rooted in nearby northeastern Mexico yet wed to the social and economic circumstances of South Texas and its hinterlands. That interpretation provides the basis for further support of my thesis that Mexican South Texas is a unique Mexican American cultural province, similar to but unlike Mexican American regional cultures in other borderland areas.

In Chapter 5, I evaluate place at the scale of lived spaces like the rancho, plaza, urban barrio, and colonia. These spaces have become the emblematic expressions of local Mexican American settlement in South Texas, and they figure prominently in Mexican American identification. I then investigate specific places and their landscapes as vignettes in Chapters 6 and 7. While South Texas has become a predominantly urban region, small town life continues to be significant to local identity. Chapter 6 explores three examples of Texas Mexican small towns. These are San Ygnacio on the Rio Grande south of Laredo, San Diego on the coastal plain west of Corpus Christi, and Cotulla along the railroad and highway corridor that connects San Antonio on the northern edge of South Texas to Laredo on the Mexican border. Significantly, these communities are dominated by Texas Mexicans and the towns are more than a century old, so that each has a legacy of many generations of Mexican American attachment to place.

In Chapter 7, I explore the two largest Texas Mexican cities of the region, San Antonio and Laredo. Demographically, economically, and culturally, San Antonio is the capital of South Texas. One of the oldest settlements in the borderland, San Antonio has a long association with Mexican American cultural ways, yet it has emerged most recently as the cradle of Texas Mexican identity. Laredo on the Rio Grande is almost as old as San Antonio but for much of its history has been in the shadow of the larger city. Laredo's historic gateway identity as a bridge between Mexico and Texas has been invigorated with the windfall of the North American Free Trade Agreement. Nevertheless, Laredo may be the most Mexican American medium-sized city in the country, symbolic of Texas

Mexican places that have risen from relative obscurity to subregional notoriety.

Finally, social identity among South Texas Mexican Americans is inspected through foodways and public celebrations in Chapter 8. Here Texas Mexican culture is studied through the lenses of folk and popular culture to assess how social practices become specific among Mexican Americans. In Chapter 9, I return to the thesis of regional distinctiveness and summarize how Mexican South Texas is a cultural province, connecting Mexico and the United States in a hybrid form that is unique in the borderlands.

"Mexican" and "Mexican American" are appellations used interchangeably in this book, as are "Texas Mexican" and "Tejano/a." Since these terms are fluid, distinction is made by the context in which each is used. For example, although persons referred to as "Mexican" are usually citizens of Mexico, at times they may be citizens of the United States. And while "Mexican Americans" usually refers to persons of Mexican heritage born in the United States, it may also refer to U.S. citizens originally from Mexico. "Texas Mexican" and "Tejana/o" are generally used to distinguish Mexican Americans who are Texans by birth from, say, Mexican Americans born in Arizona or California.

Throughout the text I follow the convention of using Spanish-language spellings and accents as they appear in standard and cited sources. Mexican place names generally follow the usage of topographic maps published by the Dirección General de Geografía, while Spanish toponyms in the United States follow the U.S. Board on Geographic Names. For example, I use the English spelling "Rio Grande," whereas in Mexico the watercourse is called the "Río Bravo del Norte."

Of this section of country very little is known. From the fact that the Nueces on the south side and the Rio Grande on the north side are without any consider-able tributaries it is inferred that it is mostly a dry elevated prairie.

—RICHARD S. HUNT AND JESSE F. RANDAL, *A MAP OF TEXAS*, 1839

Land beyond the Nueces

South Texas as a regional concept emerged in the nineteenth cen-tury with the Texan domination of lands south of the Nueces River and north of the Rio Grande, but its character was not well known nor carefully defined until this century. Penetrated and explored as early as the sixteenth century, and crisscrossed by dozens of travel-ers during the nineteenth century, today the region remains a popu-larly acknowledged subarea of Texas yet an enigma of sorts on our maps and in our writings.

In one standard bibliography that includes some 224 basic books about Texas, there is not a single entry with South Texas in its title.[1] Despite the clear historical and contemporary association of the region with Spanish and Mexican cultures, there is no mention of South Texas in the highly regarded *Dictionary of Mexican American History*. This source lists other regional terms like "Alta California," "Imperial Valley," and "Rio Arriba," and even includes places that most would agree are part of the South Texas region, such as "Crystal City," "Laredo," "Rio Grande Valley," and "San Antonio." Yet no mention is made of South Texas as a geographic entity.[2] *The New Handbook of Texas*, considered by many to be the definitive encyclopedia of Texana, defines the area environmentally as the "South Texas Plains" but offers no cultural or historical context for this regional definition.[3] The much heralded *Texas Almanac*, which has appeared yearly since 1868 as a "state industrial guide" and general encyclopedia, mentions South Texas in the index to its 1990–1991 edition but only in reference to specific organizations or institutions and not to the region as a whole.[4]

Standard guidebooks have also dismissed the region as a cultural geographic unit. The now classic *WPA Guide to Texas*, which first appeared in 1940 and has recently been reprinted, fails to distinguish South Texas as a separate region.[5] The multivolume *Eyes of Texas Travel Guide*, published as a companion to a popular television series in and about the state, includes parts of the region in its San Antonio/Border edition, but "South Texas" as a regional identifier does not appear in its pages.[6] One of the more recent guides to the state does include "South Texas" as a regional unit. It encompasses territory from Del Rio and Brownsville along the Rio Grande but stretches this area far north and east to include the entire arc of the Gulf Coast to Beaumont. San Antonio is, curiously, excluded from the region.[7]

In spite of these failings, Texans, according to one distinguished geographer, are said to maintain a "perceptual image" of South Texas as a directional region, and at least one prominent Mexican American historian has labeled the region between the Nueces River and the Rio Grande the "Tejano cultural zone."[8] In this chapter, I reconstruct historically and assess critically the varied geographical conceptions of the region called South Texas.[9] Travelers' accounts provide a geographic first approximation of the area, and to this will be added contemporary descriptions of the environments that make up the region. Mapped boundaries of South Texas are compiled and assessed to distinguish among variations of its changing geographical definition. This assessment is a "historical geosophy," an account of the geographical knowledge about the region from selected written sources, and it serves as an introduction to our understanding of South Texas as a Tejano cultural province.[10]

SOUTH TEXAS AS ENVIRONMENTAL REGION

South Texas was first written about by Spaniards in the sixteenth century. Clearly, the area was known by Native American groups before the Spanish arrived, but our understanding of the geography and regional character of what would become South Texas is almost completely a function of European American writings.[11] The earliest contacts were made along the Gulf of Mexico coast by maritime explorations and, inadvertently, from shipwrecks on barrier islands. Later encounters with the region commenced with overland expeditions from Tampico, Mexico, in present Tamaulipas south of the Rio Grande. The often-related navigation of the Rio Grande by Alvarez de Pineda in 1519 was not the first Spanish encounter with the river. According to one authority, the Río de Las Palmas or, as it is presently known, the Río Soto La Marina, considerably south of the Rio Grande near the Tropic of Cancer, is the river that Pineda sailed.

This initial reconnoitering generated little written evidence because terra firma in these latitudes was so poorly known. In fact, South Texas was little more than a patch of the larger coastal littoral that the Spanish named Seno Mexicano, or Mexican Gulf. This area was so called because the ocean body outline from the Florida peninsula west and south to the Yucatán peninsula appeared as a "seno" or pocket even on the first crude maps of the region.[12] Over the next two centuries, South Texas became increasingly better known as a geographic area.

Several Spanish *entradas* or overland explorations marched across the Rio Grande and South Texas during the late seventeenth century.[13] The first regular route across the region stretched along a northern arc roughly between Monclova, Coahuila, and San Antonio, Texas. This trace crosses the northwest corner of South Texas, a wedgelike region bounded on the north by the Balcones Escarpment, on the west by the Rio Grande between Eagle Pass and Del Rio, and on the east by San Antonio (FIG. 2.1). The town of Guerrero, Coahuila, located south of Eagle Pass and across the Rio Grande from the Texas hamlet of El Indio, was the fulcrum point of this travel corridor. It was the site of the Presidio del Río Grande and the mission San Juan Bautista, established in 1699 and 1700 respectively. This colonial settlement was the gateway to Spanish Texas. In 1827, the settlement name changed to Villa de Guerrero.[14] Over two fords located near this site passed most of those traveling between Texas and Mexico from the Spanish colonial period until the second half of the nineteenth century.

Along the Rio Grande in the vicinity of Eagle Pass, the elevation is nearly 900 feet, but the land surface slopes gently northeast over a distance of some 130 miles toward San Antonio, situated at almost 600 feet. This area includes the northern reach of the Nueces Basin, and the southwesternmost extension of the Blackland Prairie in Texas. The Balcones Escarpment is a rugged plateau edge to the north of this corridor, perched, as its Spanish name suggests, like a series of balconies above the coastal lowland. Only the Anacacho Mountains east of Del Rio and the upturned edges of *cuestas* or low escarpments like the Austin Chalk east of San Antonio mark any significant relief in this area. The terrain is

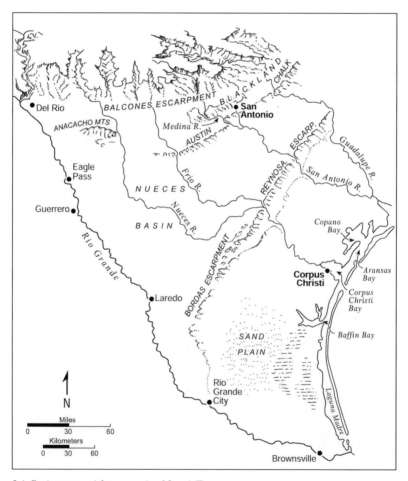

2.1. Environmental framework of South Texas.

rolling to undulating coastal plain crossed by the upper courses of several major streams, including the Nueces, Frio, and Medina as well as their numerous tributaries.

This route was blazed by José Domingo Ramón in 1716, a soldier-explorer in the service of the Spanish Crown. Later travelers who crossed and described this route included Jean Louis Berlandier, a French naturalist employed by the Mexican Boundary Commission in 1834, and Frederick Law Olmsted, a budding New York travel writer in 1857 (FIG. 2.2).[15] Olmsted described the corridor as typical of the entire South Texas area, which he called the "Mexican border frontier." This region was newly acquired as the result of the Mexican War, and Olmsted's view was not unlike that of other Anglo Americans intoxicated by the manifest destiny of the time.

> It is a region so sterile and valueless, as to be commonly reputed a desert, and, being incapable of settlement, serves as a barrier— separating the nationalities, and protecting from encroachment, at least temporarily, the retreating race.[16]

Although Berlandier on several occasions referred to the region between the Nueces River and Rio Grande as a great wilderness, his naturalist training meant his remarks were more detailed than most other travelers' and his interpretations usually more politically tempered. Dispatched to Mexico by the great Swiss botanist A. P. de Candolle, Berlandier traveled extensively across northeastern Mexico and southern Texas, collecting plant specimens and filling notebooks with his pointed observations. His account remains one of the best descriptions of the natural environment in South Texas.

In June 1834 Berlandier made an overland transect between San Antonio and Guerrero. He noted the limestone *cuesta* outcrops along the Austin Chalk that a traveler encounters below San Antonio, as well as the hilly countryside he called "Tierritas Blancas" near the Anacacho Mountains. In the course of eighteen travel days, Berlandier traversed some twenty different streams, which testify to the riparian nature of this northwestern wedge of South Texas. At the Medina River he was forced to wait several days for the high water to subside. South and west of the Nueces River, Berlandier remarked upon the changed vegetative landscape, comparing it to the oak woodland crossed between San Antonio and the Medina River.

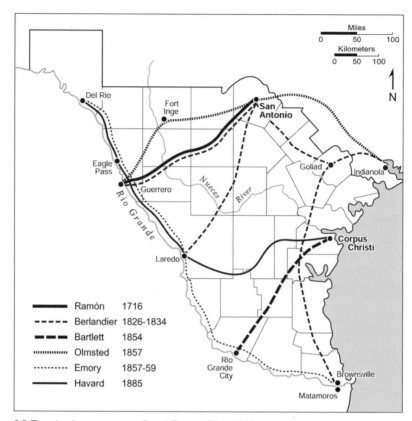

2.2. Travelers' routes across South Texas, 1716–1885.

As soon as we had gone by the Cañada del Negro we observed a great change in the vegetation, but that change was much more perceptible after the Nueces ...The streams became much farther apart; the forests disappeared at each step; and the grass-covered prairies offered only a dry herbage where divers wild animals grazed ...The oak and the nut tree which constituted a considerable part of the aborescent vegetation of Texas disappeared between the Nueces and the Río Bravo del Norte [Rio Grande]. In that region, however, on the banks of streams remarkable for their verdure one finds willows, elms, ash, and some shrubs.[17]

The Guerrero–San Antonio corridor remained a principal link between Mexico and Texas until railroads entered the region in the late nineteenth century and created a travel corridor between San Antonio and Laredo. The preference for routes across this northwest wedge, and the consequent neglect of more southerly routes via the horn of the region, resulted from the historical connections and short distance between the Coahuilan capitals of Monclova and Saltillo and the Spanish Texas and Mexican provincial capital at San Antonio. Environmental conditions, however, also differed in the southern part of the region and thus isolated it from the well-traveled corridor of the northwest.

The horn of South Texas pivots on Laredo on the west, Corpus Christi to the east, and Brownsville on the south (FIG. 2.1). It encompasses the drier southern part of the Nueces Basin, the South Texas Sand Plain, and the Lower Rio Grande Valley as well as two extensions from the northeast—the Bordas Escarpment and the Texas coastal bend including offshore barrier islands.

The highest elevations in this part of South Texas are along the Bordas Escarpment that stretches northeast to southwest below the Nueces River east of Laredo. This escarpment or *cuesta* is sharper in relief on its northwest face and slopes more gradually toward the Gulf of Mexico on the southeast. At Laredo on the Rio Grande, elevation is just below 500 feet; yet near Mirando City, some 25 miles east on the edge of the Bordas Escarpment, the elevation is slightly above 1,000 feet. At Hebbronville, some 30 miles farther east, the elevation drops to near 550 feet, and it declines to circa 35 feet above sea level near Sarita where Los Olmos Creek empties into Baffin Bay. The nature of this plateau was described in 1834.

> After traveling several miles to-day, we ascended a high ridge, about three hundred feet above the plain that we had left. This ridge is the highest land between the *Rio Bravo del Norte*, and the *Rio de las Nueces*. From its summit, one may see in a clear day, to a distance of near one hundred and twenty miles.[18]

Although average annual rainfall in the horn of South Texas is greater than in the northwest wedge, there is a decidedly drier aspect to the landscape, in part a result of greater rainfall variability and also because of fewer streams.[19] Only the Nueces River along the northern edge and the Rio Grande on the southern periphery are perennial watercourses. Interior drainage marks some parts of the area, especially in the Sand Plain, a zone of ancient sand dunes, and south of the Sand Plain at El Sal del Rey, a salt playa near Raymondville. This scarcity of surface water, especially in the summer months, caused some early travelers to journey a more northerly route.

Many travelers who crossed the Sand Plain described the region as a "wild horse desert," a term first attributed to William Kennedy, who published an account of Texas in 1841 and identified the large herds of mustangs that roamed this arid expanse.[20] Following this early reference, the toponym Wild Horse Desert became standard on many maps of the region. Naturalist travelers, however, were more discriminating in their interpretations of the "desert." Having crossed between Laredo and Corpus Christi in 1885, Havard (FIG. 2.2) made this observation:

> The great Texano-Mexican Desert, [is] a vast expanse of plains and prairies, scarred by arroyos, where streams are few and very far apart, and timber, if there be any, confined to water-courses and mountains. The epithet of desert has only reference to the scarcity of timber and water, which imparts a bald, barren aspect to the face of nature; shrubby and herbaceous vegetation fairly covers this immense zone which in many districts is admirably adapted to the raising of live stock.[21]

In 1834, Berlandier journeyed across the Sand Plain en route from Matamoros to Goliad. He remarked that the road was almost deserted and that the countryside consisted of a succession of immense plains with no drainage for water (FIG. 2.2).[22]

The Lower Rio Grande Valley portion of the South Texas horn is, technically, an inland delta or embayment that emerged with sea level changes in the distant past.[23] In its lower course, the riverine landscape is marked by meanders and oxbow lakes, known locally as *resacas,* and dense tropical vegetation including native Texas palms that impart a jungle ambiance.[24] William H. Emory of the U.S. Topographical Engineers gave this account of the Lower Valley in the vicinity of Brownsville, based on observations made during his survey of the U.S.–Mexico boundary in the 1850s (FIG. 2.2):

> From this point [the mouth of the river] upward to Brownsville the river makes a great bend to the South, and is so winding in its course that frequently the curves almost touch. The land on each side is

level, and covered with a dense growth of heavy mezquite [*sic*] . . . It is generally too high for irrigation, and the climate too arid to depend with certainty upon rain for the purposes of agriculture. The vegetation is of a semi-tropical character, and the margin of the river, which is exposed to overflow, abounds in reed, canebrake, palmetto, willow, and water-plants, and would no doubt produce the sugarcane in great luxuriance.[25]

As one proceeds upriver from Brownsville to Rio Grande City, the land surface begins a gradual ascent, rising from 57 to 190 feet above sea level over a distance of some 75 miles (FIG. 2.1). However, this distance is some 241 miles if measured by the curving course of the river, emphasizing the meandering nature of the Rio Grande in its lower course. Between Rio Grande City and Laredo, the terrain is rather hilly and unlike the flat delta lands to the east. In the nineteenth century, the Rio Grande was commercially navigable from Brownsville to Roma, just upriver from Rio Grande City. Shallow watercraft could navigate above Roma, but the presence of falls like Las Isletas above Laredo and numerous sand shoals made for treacherous conditions.[26]

The final subregion of the mosaic that makes up South Texas is a triangular transition zone. It stretches southeast from San Antonio along the San Antonio River to its mouth at San Antonio Bay above Copano Bay, then falls south to Corpus Christi Bay and extends west to the vicinity of Laredo (FIG. 2.1). The zone cuts across several different environments of the coastal plain, including the coastal bend which is made up of estuaries and bays, a prairie-woodland transition inland from the coast, and a piece of Blackland Prairie that surrounds San Antonio.

This transition zone is a riparian landscape scrawled upon by the generally northwest to southeast flow of the Nueces, Medina, San Antonio, and Guadalupe Rivers. Correspondingly, elevation descends gradually from near 600 feet at San Antonio to sea level along the coast where rivers merge with bays that form estuaries enclosed by offshore barrier islands.[27]

This subarea was not usually attractive to travelers because of poor drainage on the level terrain that complicated movement across the zone (FIG. 2.2). From ports such as Indianola on Matagorda Bay immediately north of Copano Bay, travelers made their way inland toward higher ground near towns like Victoria and Goliad. Olmsted gave this account of the coastal prairie in 1853, noting that the land rose and fell over *cuestas* as one approached San Antonio:

We looked out in the morning upon a real sea of wet grass . . . The greater part of the time, our view was entirely uninterrupted, across a nearly level, treeless space around three quarters of the horizon. Objects loomed into vagueness, as at sea. Part of the prairie was hog-wallow, very distressing to the laboring horses, and now and then came a slightly elevated long roll . . . The road from Indianola strikes the uplands along the Guadalupe, twelve miles below Victoria, and thence the road was good and dry.[28]

From Goliad inland toward San Antonio, the land rose and fell gradually as travelers crossed upland prairies interrupted by gallery forests. Berlandier traversed this route several times between 1829 and 1834, and gave this account of the landscape (FIG. 2.2):

Should we cast a general glance at the route from Goliad to the capital of Texas [San Antonio], we would find a road laid out over immense plains which are broken by small hills covered with grasses and forests, rich in vegetation and watered by numerous streams . . . There is no resemblance to the coastal regions, for it is a succession of hills covered with verdure. Here and there are scattered small forests of oaks and various shrubs, forming isolated groups in the midst of the prairies . . . The San Antonio River . . . is recognized by the large trees which cover its banks . . . the countryside is covered with a thick layer of black, organic soil of a remarkable fertility.[29]

Along the southern edge of this transition triangle, the lower Nueces River is a significant boundary of the natural landscape.[30] Berlandier remarked how different the vegetative cover appeared on either side of this divide, with mesquite to the south and oaks to the north.

From Matamoros to the Nueces only eight streams are numbered, whereas from that latter locality to Goliad there are seven on a stretch less than half as long. The vegetation is also much less rich on the Tamaulipas [south of the Nueces] portion of the route, for in the south, as far as the stream called Arroyo Colorado, the predominant tree is Mimosa pseudo-schinus . . . Beyond the stream named Aransas a lovely forest of oaks exists on a sandy terrain.[31]

In retrospect, travelers who crossed South Texas during the nineteenth century described a set of subareas rather than a single region, distinctive by environmental perception as well as natural condition. Still, to the average nineteenth-century visitor, the region was fundamentally the land beyond the Nueces River. Berlandier offered this summary of this "wilderness" on either side of the boundary and its human potential:

> If, retracing our steps, we cast a general glance over the vast wilderness which we have just crossed, we can make some small observations about the chances of populating these solitudes, full of wild animals. The southern part—between the Rio Grande and the Nueces—is the most barren and the least suitable for receiving colonists . . . the terrain consists only of rather infertile prairies and is completely deprived of forests . . . There are only a few streams, which are often dry; water is more abundant in the small marshes, which last all year there . . . The part of the wilderness situated to the north of the Nueces belongs to Texas and is the most fertile and most suited to agriculture. It is watered by numerous streams, endowed with a very lovely vegetation, and rich in forests so useful for the construction of new colonies . . . We should not attribute these very different physical characteristics to the differences in latitude or to the height above sea level; they are due rather to the presence of streams, or perhaps to a better soil.[32]

RECOGNITION OF THE CULTURAL REGION

Perhaps the first assessment of South Texas as a distinctive human geographic region in the twentieth century was a history in two volumes published in 1907. The territorial basis for the work was given to be "all that part of the state southwest of the Guadalupe River," with San Antonio "being the metropolis and historic center."[33] The Hispanic presence in the region, by then more than a century old, was denied and suppressed.

Before this time, the regional geography of Texas was largely based on geological, soil, and topographic conditions. For example, a textbook published in 1905 distinguished South Texas as the "Rio Grande Plain," a topographic descriptor for land below the Balcones Escarpment and west of the Gulf coast, but imprecise about its northeastern limits.[34]

Some three decades later in 1931, South Texas was still identified chiefly as a natural region now called the "South Texas Plains," except that its northeastern limits were set roughly at the Texas Colorado River.[35] In 1948, this same area was delimited as a geographic region, the "South Texas Plain," with the northeastern boundary adjusted southwest based upon the transition in rainfall and temperature conditions which mark the area below the San Antonio River and along the lower drainage of the Nueces River (FIG. 2.3).[36]

In 1950 the South Texas region became refined by other environmental criteria.[37] The Tamaulipan Biotic Province resembles the topographic limits of the South Texas Plain. Its northern boundary stretches along the Balcones Escarpment, but its northeastern edge swings east to distinguish the brushlands to the west of this line from the oak-hickory prairies to the east. This border also parallels the divide between major soil groups in this part of Texas (FIG. 2.3).

Hispanic South Texas was finally acknowledged in 1948 when Carey McWilliams pointed historians to the significance of this borderland and in 1955 when Robert Talbert first mapped the Spanish-surname population in the region.[38] The first to divide Texas according to culture areas rather than physical boundaries was geographer Donald W. Meinig, in 1969.[39] He outlined the "stronghold" nature of Hispanic South Texas based on counties with greater than 50 percent Spanish-surnamed population in 1960. Meinig's South Texas is the horn-shaped southernmost reach of the state bordered by the Rio Grande between Brownsville and Del Rio and pivoting on San Antonio to the north and Corpus Christi along the Gulf of Mexico littoral; the northeastern boundary roughly parallels the San Antonio River drainage (FIG. 2.3).

Over the last decade and a half, South Texas regional delimitation has been decidedly cultural. However, the borders of these regions are largely functionally defined, rather than formally enclosed. A formal culture region is a uniform area inhabited by people who have one or more cultural traits in common.[40] Jordan's delimitation of the Hispanic Borderland that includes South Texas is such a formal culture region (FIG. 2.3).[41] Another type of culture area is called a perceptual region, where the boundaries of the region are based on perceptions held by residents. Jordan's perceptual region of South Texas is such a region (FIG. 2.3). A functional culture region, on the other hand, is generally not culturally homogeneous. Rather, the area is organized to function politically, economically, or socially.

In 1973, the State of Texas created the Cultural Basin Act, which empowered the governor's office to design culture areas that would exist

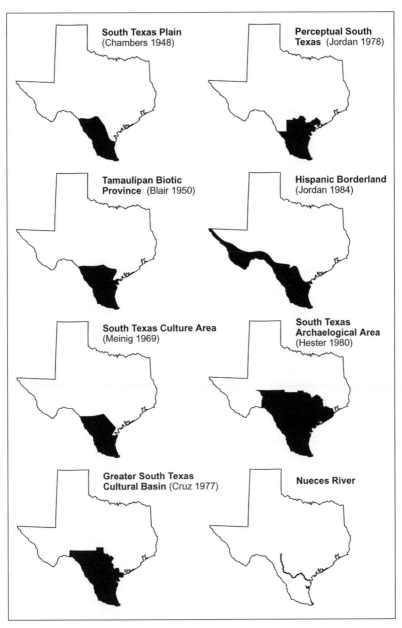

2.3. Regionalizations of South Texas.

as regional units to implement economic development programs.[42] Guide-lines for the creation of the cultural basins (functional units) included a commonalty within a geographic area culturally, historically, and eco-nomically. The Greater South Texas Cultural Basin, a region comprising forty-one counties, was the pilot for what was intended to be a statewide program (FIG. 2.3). An even larger functional culture region of South Texas has been defined by archaeologists, one of whom included some seventy-one counties that stretch from the Brazos River in the east to the Pecos River in the west (FIG. 2.3).[43]

The regional identities of South Texas were, therefore, many rather than one for much of the twentieth century. In most assessments, how-ever, the major geographical divide that separates South Texas from West Texas is the Balcones Escarpment, and the boundary between South Texas and Central Texas is a transition zone between the San Antonio and Nueces Rivers. Absent from many standard geographies of the region was any association with Hispanic influence. This compounds what historian Armando Alonzo calls the "Anglo mythic history of Texas," in which South Texas is viewed historically as unoccupied and vacant.[44]

In the next chapter, I chart the evolving historical geography of Mexican South Texas and its emergence as a Hispanic cultural zone.

To the north of Nuevo Santander is found the province of Texas, but one must cross a great desert or remote lands between the last populations of this colony and the first settlements of that one.

—JOSÉ TIENDA DE CUERVO, 1757

Territory Shaped

For most of the three centuries of Spanish colonial rule, northeastern Mexico and southern Texas were poorly defined parts of the north of New Spain.[1] This realm today includes chiefly the southern reaches of Texas in the United States and the Mexican states of Coahuila, Nuevo León, and Tamaulipas (colonial Nuevo Santander). Yet, its contemporary political geography disguises the considerable uncertainties about boundaries that existed for much of this domain, especially the Rio Grande and Nueces River frontiers. These boundaries were shaped through individual ambition, imperial rivalry, and civil and international conflict.[2] South Texas is the most recent cultural-political configuration in this framework of changing regional geography.

In this chapter I begin by outlining the political geographic history of this region. A considerable emphasis is placed on the question of shifting boundaries, particularly among Spanish Texas, Coahuila, and Nuevo Santander. This reconstruction is essential to understanding how and why South Texas is a distinctive subcultural area and one rooted in New Spain (Mexico).

Defining territory by political demarcation and settling the same area are, however, two separate processes. Spanish colonial officials were remarkably bold in expressing claims to parts of New Spain, even if their maps were imprecise about the exact outlines of that grand area. Colonizing these same frontiers was not a simple exercise. To be sure, mineral riches and slave raiding inspired individuals to stake their claims to parts of the Mexican north, but forging a community and sustaining settled life in this distant land, perceived as wilderness, amidst often combative aboriginals and a harsh environment were a constant challenge.[3] It is ironic and yet instructive to recall that in these frontier provinces the estimated population settled at the close of the colonial period in 1821 was less than the total number of native inhabitants in the respective districts at the beginning of Spanish reduction in 1519.[4]

Largely, Spanish success was measured by the dozens of towns and ranches founded in this region, many of which are still on the map. The second purpose of this chapter, then, will be to assess the historical geography of early settlement. The concern is to understand where, when, and how these footholds were organized and founded, and how they survived to become the system of nodes that would give human geographic structure to the region in the twentieth century.

When the Treaty of Guadalupe Hidalgo was signed in 1848, Mexicans and other residents of Spanish heritage in South Texas were confronted with a new formal political allegiance. In less than five decades, what had been for several centuries chiefly a thinly populated Spanish-colonial frontier was transformed by non-Hispanic colonization in the nineteenth and early twentieth centuries into a Mexican American frontier. The number of viable communities established increasingly included Anglo Americans and exceeded many times the framework of Spanish settlements. South Texas persisted nevertheless as a Mexican American cultural zone through the end of the nineteenth century, and this chapter closes with a broad sketch of that human geography.

BOUNDARIES

The northern frontier of New Spain evolved as a set of *gobiernos* or administrative units, each ruled by a governor who reported to the viceroy in Mexico City during the colonial era from 1519-1775. In the northeast, five separate jurisdictions emerged: Pánuco, Nuevo León, Coahuila, Texas, and Nuevo Santander. In the later years of the colonial era, beginning in 1776, administrative control of the north passed to a series of military divisions headed by a *comandante general* or commander-general. These *provincias internas* or interior provinces were reduced in 1787 to Occidente (western) and Oriente (eastern) commands; the latter included Coahuila, Nuevo León, Texas, and Nuevo Santander. Because authority among the viceroy, governors, and commanders-general shifted back and forth during the later years of Spanish colonial administration, jurisdictional disputes over territory were common and exact political boundaries were not always clear. Ecclesiastical and missionary administrative units that were separate from these civil and military organizations did not directly impact political boundaries and therefore will not be considered in this discussion.

Northeastern New Spain was first given formal administrative authority as the *gobierno* of San Esteban de Pánuco in 1523. Its assumed boundaries were the Río Tuxpan on the south and the Río Pánuco on the north; it extended from the Gulf coast inland to the Sierra Madre Oriental.[5] Presumably, its jurisdiction stretched north into what would become Nuevo Santander, but the boundary was ill defined at this time. This was largely the region known as the Huasteca, the homeland of an aboriginal agricultural people who occupied the north-easternmost reach of pre-Columbian high culture in Mesoamerica.[6] The Pánuco was a notorious slaving area ravaged for its Native American labor by Nuño Beltrán de Guzmán. When Guzmán transferred to Nueva Galicia, the Pánuco was absorbed as a political unit by the *gobierno* of Nueva España in 1534. The Spanish interest in the region waned for nearly fifty years, until 1580 when Nuevo León was organized.

Nuevo León was an ambitious territorial design that initially claimed as its domain much of northeastern Mexico east of the Sierra Madre Oriental to the Gulf of Mexico.[7] The administrative boundaries were finally compressed to the approximate outlines of the contemporary state of the same name (FIG. 3.1). The limestone massif of the Sierra Madre Oriental is the western backbone of the province, and this mountain range stretches southeast beyond the boundary with Nuevo Santander (present Tamaulipas). Its northeastern periphery is coastal plain spread between the Ríos Salado and San Juan that drains to the Rio Grande, while its southwestern edge pressed against the borders of Nueva Galicia and Nueva Vizcaya (present-day San Luis Potosí) that are part of the Mesa del Norte.[8] In the colonial era, Nuevo León was a mining and ranching frontier within a mixed aboriginal realm that included hunting and gathering groups like the Bocalo and Coahuiltecan, as well as others. The near constant trafficking in Native American slaves resulted in long periods of conflict, and created a vacuum that led to the importation of native groups from the south and later incursions by Apache from north of the Rio Grande.[9]

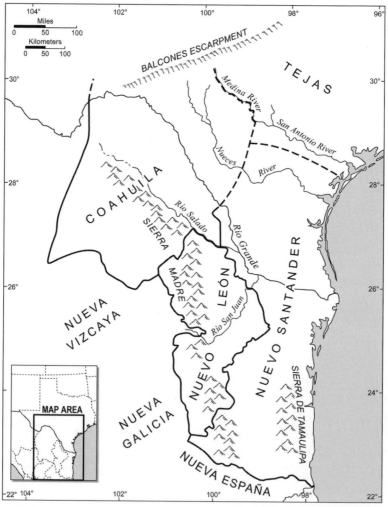

3.1. Colonial administrative boundaries of Northeast New Spain and South Texas.

Coahuila, also known as Nueva Extremadura, a region penetrated in the sixteenth century and claimed by rival provinces—Nuevo León to its east and Nueva Vizcaya to its south and west—was a vaguely defined territory even after it was declared a separate *gobierno* in 1687. On its northern edge, its borders were roughly the Medina River, west of San Antonio, and a line that reached from that boundary south until it intersected the Rio Grande northwest of Laredo (FIG. 3.1). To the northwest, the territory was poorly defined but was presumed to include the San Sabá settlements on the Edwards Plateau and to extend northwest until Nuevo México. On the southwest, the province bordered Nueva Vizcaya, and in 1787 its southern flank was expanded to include the towns of Saltillo and Parras.[10] A series of folded ranges trending northwest to southeast divides Coahuila into a northeastern coastal plain and a southwestern upland that is part of the Mesa del Norte.[11] The Río Sabinas drains the region southeast to the border with Nuevo León, where the stream feeds the Río Salado. The coastal plain lands were the western edge of the greater Coahuiltecan realm, while the more arid interior west of the Sierra was only sparsely populated with native groups. While missionaries attempted to settle and organize some of the Coahuiltecan populations, the settlements like Saltillo that were populated with Tlaxcaltecans from the south were more successful.[12]

Although explored and even partly settled in the late seventeenth century, Texas (Tejas) was politically an extension of Coahuila until 1722. Officially, the province was known as Nuevo Reino de las Filipinas, or Nuevas Filipinas.[13] Besides the arc of the Gulf coast on the east, jurisdictional boundaries were said to be the Medina–San Antonio Rivers on the south and the Red River on the north, but neither limit was firm. On the south, an unsettled zone stretched across the trans-Nueces frontier to the Rio Grande until this area began to be colonized as Nuevo Santander in the mid-eighteenth century. To the north, the divide between New Spain and New France was vague until the Adams-Onís Treaty in the early nineteenth century. Toward the interior and above the Balcones Escarpment, borders were uncertain because settlement did not much penetrate beyond the pivot points of San Antonio or Los Adaes (near present-day Robeline, Louisiana), each located on the coastal plain.[14] This condition led historian Herbert Eugene Bolton to proclaim Texas "a buffer province" during the critical period of the eighteenth century separating northern New Spain from French territory in the Mississippi River drainage.[15] Aboriginal populations in the southern reaches of the province consisted primarily of Coahuiltecan hunter-gatherers both in the interior and along the coastal littoral.[16]

The last *gobierno* created in the northeast of New Spain was Nuevo Santander in 1748. This province was bordered on the south by Nueva España and on the west by Nuevo León. Each of these areas had been settled earlier, so claims to territory were especially sensitive, although they were ultimately resolved in favor of Nuevo Santander.[17] Nevertheless, it was chiefly on the north—a *despoblado* or unpopulated zone where Nuevo Santander abutted Texas and Coahuila—that boundary questions persisted late into the colonial period. Topographically, Nuevo Santander is chiefly a coastal plain that stretches for approximately six degrees of latitude from near the Río Pánuco on the south to the San Antonio River on the north, and is roughly divided by the Rio Grande (FIG. 3.1). On the south, rivers like the Purificación–Soto La Marina and Conchas–San Fernando drain eastward from the Sierra Madre, while streams like the Nueces on the north flow easterly from the Balcones Escarpment. These rivers empty into the Gulf of Mexico via numerous estuaries and bays of the barrier-island coastline. The only significant uplands in the province are the isolated Sierras de San Carlos and de Tamaulipas in the southern portion of the area below the Rio Grande. While the region was said to be part of the Coahuiltecan domain, recent studies suggest that the diversity of groups in this zone may have been significantly more complex than earlier assessments realized.[18]

Of particular concern to an understanding of the historical political geography of this province is the issue of the changing assessment of its northern boundary with Texas. In 1721, the Marqués de Aguayo, governor of Coahuila, Nueva Extremadura, Texas, and Nuevas Filipinas, acknowledged that the Medina River was the boundary between Texas and Coahuila, and the Nueces River the divide between Texas and Nuevo Santander.[19] One the earliest detailed maps of what would become Nuevo Santander is attributed to Ladrón de Guevara in 1736.[20] This map shows the coastal lands between the Río Pánuco and the Río Bravo (Rio Grande) as well as lands north into the province of Texas, indicated as lying north of a mountain range situated well above the Río Bravo. Across the horn of present South Texas and extending as far south as the Río Pánuco is scrawled "País despoblado hasta la costa" (Uninhabited land as far as the coast). When José de Escandón explored these lands in 1747 in preparation for the colonization of Nuevo Santander, he added significantly to Guevara's map by indicating that, in fact, the coastal zone was not "despoblado" but included various aboriginal groups. Importantly, Escandón's *Mapa de la Sierra Gorda y costa de el Seno Mexicano* also designated jurisdictional boundaries for neighboring *gobiernos*.[21] The lands north of the Río Nueces are clearly assigned as *"Parte de la jurisdicción de Texas,"* suggesting in no uncertain terms that Escandón believed this to be the boundary between Texas and what would become Nuevo Santander.

In 1757 José Tienda de Cuervo conducted an inspection of the Mexican north. His report was unequivocal about the northern boundary of Nuevo Santander being the southern reach of the province of Texas, but he was uncertain about the frontier between Texas and the Rio Grande because he had not traveled that territory (see the epigraph at the introduction to this chapter). Agustín López de la Cámara Alta, official engineer, signed the principal map that resulted from the inspection in 1758. This map and others made from it, like the one drafted by Francisco José de Haro, show the northern boundary of Nuevo Santander as the San Antonio River, not the Nueces River that had earlier appeared on Escandón's 1747 map.[22]

Further confusion arises from the 1771 map that resulted from the *relación* or report produced by Nicolás de La Fora as part of the 1766 brief inspection of the northern frontier by the Marqués de Rubí.[23] La Fora's account and map suggest that the boundary between Nuevo Santander and Texas is the Nueces River, not the San Antonio River, although the Nueces is not formally labeled on his map. His map shows Nuevo Santander below a line that appears to be the Nueces. In the text of his report, however, he notes that the colony of Nuevo Santander "extends from Laredo following the course of the Río Grande del Norte to the Gulf of Mexico, as shown on the general map" and thus further confuses the boundary issue.[24]

In 1804, the great German geographer Alexander von Humboldt published his highly regarded *Political Essay on the Kingdom of New Spain* in several volumes, including an atlas. A single map in this atlas is titled "Carta general del reino de la Nueva España." It shows the boundary between Texas and Nuevo Santander as a line that starts near the Mission Espada (south of San Antonio Valero, the Alamo) and then intersects the Nueces River near 28° north latitude and then follows the river along its south bank to its mouth. Humboldt did not survey this terrain firsthand but relied on materials available to him in the archives in Mexico City. In the introduction to his *Political Essay*, Humboldt admits that he was unable to uncover sufficient data in the Mexican archives to compose the Texas portion of the Mexico map. Instead, he drew the Texas map based upon information provided by U.S. General James Wilkinson, commander of United States forces in New Orleans, whom he met in Washington upon his return from Mexico.[25]

An official decree in 1805 to the *comandante general* of the Provincias Internas de Oriente, Joaquín de Arredondo, resulted in the drafting of a map to show the boundaries of this province that includes Coahuila, Nuevo León, Texas, and Nuevo Santander. This map, published in 1815, shows plainly that the boundary between Texas and Nuevo Santander is the middle and lower Nueces River, starting at between 28° north latitude and 101° west longitude and running southeast toward the mouth of the river.[26] Félix Calleja, then the viceroy of New Spain, approved the map in October of the same year. When Mexico rebelled against Spain and declared itself independent in 1821, the Nueces River became the official divide between the state of Coahuila y Tejas and Tamaulipas, formerly Nuevo Santander.

By the 1830s, Texas geography, as viewed from the north, had become a matter of some speculation. Stephen F. Austin's early maps became the basis for several commercial maps produced during this period. The least derivative and reputed to be the best of these was that produced by David Burr, geographer to the U.S. House of Representatives. Burr's map of 1833 was published by J. H. Colton of New York and was quickly imitated by others like J. H. Young, who published in 1837 *New Map of Texas with Contiguous American and Mexican States.*[27] Like the Burr map before it, Young's map shows that the middle and lower Nueces is the boundary between Texas and Tamaulipas.

After Texas gained independence from Mexico in 1836, the lands south of the Nueces and north of the Rio Grande were disputed. Texas claimed this territory by right of the Treaty of Velasco that was signed by Santa Anna after his defeat at the Battle of San Jacinto, but Mexico refused to concede. Mexico held that the territory had been part of neither Spanish nor Mexican Texas, because the area encompassed first Nuevo Santander, then Tamaulipas—never Texas.[28] Furthermore, Mexico insisted that the provisions of the Treaty of Velasco that relinquished the area to Texas were null and void because they were unacknowledged by the Mexican Congress. This boundary discord persisted until the United States' annexation of Texas, which precipitated the U.S.-Mexican War and ended in the Treaty of Guadalupe Hidalgo setting the boundary as the Rio Grande in 1848.

The old and new boundaries are illustrated on the map of Tamaulipas published by Antonio García Cubas in 1858 as part of his monumental *Atlas geográfico, estadístico e histórico de la República Mexicana*.[29] This map shows the Nueces River as the "Antiguo límite de Tamaulipas," starting northwest of Laredo at 28°30' north latitude and 100°29' west longitude and running southeast to Corpus Christi Bay (FIG. 3.2). The 1858 boundary is the Río Bravo (Rio Grande) northwest of Laredo, at 27°40' north latitude and running southeast to the Boca del Río Bravo at the southern tip of Padre Island. The boundary is labeled "Límite actual entre la República y los Estados Unidos con arreglo al tratado de Guadalupe en 1848."

By the mid-nineteenth century, it was clear that the boundary dispute between Texas and Tamaulipas had finally been resolved through international agreement. However, an academic footnote to this story appeared in 1915, when the eminent borderland historian Herbert Bolton cited the La Fora map as the source for his map, which designated the Nueces as the boundary between Texas and Nuevo Santander.[30] Bolton, however, drew his boundary along the Nueces, but not to its mouth at present Corpus Christi Bay as previous maps from Escandón to García Cubas had done. Rather, Bolton's map shows the boundary to veer southeast from the Nueces toward the Aransas River (close to 30° north latitude) and then follow that drainage to Aransas Bay. Why this would be so is not clear, because La Fora's map does not show this level of detail, nor does it label the Aransas River or Bay. Bolton claims that the La Fora map he inspected was housed in the Archivo General de México. Assuming, for the moment, that it is unlikely that Bolton misreported from an archival map, one possible explanation is simply that there exist various copies of the same map. In fact, the distinguished Mexican historian Vito Alessio Robles, who published his version of the La Fora account from a copy in the Ministry of War in Madrid, admits that there are several separate accounts of the document known to exist in Spain, Mexico, and the United States.

The changing perception of boundaries between colonial Nuevo Santander (later Mexican Tamaulipas) and Texas are summarized in Table 3.1. What is clear from the documents is that the region generally south of the Nueces River was, from the mid-eighteenth century, a separate administrative unit of colonial New Spain and later the Republic of Mexico, despite claims to the contrary by the Republic of Texas. In 1848, the issue became resolved through political expediency following the U.S.-Mexico War and the United States annexation of Texas, which had been initiated in 1845. These early struggles would define the southern

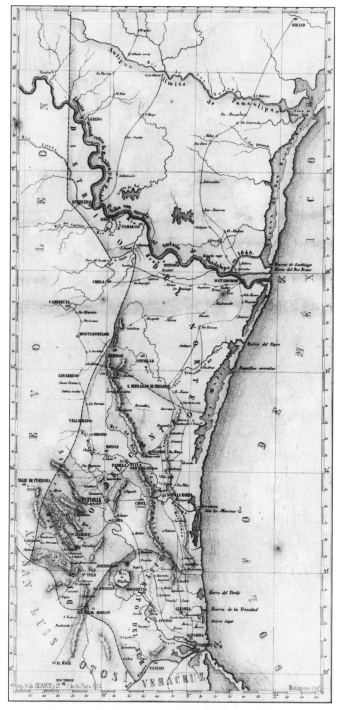

3.2. Tamaulipas boundary along the Nueces River.

TABLE 3.1 Changing Definitions of the Nuevo Santander–Texas Boundary

SOURCE/DATE	RIVER BOUNDARY	MAP
Escandón (1747)	Nueces	*Mapa de la Sierra Gorda*
Tienda de Cuervo (1757)	San Antonio	*Mapa General Ychnographico de la nueba Colonia Santander*
La Fora (1771)	Nueces–Rio Grande	*Mapa de la frontera del vireinato de la Nueva España*
Humboldt (1804)	Nueces	*Carta general del reino de la Nueva España*
Arredondo (1815)	Nueces	*Mapa de las provincias internas de Oriente*
Young (1837)	Nueces	*New Map of Texas with the Contiguous American and Mexican States*
García Cubas (1858)	Nueces	*Tamaulipas*
Bolton (1915)	Nueces–Aransas	*Map of Texas & Adjacent Regions in the Eighteenth Century*

horn-shape outline of South Texas and give temporary alignment along a northern fringe of the Nueces River. The precise dimensions of Mexican and United States South Texas, however, require consideration of human settlement.

COLONIZATION

Spanish colonial settlement of northeast New Spain, including what would become South Texas, extended over nearly two centuries. The first phase of this protracted experience resulted in the establishment of several foundation towns, both mining and livestock centers, west and south of the present Rio Grande; these include Saltillo (1577), Cerralvo (1583, 1625), Monterrey (1596), Cadereyta (1637), and Monclova (1689).[31] These settlements were colonized via Durango to the south (FIG. 3.3).

The colonization of Texas occurred during the first half of the eighteenth century, launched chiefly from Saltillo and Monclova, the principal dispersal centers.[32] The strategic pivot point linking Coahuila and Texas was San Juan Bautista (1699–1700), near present-day Villa Guerrero and Eagle Pass and proximate to a ford on the Rio Grande.[33] Later settlements were established at San Antonio de Béxar (1718–1731) on a spring-

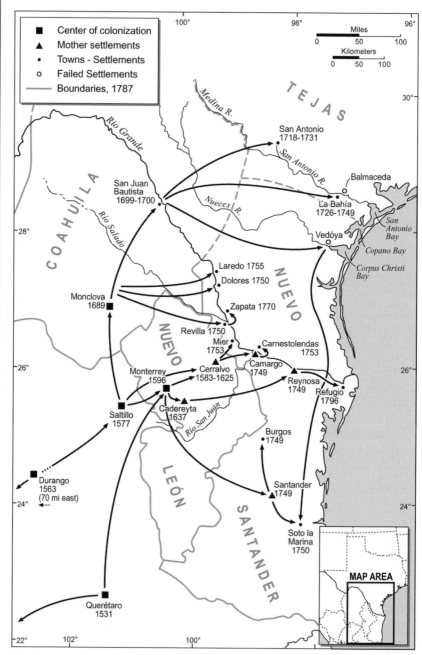

3.3. Colonial settlement of Northeast New Spain and South Texas, with founding dates.

fed river below the Balcones Escarpment and at La Bahía del Espíritu Santo (1726-1749) on the San Antonio River along the lower coastal plain.[34] These early nodes were mission and presidio settlements involving ecclesiastical orders and spare military garrisons. San Antonio, with five missions, a presidio, and a civil settlement or *villa* by 1731, was a major center of the frontier, and that concentration of varied institutions at one general location made the settlement unique in the Spanish borderlands. The *villa* was known as San Fernando, but the presidio name, San Antonio de Béxar, usually shortened to Béxar, persisted throughout the Spanish period. San Antonio became the provincial capital of Spanish Texas in 1772 and was elevated to city status in 1811, making it the political equal of Saltillo and Monterrey.[35]

An early trail connected San Juan Bautista and San Antonio, and this evolved into a major conduit of travel between colonial Coahuila and Texas. This road, probably several separate paths, traversed the northwest of South Texas (see Chap. 2) through present-day Maverick, Dimmit, Zavala, La Salle, Frio, Medina, Atascosa, and Bexar Counties.[36] This *camino*, as it would come to be called, extended west and south to Monclova and Saltillo and east to the Spanish outpost of Los Adaes in present Louisiana. A shorter spur road south from San Antonio linked that settlement to La Bahía and Copano Bay on the coast.

Nuevo Santander was a later colonization effort, contracted to José de Escandón and steered initially from Querétaro through Monterrey.[37] Santander (1749; present-day Santander Jiménez), situated in central Tamaulipas, became the mother settlement for several towns in its vicinity, including Soto la Marina (1750) and Burgos (1749). The settlements along the Rio Grande were established between 1749-1796, and are linked to mother settlements in Nuevo León and Coahuila. The first of these were Camargo (1749), settled from Cerralvo, and Reynosa (1749), mothered by Cadereyta. Mier (1753) too was founded by settlers from Cerralvo, a town that rightly deserves its motto, "Cuna [cradle] de Nuevo León." Both Camargo and Reynosa in turn gave birth to settlements—to Carnestolendas (1753), a ranching settlement north of the Rio Grande, and Refugio (1796), a mission-ranching node south of the Rio Grande and the precursor settlement for the town of Matamoros. From ranching settlements in Coahuila, Escandón gave authority to found and settle Revilla (1750) on the west bank of the Rio Grande, and Dolores (1750) and Laredo (1755) on the east bank. Revilla (renamed Guerrero in 1827) was a source of settlers for Zapata (1770) and later San Ygnacio (1830), both east of the Rio Grande. Escandón intended to create a settlement on the San Antonio River near La Bahía, to be called Villa de Balmaceda, but resources to fund the undertaking were not forthcoming. A second trans-Nueces settlement, Villa de Vedóya, was planned with colonists from Coahuila and Nuevo León via San Juan Bautista, but the poorly supplied expedition and unsatisfactory site resulted in its being shifted to Soto la Marina in the far south of the province.[38]

A change of viceroy in Mexico City in the mid-eighteenth century resulted in the formation of a commission to inspect the colony of Nuevo Santander, the José Tienda de Cuervo inspection described above. The 1757 survey produced an early statistical picture of Escandón's settlements along the Rio Grande (TABLE 3.2). Over 2,200 settlers, including missionized natives, and nearly 214,000 head of livestock were counted for six settlements and their adjoining, ill-defined ranchlands. Some settlements like Camargo and Revilla were able to cultivate corn, beans, squashes, and sugarcane, while others were dependent on trading livestock for foodstuffs.

The growth of the Rio Grande settlements toward the end of the

TABLE 3.2 Population and Livestock in Rio Grande Settlements, 1757

SETTLEMENT	POPULATION (Spaniards[a] + Indians)	LIVESTOCK (Horses, Mules, Cattle, Sheep, Goats)
Reynosa	279 + 300	17,261
Camargo	637 + 245	8,000; 2,600; 72,000[b]
Mier	140[c] + 150	44,015
Revilla	357	50,000
Dolores	92[c]	9,050
Laredo	60[c]	10,211
TOTAL	2,260	213,137

SOURCES: Lawrence Francis Hill, *José de Escandón and the Founding of Nuevo Santander; Estado general de las fundaciones hechas por D. José de Escandón en la colonía del Nuevo Santander;* Florence Johnson Scott, *Historical Heritage of the Lower Rio Grande;* Oakah L. Jones, *Los Paisanos: Spanish Settlers on the Northern Frontier of New Spain.*

[a]Spanish, mestizo, or mulato.
[b]Differentiated as horses and mules; cattle and sheep; goats.
[c]Given as families; 35 at Mier, 23 at Dolores, 15 at Laredo. Computed as one family equals four individuals.

eighteenth century led to the formation of a second commission to inspect this frontier, the general visit of the royal commission to the colonies of Nuevo Santander. This inspection was especially directed to determine boundaries for private land grants and to adjudicate land disputes outside of town limits. Because settlers were concerned about access to water for livestock in this semiarid environment, the commission decided on strict definitions for a *porción* or assigned land. The allotments were long quadrangles with approximately nine-thirteenths of a mile of riverfront, and the length measured from the river between 11 and 16 miles inland. The *porciones* created a distinctive pattern of elongated land grants along the Rio Grande between an area immediately upriver from Laredo to just downriver from Reynosa (see FIG. 5.2), and along the lower courses of the Río Salado, Río San Juan, and Río Alamo between Revilla and Camargo.[39] *Porciones* were allocated to the town jurisdictions of Laredo, Revilla, Mier, Camargo, and Reynosa. Laredo included 88 *porciones* along the Rio Grande, Revilla 68 fronting the Rio Grande and Río Salado, Camargo 111 along the Rio Grande and Río San Juan, Mier 80 fronting the Río Alamo, and Reynosa 80 on the Rio Grande.[40] In addition to *porciones*, the Spanish Crown issued large grants of land to the sons of many of the original *porción* grantees, including many allotments to influential families in Camargo and Reynosa. These grants were for ranching north and east of the Rio Grande in parts of what are today Hidalgo, Cameron, Willacy, Webb, and Zapata Counties, as well as the massive José Vásquez Borrego grant downriver from Laredo.[41] In some of these locations, especially around Laredo, Camargo and Reynosa, sheep outnumbered cattle in the first half of the eighteenth century.[42]

Following Mexican independence from Spain in 1821, the settlement of Texas and Tamaulipas became priorities. Both the Mexican federal government and the states of Coahuila y Texas, as well as Tamaulipas, passed colonization laws between 1824 and 1830 to encourage settlement. In Texas, settlement was directed under the auspices of immigration agents known as *empresarios*. However, of some twenty-four *empresario* contracts issued for all of Texas between 1825 and 1832, seventeen went to foreigners, mostly Anglo Americans.[43] Only a few of these resulted in colonies between the Nueces and Guadalupe Rivers. South of the Nueces, colonization efforts were even less fruitful. Native depredations in the Nueces strip, the perception of a wilderness environment, and an uncertain political alignment largely checked successful settlement of this zone (FIG. 3.4).

In Texas, the most successful Mexican *empresario* was Don Martín

De León, native of Burgos, Spain, and onetime permanent resident of Burgos, Tamaulipas. De León moved to San Antonio around 1800 and established a cattle ranch in the vicinity, the stock from which he drove to New Orleans and sold each year. In 1824 De León was authorized to transport forty-one colonists to a site on the lower Guadalupe River known as Cypress Grove, which he renamed Guadalupe Victoria after the president of Mexico (FIG. 3.4). Victoria was platted by J. M. J. Carvajal of San Antonio in the Mexican fashion, with a grid and large public plazas for municipal, ecclesiastical, and marketplace functions. The 30,000-acre Garcitas Creek ranch, situated in tall grass prairie near Matagorda Bay, was an economic mainstay of the colony, which totaled three hundred residents in 1834.[44]

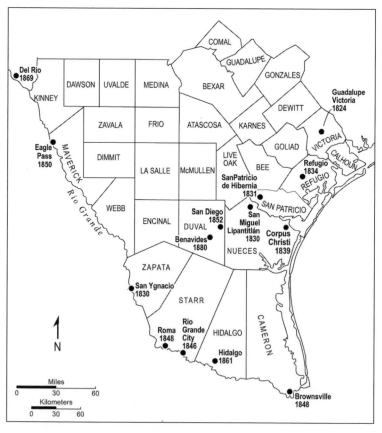

3.4. Towns founded by Mexicans and Mexican Americans, 1824–1880.

Two additional *empresario* colonies were planted north of the Nueces River, and each included Mexican as well as foreign settlers. In 1831 John McMullen and James McGloin, originally from Ireland and residents of Matamoros, were granted the right to settle a site known as Paso de Santa Margarita on the north bank of the Nueces.[45] This settlement came to be called San Patricio de Hibernia (FIG. 3.4). It was laid out in the typical Mexican manner of a grid focused on plazas, and by 1834 counted some six hundred residents.[46] In 1834, a second Irish Mexican colony was established at the Spanish mission site of Refugio on the San Antonio River upstream from La Bahía. This site had been abandoned during the 1820s and then reoccupied by various squatters, including several Irish families, before the principal colonization party arrived.[47]

In Tamaulipas, south of the Nueces, there were several ill-fated attempts to colonize, but only three new settlements proved successful, two in present-day South Texas.[48] On the south bank of the Nueces and situated where the Matamoros road crossed the river, Mexican general Manuel de Mier y Terán established San Miguel Lipantitlán in 1830, a garrison intended as defense against marauding Lipan Apache and to monitor smuggling at Corpus Christi Bay (FIG. 3.4). The settlement was short-lived and no permanent town resulted.[49] On the north bank of the Rio Grande between Laredo and Zapata, private settlers from Revilla (Guerrero) founded San Ygnacio in 1830 (FIG. 3.4) under the leadership of Don Jesús Treviño, a wealthy alderman who purchased land from the heirs of the Vásquez Borregos family.[50] San Ygnacio survived into the era before railroads as a ranching and freighting station connecting Corpus Christi with Monclova and Saltillo (see Chap. 6).

Easily the most successful town founded in the region was Matamoros in 1823, south of the Rio Grande in Tamaulipas at the site of the late-eighteenth-century mission Congregación del Refugio and facing what would become Brownsville north of the river in 1848 (FIG. 3.4). Before 1848, Matamoros was a central place for ranchers north of the Rio Grande and was visited for supplies as well as seasonally during the winter holidays. Matamoros and its Gulf port satellite of Bagdad would become a major pivot point for the Confederate cotton trade during the Civil War, and this notoriety attracted a substantial cosmopolitan population numbering perhaps fourteen thousand at its nineteenth-century apex.[51]

While towns were the principal nodes and largest concentrations of Mexican settlement in the South Texas region, ranchos were more numerous as individual homesteads, although the success of these varied by era. For example, in the first half of the nineteenth century, ranch economies and lifestyles suffered greatly as a result of civil conflict and native raiding.[52] In 1834, Almonte recorded only five thousand cattle and sheep for the entire Department of Bexar, which included the settlements of San Antonio, Victoria, San Patricio, Refugio, and Goliad (La Bahía).[53] After Santa Anna relinquished the Nueces strip in 1836, many Mexicans withdrew from the area to towns and ranches south of the Rio Grande. After 1848, however, ranches became reoccupied and the numbers of livestock, especially sheep and cattle, increased markedly.[54] By 1882, cattle were most densely concentrated in counties along the San Antonio River where grasses were abundant, while sheep came to dominate much of the trans-Nueces, a distinctively drier zone, particularly Webb, Encinal, Maverick, and Duval Counties (FIG. 3.5). A Mexican boundary commission report issued in 1875 counted 157 ranchos along the north side of the Rio Grande between San Felipe del Río (Del Rio after 1869) and the mouth of the river below Brownsville.[55]

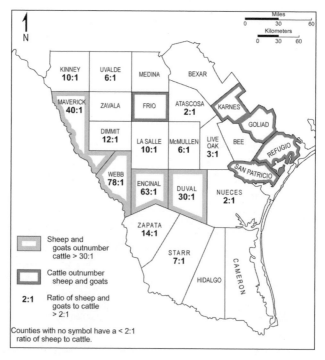

3.5. Sheep and goats versus cattle in South Texas, 1882.

MEXICAN AMERICAN TERRITORY

At the close of the nineteenth century, the population of South Texas was chiefly concentrated in two settled areas, which were predominantly Mexican American. These were the urban node of San Antonio (Bexar County), and a ten-county zone in deep South Texas that included Cameron, Hidalgo, Starr, Zapata, Webb, Encinal, Duval, Nueces, La Salle, and Maverick Counties.[56] Between 1850 and 1880, the population of Mexican Americans in these counties increased from 30,040 to 43,397, and in half of these counties over 90 percent of the population was Mexican American.[57] By comparison, the Mexican American population of San Antonio was 1,642 in 1850, some 46 percent of the city's population, but that percentage dropped to 41 percent in 1880, although the number of Mexican Americans grew to 8,425.[58]

These relative changes in population and the proportion of Mexican Americans suggest something of the geographic shift that occurred in the second half of the nineteenth century in the region. Mexican-origin populations continued to migrate to counties along the Rio Grande from Mexico, as well to interior counties of the region, but there was beginning to emerge a consequent Anglicizing of counties along the northern edge of South Texas, especially north of the Nueces River (FIG. 3.6). To the north and west of the river were Zavala, Frio, Medina, and McMullen counties, where the principal immigrant groups were southern Anglo Americans from Missouri, Arkansas, and Louisiana. Counties north and east of the river like Wilson, Karnes, Goliad, Victoria and part of Bee were being populated by immigrants from Alabama, Louisiana, and Arkansas.

Even in counties that persisted as predominantly Mexican American, Anglo American immigrants were significant in organizing new towns. Corpus Christi was founded as a trading center in 1839, before the Mexican War, and many of the river towns such as Rio Grande City, Roma, Brownsville, Eagle Pass, Hidalgo, and Del Rio date from near the end of the war or shortly thereafter (FIG. 3.4). All except Roma, Hidalgo, and Del Rio were first organized as federal forts.[59] Anglo Americans like Charles Stillman, Henry Clay Davis, and John Twohig were instrumental in founding these settlements, yet the towns remained chiefly Mexican American places where Spanish language and Mexican cultural ways and environments prevailed. John G. Bourke, certainly one of the region's most pointed

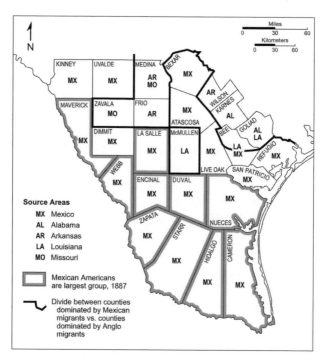

3.6. Sources of migrants to South Texas counties, 1865–1885.

observers, remarked in 1894 that the lower valley along the Rio Grande was terra incognita to the rest of the United States:

> Twice the waves of North American aggression have swept across this region, bearing down all in their path; but as the tempest abated the Mexican population placidly resumed its control of affairs and returned to its former habits of life, as if the North American had never existed.[60]

Interior settlements founded later, like San Diego and Benavides, established in 1852 and 1880 respectively, remained effectively Mexican American communities with small Anglo American and European minorities (FIG. 3.4).[61]

In the course of nearly two centuries, and especially since the middle of the eighteenth century, South Texas took shape as a Hispanic cultural region. The evolving course of this region over the most recent century will be charted in the next chapter.

The beginning of the twentieth century brought a renaissance to the Texas border, an awakening in every sense of the word. For nearly two hundred years the Texas-Mexicans had lived in the border counties, knowing very little and caring less of what was going on in the United States. They looked southward for all the necessities and pleasures of life. Mexican newspapers brought them news of the outside world, their children were educated in Mexican schools, Spanish was their language, Mexican currency was used altogether. When the Texas-Mexicans traveled, they went to Mexico; when the women yearned for finery, it was acquired across the river.   —JOVITA GONZALEZ, "AMERICA INVADES THE BORDER TOWNS," 1930

Homeland Forged

When the ranches were being rapidly cleared of brush and planted to cotton, and towns were springing up about 1910, Texas-Mexicans and Mexicans also came in from San Diego, Alice, Aguilares, Cotulla, Encinal, Laredo, Brownsville, and other places lying south and west of Nueces County. A very few Texas-Mexicans have come to Nueces County from central Texas and other points north, but in the main, the resident Mexican population has been built up by more or less continuous migration from the south and southeast whence the first Mexican settlers came.   —PAUL S. TAYLOR, AN AMERICAN-MEXICAN FRONTIER, 1934

In 2000 California and Texas were home to 13.4 million of the nation's 20.6 million people of Mexican heritage. Although the Golden State counted some 8.4 million Mexican Americans, 3.4 million more than Texas, California has only recently achieved its rank as the state with the greatest Mexican origin population. Before 1950, Texas was the undisputed demographic focus of Mexican Americans in the United States.

Despite the growth of the Mexican population in California, in only one county in that state are those with Mexican ancestry greater than half its population (FIG. 4.1). In neighboring Arizona and New Mexico, the number of counties that are predominantly Mexican is similarly few. Along the Texas border, by comparison, no less than thirty-two counties are more than 50 percent Mexican American, and in twenty of these more than 70 percent are of Mexican ancestry.[1] This proportional concentration of a single group over so vast a geographic area makes the Texas borderland the largest ethnic subregion in the United States, a veritable Mexican American rimland enclave along the south-central border.

The southern extent of this rimland contains a subregion of thirty-two counties that is the demographic homeland of Texas Mexicans or

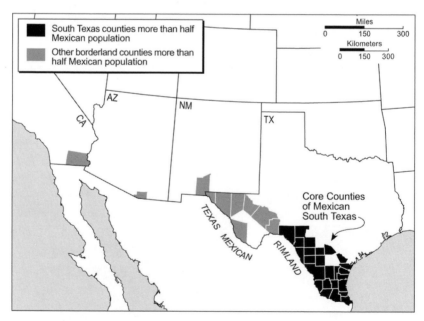

4.1. Texas Mexican rimland. South Texas is the state's largest ethnic subregion and has the highest concentration of Mexican Americans along the borderland.

Tejanos, as many today call themselves. How and why did this area come to be dominated by Texas Mexicans? In this chapter I examine the spatial spread of Texas Mexicans from the early to late twentieth century, and assess the process of population expansion in the region over nearly a century of growth. This examination proceeds by a study of four demographic cross sections: 1910, 1930, 1950, and 1990. In each, I chart the geographic growth and distribution of Texas Mexicans by counties. This chapter presents a geographical understanding across time of core and periphery influences in the subregion.

EXPANSION AND LAND USE CHANGE: 1910

Between 1887 and 1910 the population of Texas nearly doubled. Yet the number of Texas Mexicans nearly tripled, approaching one-quarter million. More than half of all Texas Mexicans in 1910 resided in South Texas counties, where they represented 37 percent of the region's population (TABLE 4.1).

Until 1909, only a nominal number of Mexican immigrants came

TABLE 4.1 Texas Mexican Population Changes

DATE	TEXAS	TEXAS MEXICAN	PERCENT TEXAS MEXICAN	SOUTH TEXAS[a] MEXICAN	PERCENT SOUTH TEXAS[a] MEXICAN
1910	3,896,542	232,920	6	135,232	37
1930	5,824,715	683,681	12	371,486	46
1950	7,711,194	1,027,455	13	669,898	49
1990	16,986,510	3,890,820	23	1,741,685	71

SOURCES: *1910:* U.S. Bureau of the Census, *Thirteenth Census of the United States, Abstract of the Census with Supplement for Texas,* Table 5, Foreign White Stock by Nativity, 1910, and Foreign Born, 1910. *1930:* U.S. Bureau of the Census, *Fifteenth Census of the United States: 1930,* Table 17, Population—Texas Composition and Characteristics, 1014–1015. *1950:* U.S. Bureau of the Census, *1950 U.S. Census of Population, Special Reports, Persons of Spanish Surname,* Table 7, Citizenship and Country of Birth of White Persons of Spanish Surname, for Counties and Urban Places of 10,000 or More in Selected Southwestern States: 1950. *1990:* U.S. Bureau of the Census, *1990 Census of Population, General Population Characteristics, Texas,* Table 4, Race and Hispanic Origin: 1990.

[a]South Texas included thirty-two counties in 1990: Atascosa, Bee, Bexar, Brooks, Cameron, Dimmit, Duval, Frio, Goliad, Hidalgo, Jim Hogg, Jim Wells, Karnes, Kenedy, Kinney, Kleberg, La Salle, Live Oak, McMullen, Maverick, Medina, Nueces, Refugio, San Patricio, Starr, Uvalde, Val Verde, Webb, Willacy, Wilson, Zapata, Zavala. In 1910, the region consisted of 26 counties because Brooks, Jim Hogg, Jim Wells, Kenedy, Kleberg and Willacy were carved out of Nueces, Starr, Hidalgo, and Cameron Counties.

to the United States, but the Mexican Revolution in 1909-1910 changed this abruptly, and Texas quickly became the major recipient of Mexican immigrants.[2] Push factors like the revolution in Mexico evolved at the same time pull factors developed like the rise of farming economies in South and Central Texas. For example, during the 1880s cotton cultivation expanded in northern Mexico, especially in Torreón, Coahuila, the so-called La Laguna district, and in Central Texas cotton moved especially into the string of counties stretching between San Antonio and Dallas.[3] By the 1890s Mexican laborers from La Laguna began to migrate into Central Texas as the cotton crop matured.[4] Most of this workforce, however, returned to Mexico at the close of the harvest. As a result, the geography of Texas Mexicans in South Texas changed little, although the density and concentration increased with growth. The only serious advance occurred along the northwest periphery of the region.

The 1910 map of the Mexican population in South Texas counties shows an increase in the concentration of stronghold (greater than 70 percent) counties, where impress of the subculture, compared to 1887, became substantial (FIG. 4.2).[5] By 1910, a concentration of eight stronghold counties stretched from the towns of Eagle Pass to Brownsville along the Rio Grande, and pushed northeast to Cotulla in La Salle County on the north bank of the Nueces River. Dimmit and Frio Counties, where the Mexican population was insignificant in 1887, became in 1910 part of a Mexican South Texas domain where the subculture dominated the area, albeit with less intensity than in stronghold counties. All other counties of the region were significantly less Mexican—below 25 percent except for Zavala, which registered 27 percent Mexican in 1910.

Geographer Robert Spillman speculates that the Mexican population increases in these peripheral counties, as well as in La Salle and eastern Webb Counties, may have been spurred by the construction of the International and Great Northern Railroad that connected San Antonio to Laredo in 1882. His map of population distribution clusters for 1910 reveals a striking alignment with the railroad corridor, especially around the settlements of Pearsall, Dilley, Cotulla, and Encinal.[6] A contemporary account of the Mexican quarter in the latter town imparts something of the shantytown flavor of that place, as reported in 1897.

> Not far from where the Old Comanche Trail crosses the Nueces lies the little town of Encinal in Western Texas, county of La Salle, upon the International and Great Northern Railway track ... Across

the creek straggled the quarter of Mexicans known as Chihuahua. Entering its purlieus, one came upon another world. The houses either made of adobes, or else mere huts, a cross between an Indian "wickey-up" and a Mexican Jacal, were made as nests of prairie dogs are made, of everything that came to hand. Kerosene-tins and hides, sides of stage-coaches, ends of railway cars, with all the wreckage of a prairie town, were used in their make-up.[7]

The railroad, however, cannot explain the growth of the Mexican populations in neighboring Dimmit and Zavala Counties, which were not tied to the International and Great Northern Railroad. Rather, towns like Crystal City, Carrizo Springs, Asherton, and Catarina were chiefly farming towns founded by Anglo immigrants. These communities succeeded because of artesian wells tapped to provide irrigation for the cultivation of onions and other vegetable crops, for which Mexican workers

4.2. Texas Mexicans, 1910.

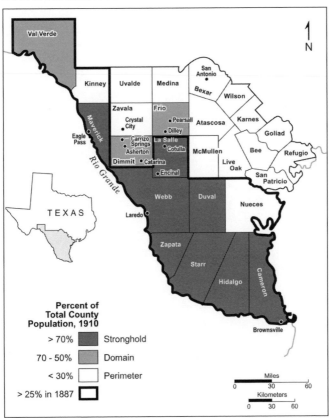

4.3. Texas Mexican workers, Cotulla, Texas, around 1907.

were the critical labor supply that planted, maintained, and harvested (FIG. 4.3).[8]

Val Verde County in the northwest corner of South Texas was greater than 25 percent Mexican in 1887, in part because the Southern Pacific Railroad brought in Mexican railroad workers as it passed through Del Rio on its way east to San Antonio in 1878. By 1910, the county was part of a Texas Mexican domain on par with Frio and Dimmit. Agricultural production and service—particularly irrigated corn farming and Del Rio's role as a center for the sheep- and goat-ranching economy of the Edwards Plateau lands—were significant factors in attracting Mexican labor to the area.[9]

Nueces County was the only county in South Texas in which the proportion of Mexicans declined between 1887 and 1910. In 1887 more than half the county was Mexican, but this condition reversed dramatically when the county population doubled to almost 22,000 between 1900–1910, causing the proportion of Mexicans to fall to only 13 percent. The infusion of Anglos into Nueces County spurred a frenzy of platting subdivisions and founding towns, including the farming settlements of Robstown (1907), Agua Dulce (1907), Clarkwood (1909), Bishop (1910), Driscoll (1910), and Calallen (1910).[10]

In 1910 the leading edge of Mexican South Texas had not moved much farther north than the divide that existed in 1887 (FIG. 4.2). Mexicans had encroached into Dimmit, Zavala, and Frio, but an array of fifteen counties from Kinney to Bexar to Refugio was still predominately Anglo with Mexican minorities.

The land use change emerging in South Texas during this transi-

tion era, especially the incursion of farming into what had been principally a ranching region, signaled the economic transformation that was
underway (FIG. 4.4). Only the Rio Grande counties of Maverick, Zapata,
Starr, and Cameron were ranch counties by 1910, where more than
60 percent of their lands were in ranches. Bexar and Karnes Counties
along the northern edge of the region following the San Antonio River
were steadfastly farm counties, with greater than 90 percent of their lands
in this use. Even Nueces River counties like La Salle and Nueces had
become predominately farmland, with more than 95 percent of their
lands under cultivation by 1910. Most of the counties in the region had
mixed farming and ranching economies.

The consequence of this change from ranching to farming altered
the population geography of the region in profound ways. Mexicans increased in absolute numbers throughout the region, yet increasingly they
became an underclass of workers without political clout. Anglo farmers
came to dominate the South Texas regional economy, and the growing

4.4. Farm and ranch counties in South Texas, 1910.

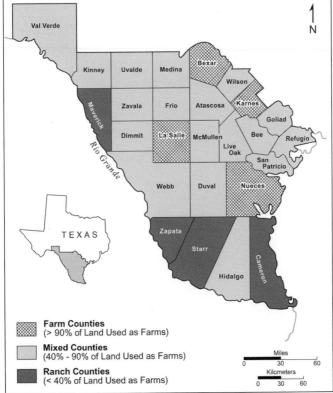

number of non-Hispanic immigrants to the region, combined with the onset of the Great Depression, changed the proportion of Mexicans to Anglos in several core counties.

EBB TIDE OF THE IMMIGRANT WAVE: 1930

Between 1910 and 1930, the population of Texas grew by 67 percent. While the Mexican population increased by only one-half of that percentage, Mexicans doubled as a percent of all Texans. In South Texas, however, the Mexican population nearly tripled from two decades earlier and the percentage of Mexicans in this region represented almost half of all Texas Mexicans (TABLE 4.1).

In the decades before 1930, Mexican immigration to the United States and to Texas peaked, although the proportion of Mexican immigrants to the state dipped slightly as migrants redistributed to other border states and as a result of deportations and repatriations during the early years of the Great Depression.[11] Max Sylvius Handman described the Mexicans in Texas to a national conference of social workers in 1926. He outlined three groups: an elite immigrant population of chiefly political refugees; the Texas Mexicans or "Texanos" who were descendants of earlier Mexican immigrants to Texas; and the Mexican "casual laborers" who were the largest proportion of the most recent immigrants. Handman declared Texas to be "the corridor and clearing house for the majority of the Mexican casuals who are distributed over the country."[12] In fact, Texas, especially San Antonio, became the primary node for Mexican labor into the Central Plains, as well as throughout Texas.[13] In 1930 the Mexican stock population of Texas (foreign-born and native-born combined) totaled 46 percent of all Mexicans counted in the United States; California's share of this population was 29 percent. In that same year, the Mexico-born population in Texas reached a new record for the century: it represented 74 percent of the total Texas foreign-born population.[14]

The largest numbers of Mexican immigrants to the United States during the 1910–1930 period came from a central Mexico sending region, especially the states of Michoacán, Guanajuato, and Jalisco.[15] However, the majority of immigrants to South Texas came directly from neighboring states like Nuevo León, Coahuila, and Tamaulipas (FIG. 4.5). In Zavala, Maverick, and Val Verde Counties, for example, an average of greater than three-fourths of the Mexico-born birth parent population hailed from Coahuila, while in Zapata, Jim Hogg, and Starr Counties more than two-thirds de-

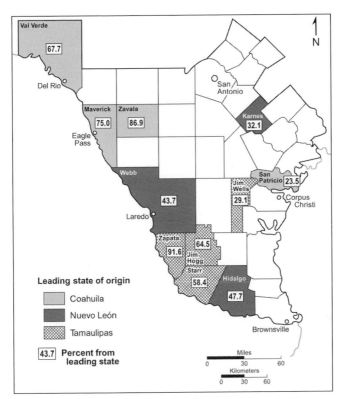

4.5. Mexico-born birth parent populations in South Texas, 1930.

rived from Tamaulipas. The generally higher values for those counties near-est the border reinforce the importance of a hinterland effect. For counties farther removed from the border, like Karnes, San Patricio, and Jim Wells, the lower birth parent counts point to the greater plurality of source states with greater distance from the international boundary. In Jim Wells County, one in five of the immigrants came from Guanajuato, while in San Patricio County one in six came from San Luis Potosí; both of these states are in north central Mexico and each is some distance from the border.[16]

The persistence of ranching in selected counties and expansion of farming in South Texas became major pull factors for Mexican immi-grant labor.[17] Based on the value of crop and stock production, South Texas counties were still decidedly rural economies during this era. After 1920 when farming increasingly displaced ranching in the region, winter truck crops, summer cotton, and citrus cultivation came to dominate the best lands.[18] Much land became cultivable between 1911 and 1931 when irrigation expanded in the Lower Rio Grande Valley alone from 53,100 to 257,800 acres.[19]

The map of Mexican percentages by county in South Texas is filled in considerably by 1930 (FIG. 4.6). The heretofore northern fringe counties from Kinney to Bexar to Refugio, as well as the cluster of eight counties between Atascosa and Kleberg, were now firmly part of a perimeter of Mexican South Texas; greater than one-quarter (but less than one-half) of each county was of Mexican origin. Karnes, San Patricio, and Jim Wells were now clearly counties of the domain, with greater than half their populations Mexican. This advance north is the result of a push of cotton cultivation into these counties and the consequent draw of Mexican labor. In 1929, Uvalde, McMullen, San Patricio, Refugio, Jim Wells, Kleberg, and Nueces Counties each registered cotton production where none had existed two decades previously.[20] The spread of cotton to Central Texas allowed six counties beyond the historic San Antonio River border to become part of an outland or far periphery in 1930. These included Comal, Hays, Guadalupe, and Caldwell along the blackland prairie corridor northeast of San Antonio, and DeWitt and Victoria along the coastal plain east of Karnes and Goliad Counties.[21] In Nueces County, Paul Taylor found that the rise of cotton culture directly correlated with the growth of the Mexican population. In 1910, when the Mexican population was 2,828, Nueces County produced only 8,566 bales. In 1930, cotton production climbed to 148,442 bales, a 577 percent increase, and the Mexican population rocketed to 23,276, a 1,215 percent increase from 1910.[22]

In what had been a core of stronghold counties in 1910, there was now considerable shuffle, with both expansion and erosion. In the northwest, Zavala and Dimmit Counties became strongholds. Farther south, Cameron, Hidalgo, Zapata, and Duval, as well as the new counties carved out of this cone of South Texas after 1911, represent a new domain and perimeter with lower concentrations by 1930. Kenedy County, which was created from parts of old Cameron and Nueces Counties, remained a stronghold outlier focused on the ranching empire of the King family.[23] Along the Rio Grande, Maverick, Webb, and Starr Counties persisted as stronghold parts of the 1910 distribution (FIG. 4.6).

The change from stronghold to domain and perimeter for these counties is somewhat deceiving, because the absolute population of Mexicans actually increased for each of these units between 1910 and 1930.[24] County boundaries and Anglo immigration changed, however. Cameron County, for example, became reduced to three separate counties, and only the northern portion configured as Kenedy County persisted as a ranching hearth with an overwhelmingly Mexican population. In the south, Willacy County

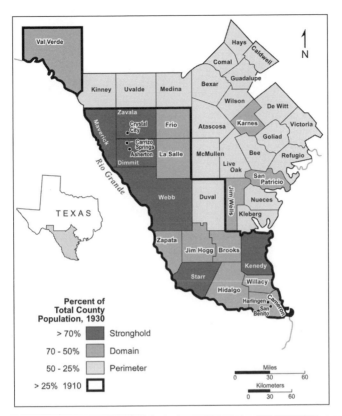

4.6. Texas Mexicans, 1930.

and the new Cameron County were largely invaded by Anglos between 1910 and 1930, many of whom gravitated to new towns like Harlingen (1904), San Benito (1904), and Raymondville (1903), as well as to Brownsville. These communities and others benefited from the introduction of irrigation agriculture and proximity to the Missouri Pacific, St. Louis, Brownsville, and Mexico Railroads. Successful farming and access to rail for export fostered a boom during the first two decades of the century.[25]

This concentration of Mexicans in towns, however, belied the rural nature of the economy in South Texas during this period. This was especially true in Dimmit County and neighboring Zavala County, heart of the so-called Winter Garden district, where farmers grew winter vegetables for the north and northeast United States. Paul Taylor noted in 1929 that the distribution of the Mexican population was determined principally by the location of irrigated crops because they created a demand for labor. Towns like Asherton, Carrizo Springs, and Crystal City whose populations were predominantly Mexican were "fluid reservoirs

of agricultural laborers who ride out in the morning on trucks in what-
ever direction their work may lie on that day."[26]

MIGRANT CYCLES: 1950

The population of Texas grew by almost 2 million between 1930 and
1950. The number of Texas Mexicans surpassed 1 million, growing 67
percent in two decades, although the Texas Mexican percentage statewide grew only slightly during this same interval. The number of Texas
Mexicans concentrated in South Texas counties increased to almost half
the region's population, a total nearly equal to the number of Texas Mexicans in the entire state in 1930 (TABLE 4.1).

The subregional concentrations of Texas Mexicans changed slightly
between 1930 and 1950. As in 1910, there were chiefly stronghold counties where the Texas Mexican concentration was greatest along the Rio
Grande (FIG. 4.7). Two zones of counties, a domain and a perimeter with
lower concentrations of Texas Mexicans, respectively, were situated inland from the Rio Grande up to the historic San Antonio River border.
Some counties in the subregion lost Texas Mexicans during this era. In
part this reflected the shift in Texas cotton culture toward the Panhandle
and away from the south and central parts of the state.[27] This shift is
illustrated by the decline in the percentage Mexican to less than 25 percent in Nueces, Kleberg, and Karnes Counties, which had been vital
cotton districts just two decades previously (FIG. 4.7).

This changing distribution is explained in part by shifting populations as well as the economy. While the number of Mexico-born persons
in Texas reached a peak in 1930, this total declined as a proportion of
other foreign-born Texans between 1930 and 1950.[28] Counties that maintained significant percentages of populations born in Mexico were those
along the Rio Grande, especially those next to a large Mexican border
city; for example, Maverick—Piedras Negras, Hidalgo—Reynosa,
Cameron—Matamoros, and Webb—Nuevo Laredo (FIG. 4.8). Mexican
border cities were staging areas for Mexican immigrants to the United
States from the 1940s and 1950s as migrant worker programs gained popularity.[29] Other inland counties such as Zavala, Dimmit, and Willacy persisted as farming areas, and Mexican labor demand remained high. As a
result, Mexico-born population percentages were greater in these counties than in most other parts of the subregion (FIG. 4.8).

By 1950 almost 30 percent of employment in sixteen selected South

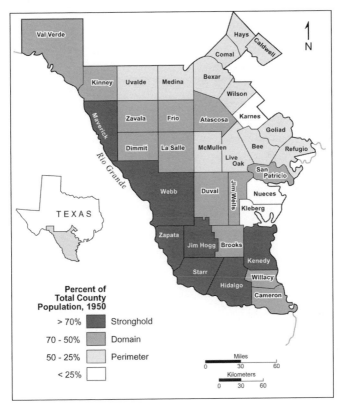

4.7. Texas Mexicans, 1950.

Texas counties was farm labor. Migration was a way of life for South Texas Mexicans, who moved with crops and season from vegetable harvests in the Winter Garden to cotton in the Texas Panhandle. Some ventured on to Montana, Colorado, and Michigan for sugar beets and then back to Texas, with stopovers in Denver and San Antonio.[30] In 1942 Carey McWilliams described the Texas portion of this circle of migration and labor as the "the big swing."

> "The big swing" of workers in the cotton harvest starts in the southern part of the state in June or July. From there it sweeps eastward through the coastal counties and then turns west for the central portions of the state. After the cotton has been picked in central Texas, the army splits into three units: one moves into east Texas; another proceeds to the Red River country; and a third treks westward to the San Angelo–Lubbock area. Most of the migrants who make the entire circle are Mexicans from the southern counties of

the state. They tend to move west, rather than north, and skirt the old plantation area in which most of the Negro labor is concentrated. From the West Plains area, in late November or December, the movement doubles back toward the southern counties for winter vegetables and produce crops. The migration pattern may be likened to an imperfect circle, a circle that is somewhat flattened out and that bulges toward the west. It is this pattern which is referred to in Texas as "the big swing."[31]

The 1940s in South Texas may represent a transition period in which Mexican emigrants begin to arrive from distant interior locations, away from the northeast border-states identified as primary source areas in 1930. A 1950 survey of 2,364 Mexican aliens deported through the Hidalgo, Texas, office of the U.S. Immigration and Naturalization Service found that 36 percent came from Nuevo León, Coahuila, and Tamaulipas. Some 60 percent hailed from central Mexico sending states, including Guanajuato, San Luis Potosí, Jalisco, Michoacán, Zacatecas, Durango, and Aguascalientes.[32]

4.8. Mexico-born populations in South Texas, 1950.

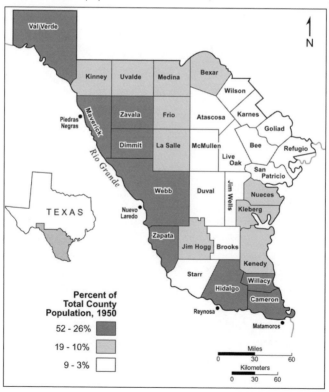

A separate survey performed at the McAllen detention center in the same year asked 160 deported Mexican aliens from Texas how many times they had entered the United States, by which mode of transportation from residence to the border, and the method used to cross into Texas. Over half of the respondents had entered on multiple occasions and most had traveled by bus to the border. However, once on the Mexican side of the border, some 82 percent indicated that they waded or swam across the Rio Grande into the United States, explaining why Texans during this era were wont to refer to Mexican immigrants as "wetbacks."[33]

While it has been assumed that much of this labor was drawn to South Texas for crop harvests and field work in cotton, citrus, and vegetables, there was a considerable industrial component to this agriculture as well, what Carey McWilliams called "factories in the fields." In the Lower Rio Grande Valley alone in 1950, there were some three hundred fruit and vegetable packing plants, which, by virtue of a special ruling that classed them as agricultural, were thereby able to hire those from Mexico without regard to the provisions of the federal minimum wage law.[34]

One important geographical consequence of the immigrant Mexican labor presence in the Valley was that it prompted many Texas Mexicans to seek farm labor employment away from the border counties and out of Texas, where wages were generally higher than those paid to Mexican labor in South Texas. In 1946, Pauline Kibbe described this cycle of migrant labor in the state, referring to the Texas Mexicans as "Latin Americans" to distinguish them from the immigrant Mexican population.[35]

In addition to the Lower Rio Grande Valley, the Texas Winter Garden district—centered at Crystal City and encompassing Zavala and Dimmit and parts of Maverick, Webb, La Salle, and Frio Counties—still represented an important concentration of Texas Mexican migrant labor. A 1941 Works Progress Administration study of three hundred Texas Mexican families found that more than 90 percent worked in spinach during the winter harvest for this crop, between November and March, before moving on to other areas and harvests.

When all the spinach was cut and shipped, nineteen out of twenty families migrated north or east to work other crops. Almost a third got in a few weeks' work in the Texas cotton harvest before going on to beets or cotton elsewhere. Over 60 percent of the families worked in the sugarbeet fields throughout an area extending from Michigan to Montana. A third of all the family groups worked at picking cotton from July until late autumn. Almost half of this latter group also found work chopping cotton before the picking season started.[36]

Unlike migrant Mexican labor in the Valley, which was typically too poor to afford its own transportation, Texas Mexican migrants usually traveled in their own cars and trucks, although some were transported out of state by labor contractors.[37]

A final theater of Texas Mexican migrant labor of this era was that associated with sheep and goat shearing, an activity that dates to the nineteenth century in the region. Although shearing machines had replaced hand shears as early as World War I, the labor in this economy was still Texas Mexican. Val Verde and Uvalde Counties were the centers of this industry, which serviced a sheep- and goat-raising area that spread into adjoining counties of the Edwards Plateau. Most shearers resided in Uvalde, Del Rio, and San Angelo. The shearing season rotated south to north and back. Sheep and goat shearers in counties below the Edwards Plateau typically clipped first in March. By April, crews traveled north and west into the plateau counties, north as far as Bosque and west as far as Upton, completing the cycle by May and June. In September workers repeated the process for goats and then for sheep until late December. Unlike Texas Mexican migrant workers who typically traveled as families, sheep and goat shearing was traditionally a male enterprise organized by a *capitán* or headman who owned the necessary shearing machines and trucks and contracted with ranchers to perform the work. Crew sizes varied from five to sixteen. At the end of the clipping season, the crew would continue under contract for the *capitán*, in fence building, prickly pear grubbing, cedar chopping, and other ranch work. Because sheep and goat workers were skilled laborers who had established themselves within the region's ranching economy before the great immigrant waves from Mexico commenced in the early twentieth century, these migrants were generally better paid and enjoyed a certain degree of acceptance in the community.[38]

TEXAS MEXICAN HOMELAND: 1990

Texas' population more than doubled between 1950 and 1990. The Texas Mexican population nearly quadrupled in the same period, so that nearly one of every four Texans was of Mexican ancestry. In South Texas, where close to half of all Texas Mexicans resided, 71 percent of the region's population was Texas Mexican, giving the area the most extensive regional concentration of Mexican Americans in the United States (TABLE 4.1).

A stronghold of seventeen counties, which were part of a thirty-two-county South Texas Mexican homeland in 1990, constituted a nearly contiguous territory from Del Rio to Brownsville along the Rio Grande, with interior points at Frio, Jim Wells, and Kenedy Counties (FIG. 4.9). In four of these stronghold counties, the Mexican-origin population was greater than 90 percent, while in eight others it registered between 81 and 89 percent in 1990 (TABLE 4.2).

Seven counties from Kinney to Atascosa to Kleberg were part of a narrow domain of Mexican South Texas in 1990. Eight additional counties stretching from Menard through Bexar and southeast along the San Antonio River divide to Refugio, as well as two inliers—Live Oak and

TABLE 4.2 Stronghold Counties of Mexican South Texas

COUNTY	POPULATION	MEXICAN	PERCENT MEXICAN
Starr	40,518	39,390	97.2
Webb	133,239	125,069	93.8
Maverick	36,378	34,024	93.5
Jim Hogg	5,109	4,659	91.1
Zavala	12,162	10,875	89.4
Brooks	8,204	7,338	89.4
Duval	12,918	11,267	87.2
Hidalgo	383,545	326,972	85.2
Willacy	17,705	14,937	84.3
Dimmit	10,433	8,688	83.2
Cameron	260,120	212,995	81.8
Zapata	9,279	7,519	81.0
Kenedy	460	362	78.6
La Salle	5,254	4,068	77.4
Frio	13,472	9,749	72.3
Jim Wells	37,679	27,201	72.1
Val Verde	38,721	27,299	70.5
TOTAL	1,025,196	872,412	85.0

SOURCE: U.S. Bureau of the Census, *1990 Census of Population and Housing, Texas.*

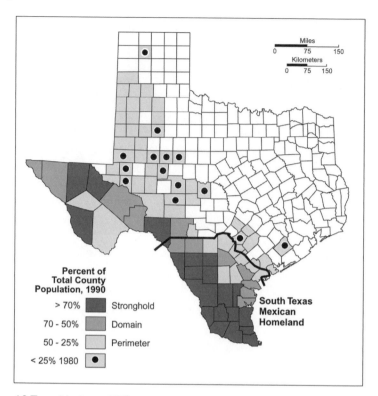

4.9. Texas Mexicans, 1990.

McMullen—were counties of the subregion's perimeter (FIG. 4.9). Bexar County, focused on San Antonio, was just less than 50 percent Mexican and therefore mapped as part of this perimeter in 1990. However, it alone included almost 600,000 Mexican Americans, the largest single county concentration in the entire South Texas region and testimony to the rapid urbanization of Texas Mexicans since 1950. At the low end, McMullen County, which called itself "The Free State," a kind of non-Hispanic outpost along the entrenched stronghold front of Mexican-dominated counties, counted a mere 320 Texas Mexicans in 1990.[39]

The Mexico-born population of South Texas in 1990 was particularly concentrated, not only in the most populated counties like Bexar, but also in counties along the border like Cameron, Hidalgo, and Webb, each with a major urban core—Brownsville, McAllen, and Laredo, respectively (FIG. 4.10). An important change that occurred in Mexican immigration to Texas and to the borderlands and nation in general between 1950 and 1990 was the greater attraction of labor to service sector employment in urban and suburban centers.[40]

Northeast of the San Antonio River divide seven counties, six contiguous to the South Texas Mexican homeland and one outlier, represented an extended outland in 1990 (FIG. 4.9). These included the blackland prairie counties of Caldwell and Hays that were outland concentrations in 1950, plus two additional nearby counties, Guadalupe and Gonzales. Along the lower coastal plain, Victoria and Calhoun Counties, as well as Wharton County on the southwestern edge of metropolitan Houston, were counties of the outland. Most of these counties represented farming, ranching, and small town subareas, with Victoria the only metropolitan center and Wharton a suburban outreach.

Precisely what contributed most to the Mexican population growth in these counties is not clear. A recent survey for an eighty-eight county zone, stretching from Odessa in West Texas to Waco in North Central Texas and including South Texas, concluded that undocumented Mexican aliens

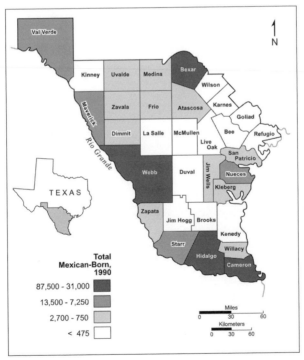

4.10. Mexico-born populations in South Texas, 1990.

here came chiefly from Guanajuato, San Luis Potosí, Zacatecas, and Durango—Mexican states distant from the northeast border states sending undocumented aliens identified in 1930. The study also noted that towns and cities along the urban axis between San Antonio and Waco had become an increasingly important migrant corridor, especially smaller outlying communities where immigrants are "well integrated into the society and unrecognizable from resident Mexican Americans."[41]

To the northwest, along the West Texas edge of the Texas Mexican rimland, long-standing Mexican populations in many counties have become more concentrated. The most remarkable growth, however, has been in counties of the Trans-Pecos and northern Panhandle; thirty-eight had Mexican populations greater than 25 percent in 1990, while only two of these did in 1950 (FIG. 4.9). Part of this transformation resulted from the expansion of cotton cultivation into the Panhandle counties during the 1950s and 1960s, but the more recent intensification may be the result of service sector employment demand in the region's small towns, as well as population growth in places.[42] At present, however, because a detailed study of the population origins of Mexicans in this region is lacking, we do not know if this represents a geographical periphery of Mexican South Texas or a region populated chiefly by generations of migrants from the interior of Mexico. It has been asserted, for example, that Texas Mexicans of West Texas are culturally and historically distinctive and not directly related to Texas Mexicans of South Texas.[43]

EPILOGUE

The South Texas Mexican homeland is a thirty-two county area larger than the state of Pennsylvania where Texas Mexicans hold sheer demographic dominance. This subregion of Texas consists of a stronghold where Texas Mexicans exceed 70 percent of the population, a domain where they are greater than half the population, and a perimeter where Texas Mexicans are more than one-quarter of the population. The homeland may be spreading northeast into an outland of seven discontiguous counties along the Texas coastal plain between San Antonio and Houston.

The homeland supports a Texas Mexican subgroup that is culturally distinctive and geographically separate from other Mexican American subregions of the borderland. In Chapter 5, I turn to a closer inspection of the geography of Texas Mexican spaces, the places that have sheltered and can be called home to these populations.

New Lots is a city bisected by the railway of the Missouri Pacific. In 1921, the town's first year, the north side of the tracks was allocated by municipal ordinance to the residences and business establishments of Mexican-Americans, and to industrial complexes. Mexican Americans refer to the north side of the tracks as Mexiquito, *el pueblo mexicano*, *nuestro lado*; even the traffic light north of the tracks is referred to as *la luz mexicana*. The other side of the tracks is spoken of as *el lado americano*, *el pueblo americano*, and other similar terms. Those who live south of the tracks also distinguish the two sides: "this side" and "the other side," "our side," and "their side," and "Mexican town" are all descriptive terms heard in the city of New Lots.

—ARTHUR J. RUBEL, *ACROSS THE TRACKS: MEXICAN AMERICANS IN A TEXAS CITY*, 1966

Texas Mexican Spaces

The word *settlement* encompasses all human-made arrangements that result from the process of living in space.[1] In South Texas, lived spaces can include a ranch, a town, or a suburb of a city, among others. The cultural landscape is the artificially built and modified environment humans create, remaking nature to suit our needs and wants.[2] The function and form of a lived space, as well as its landscape, are expressions of cultural difference. Beyond group tradition, social institutions and political will can shape lived spaces. As described above for a town in the Lower Rio Grande Valley, segregation has been a common fact of life for Texas Mexicans since the creation of Anglo American settlements in the region. As a consequence, Texas Mexican communities that exist side by side with

Anglo Texan communities have developed separate land uses and social spaces, and in some cases are enclave towns within towns.

In South Texas, three lived spaces and their landscapes have been especially significant indicators of Mexican cultural tradition and thus Texas Mexican identity: the rancho, the plaza, and the barrio and colonia. This chapter examines these spaces, especially their historical evolution, geographical distribution, and landscape character in Mexican South Texas.

RANCHO

The rancho was a fundamental settlement form carried to South Texas and to much of the borderland area by Spanish and Mexican colonizers. The Spanish word *rancho* means a mess, or food served to a group of people. In Mexico, *rancho* and *ranchería* are used to refer to a stock farm or a group of huts, and thus the words connote a lived space.[3]

In South Texas, the rancho was typically, but not exclusively, a settlement based upon the maintenance of livestock—horses, cattle, sheep, and goats—and was a dispersed form found outside of, but not too distant from, towns. In fact, until the late nineteenth century when native raiding in the region diminished, most viable ranchos north of the Rio Grande were located near towns for protection, including settlements like Reynosa and Camargo south of the river. At one time in the 1840s, only seven of forty-seven ranchos in the vicinity of Laredo were occupied, because of Apache hostilities.[4]

This explains a common misconception about the geography of early rancho settlement in South Texas. While historical maps display the boundaries of dozens of land grants within the region, a land grant on paper did not always equate to a viable settlement or rancho.[5] Before the late-nineteenth-century introduction of the windmill, which facilitated deep wells, access to water for cattle and sheep was a critical determinant of rancho geography. The location of springs often predicted the placement of a rancho headquarters like Los Ojuelos and Las Albercas in present Webb County.[6] Other ranchos were situated along the Rio Grande and *porciones*, long-lot land grants, gave access to precious water for livestock, not for cultivation.[7] A map of rancho cemeteries in Hidalgo County illustrates this pattern (FIG. 5.1). Because private cemeteries were common features of ranchos, their distribution mirrors the geography of rancho headquarters. Twenty-eight of sixty-one historic ranchos in Hidalgo County were concentrated along the Rio Grande and nineteen others

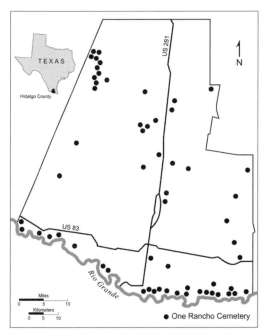

5.1. Hidalgo County ranchos.

were clustered in the north of the county, where springs are plentiful and groundwater is easily accessible.

Many South Texas communities like Laredo, San Ygnacio, and Rio Grande City were early rancho headquarters for land grants north of the river.[8] The conversion process that resulted in some Texas Mexican ranchos becoming small towns is illustrated in Starr County. In the mid-nineteenth century, 91 percent of the ranches in Starr County (373 of 408) were owned by Texas Mexicans, including Rancho San Isidro located in the northeast corner of the county.[9] Rancho San Isidro was created from an 1836 land grant to Gregorio Vela by the State of Tamaulipas. In 1877, the ranch seat was established at the site of Old San Isidro, near the present town. By 1892 when many small Texas Mexican ranchos began to be sold, San Isidro's lands were subdivided into town plots, giving rise to communities like Santa Elena and La Gloria that are proximate to San Isidro today.[10] El Sauz, a small village near the center of Starr County, also emerged from a rancho. Today, the sleepy hamlet includes a few hundred folk and is populated by four principal families descendent from the rancho: Pérez, Garza, Villareal, and Reséndez.[11]

In colonial Mexico, the word *hacienda*, a rural estate, did not become current until the eighteenth century.[12] In northeast Mexico, an hacienda was a landed estate and the owners of these properties were called *hacendados*.[13] The term *hacienda* does not appear to have gained wide currency in South Texas, although the first livestock estate created in the region—Nuestra Señora de Dolores—was formally called an hacienda.[14] In South Texas, the word *rancho* prevailed as the common term for a livestock estate, large or small. Nevertheless, as in Mexico, the rancho in South Texas mirrored a social order that comprised a landowning class and a laborer class.

On South Texas ranchos the landowning class was symbolized by the *patrón*, the near equivalent to the Mexican *hacendado* or master of the estate. The laboring class was epitomized by the *peón*, a laborer who performed work on the ranch, or a vaquero, a cowboy who managed livestock. This relationship was both a boss–worker arrangement and a social contract where the *patrón* counseled and protected his *peones*.[15] Perhaps the most celebrated surviving example of this social contract in the South Texas region is the vaqueros of the King Ranch known as "los kineños," the King people.[16]

Rancho living space mimicked social structure. The *patrón* and his family lived in a *casa grande* or *casa mayor*, a big house typically rectangular, flat-roofed, and constructed of cut sandstone or caliche block called *sillar*. Separate and usually some distance from the big house were the jacales of *peones* and vaqueros, typically made of unhewn wood and thatch.[17] As the *patrón* family extended, additional *casas mayores* would be constructed, as happened at the Randado ranch compound in Jim Hogg County around 1900.[18] On rare occasion, the ranch compound might become a wall-enclosed space in which linked rooms in an L-shape surrounded an open courtyard like that at Rancho San Ygnacio in Zapata County.[19]

The built environment of rancho compounds might include other elements: a *noria* or hand-dug, stone-lined well; a small church for visiting priests and services; a family cemetery and one for workers; a small store that supplied provisions to *peones*; various storage sheds; a *corral de leña* or livestock enclosure made of mesquite logs; and a stock tank behind an earthen *presa* or dam.[20]

Elena Zamora O'Shea recalls rancho life and the lived spaces typical of this settlement type in South Texas during the 1930s:

> The ranches were far apart, sometimes twenty and thirty miles between settlements. The rancher and his family depended on them-

selves for support, entertainment, and aid. Each settlement had a well dug for its water supply, and had a *pila* (stone and mortar tank), for reservoir, and another one for bathing. Near these tanks were small truck gardens which the women and the children peones tended, and which provided the few fresh vegetables and fruits that were consumed . . . As their trips into principal towns were made only twice a year for the purpose of disposing of their products, such as wool, goat hair, horse hair, hides, pelts, deer skins, a few *coyote* skins, wild cat, and fox, the ranchers always obtained sugar, flour, coffee, rice, and other necessities in quantities to last them . . . In the large ranches there were the *Casa Grande*, or owner's residence, and several families of peones . . . As the settlements were so far apart it was impossible to have schools . . . Those of us who learned English at the time were sent away to boarding schools . . . Every child living in the ranch learned to read and write Spanish.[21]

When Anglo Texans like Richard King and Mifflin Kenedy began to acquire ranchlands from Texas Mexicans in the nineteenth century, many of the elements of social structure and built landscape from the Spanish Mexican rancho tradition persisted. While the enclosure of rangelands and modern breeding practices prompted the use of barbed wire fencing and imported lumber replaced stone and unhewn wood in the construction of big houses and worker houses on ranches, vaqueros continued to outnumber Anglo cowhands on South Texas ranches. Today, however, on many of these surviving ranches, vaqueros live on the ranch for five or six days per week as needed and return to nearby towns and their families on weekends.[22]

The rancho, once the most common settlement form and lived space of South Texas has yielded largely to the farm as the basic rural settlement of the area, especially since the early-twentieth-century invasion of the region by Anglos (FIG. 5.2). Up to the end of the nineteenth century, ranchos in western counties like Webb, Zapata, and Starr were chiefly owned by Texas Mexicans. After Anglos began to acquire ownership and control of these lands in the 1880s, many rancho names persisted in their original Spanish designation. Surviving ranchos, those where cattle herding is still the principal means of the working ranch, are found in a line stretching from Zapata on the lower Rio Grande to Sarita near the Gulf, including parts of Zapata, Jim Hogg, Brooks, Kenedy, and Kleberg Counties. On most ranchlands in the region, however, grain production,

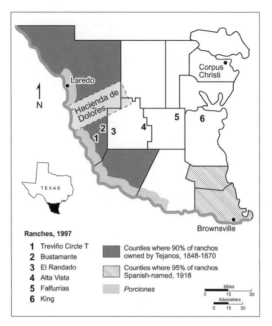

5.2. Rancho lands in South Texas.

oil leases, and sport-hunting leases—especially for deer—have replaced cattle as the chief forms of economy.[23]

While the rancho no longer survives as a settlement form for most Tejanos, its legacy is important as a symbolic representation in other ways. Western dress, especially boots and hats, folk musical styles like *corridos*, and foodways including *barbacoa* all stem from the rancho lifestyle. By the twentieth century, most Tejanos were living in towns and cities, so that other spaces became symbolic to the group in South Texas. Significant among these spaces are plazas.

PLAZA

As a physical form and social space, the plaza is a common feature of settlements throughout Hispanic America that varies by type, form, and landscape characteristics.[24] In the borderland shared by Mexico and the United States, these differences are even more pronounced because of the interactions of Hispanic and Anglo American traditions.

Although the presence of Hispanic plazas in South Texas towns is related to the Mexican heritage of the region, a substantial Mexican American population alone does not explain a plaza in a town. Outside the region, plazas were organized as part of Spanish and later Mexican town founding, so that locations as distant as El Paso in the far west, Victoria in the central coastal plain, and Nacogdoches in the eastern pine woodlands each had plazas. San Antonio, founded in 1718, boasted three plazas that were said to be the meeting places for every kind of celebration, the markets for both gossip and goods, and the civic centers for all activity, whether social, religious, political, or military. Even towns not founded by Hispanics, such as Gonzales, San Patricio, Refugio, and San Felipe, incorporated plazas into their design and layout.[25]

Still other towns in South Texas, such as Kingsville in Kleberg County, La Grulla in Starr County, and Mirando City in Webb County, presently have plaza parks that were added after the town's founding. Some of these parks function socially like Hispanic plazas, yet their landscapes combine elements such as picnic facilities and playgrounds that make them more unlike a traditional plaza, and therefore they are not included here.

On the basis of fieldwork, it was determined that twenty towns in South Texas included traditional plazas (FIG. 5.3). Ten of these towns had their first plazas built in the nineteenth century, six in the twentieth cen-

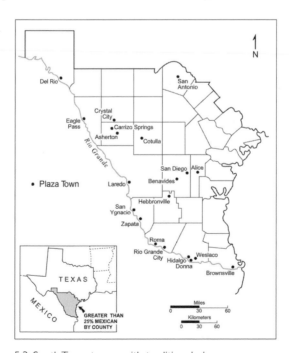

5.3. South Texas towns with traditional plazas.

TABLE 5.1 South Texas Plaza Town Characteristics

TOWN[a] Plaza	Church	Kiosco	Fountain	TYPE by Situation	Total	% Hispanic
San Antonio					935,933	55.6
Military				Central		
Main	×		×	Central		
Alamo		×		Peripheral		
Milam		×		Peripheral		
Guadalupe	×			Peripheral		
Market				Mall		
Paschal[b]						
Washington[b]						
Haymarket[b]						
Laredo					122,899	93.8
San Agustín	×	×		Central		
Market				Peripheral		
Jarvis		×		Peripheral		
School Block[b]						
Bruni			×	Peripheral		
St. Peter's				Peripheral		
Tex-Mex Depot[b]						
Zapata					7,119	81.3
Plaza[b]	×	×				
Plaza				Peripheral		
San Ygnacio					871	92.8
Blas Uribe	×	×		Central		
Uribe[b]						
Rio Grande City					9,891	96.8
Britton Avenue	×	×		Mall		
Roma					8,059	97.9
Broad Street	×			Mall		
Bicentennial		×		Peripheral		
Brownsville					98,962	90.1
Market			×	Peripheral		
Washington		×	×	Peripheral		
Eagle Pass					20,651	95.2
San Juan	×	×		Peripheral		
Hidalgo					3,292	98.0
La Cancha		×		Peripheral		
Del Rio					30,705	77.1
Brown		×	×	Segregated		
San Diego					4,983	95.4
Padre Pedro	×	×		Central		
Alcalá				Peripheral		

TABLE 5.1 continued

| TOWN[a] | LANDSCAPE ELEMENTS | | | TYPE | 1990 POPULATION | |
Plaza	Church	*Kiosco*	Fountain	by Situation	Total	% Hispanic
Carrizo Springs					5,745	83.6
Cinco de Mayo	×			Segregated		
Benavides					1,788	95.4
Plaza	×	×		Peripheral		
Cotulla					3,694	79.4
Florita	×	×	×	Segregated		
Hebbronville					4,465	92.2
Plaza	×	×		Peripheral		
Alice					19,788	72.5
Park Plaza		×		Segregated		
Asherton					1,589	99.2
Placita				Peripheral		
Donna					12,751	87.8
La Plazita Park		×		Segregated		
Crystal City					8,117	92.6
Plaza Park		×		Peripheral		
Weslaco					21,877	79.7
Park Plaza		×		Segregated		

SOURCES: Field survey by author; U.S. Bureau of the Census, *1990 Census of Population and Housing, Texas.*

[a]Towns are listed in descending order of founding.
[b]No longer a plaza.

tury, and two in the eighteenth century. The construction of a plaza in a town was based on legal ordinance or tradition. The revised Laws of the Indies issued by Philip II in 1573 established 148 ordinances for the founding of colonial towns in the Americas, and four of these concerned the construction of a main plaza.[26] The main plaza was to be the starting point for a town; it would be a square or rectangle, proportioned to the number of inhabitants, and not less than 200 feet wide and 300 feet long. Streets were to extend from the corners of the plaza as well as from the middle of each side, and around the plaza there were to be portals and sidewalks.

Eighteenth-century plazas were constructed in San Antonio (see Chap. 7) and in Laredo (TABLE 5.1). Laredo's San Agustín Plaza was decreed the focal point of the town plan of 1767, a dozen years after the town's founding.[27] Like most Spanish colonial towns, Laredo accommodated the Laws of the Indies but adapted them to local circumstances. The dimensions of San Agustín Plaza met the ordinance criteria, but no middle block streets emerged from the plaza, nor were there portals surrounding the space. The tradition of plaza space was continued during the Mexican era, so that towns founded between 1821 and 1836 in South Texas were required by law to include a plaza.[28] Again, however, the letter of the law was not strictly followed. In San Ygnacio, established in 1830, the town plaza was created on donated land almost one-half century after the town was founded. In Zapata, a Rio Grande town founded as Carrizo in 1770, the plaza was not built until shortly after the town name was changed in 1898.[29]

Most towns with plazas in South Texas, however, were founded after 1836, when Texan, not Spanish or Mexican, political authority prevailed. Although no single municipal code governed town founding or design, plazas were often included on the original plats. Several towns initially had no plaza but added one later, as, for example, Del Rio in 1908, Cotulla in 1925, and Hidalgo in 1933. At least five of the towns and perhaps others had the land for a plaza donated by wealthy Anglo American patrons. For example, John Twohig gave Plaza San Juan to the city of Eagle Pass in 1850 when the town was laid out, and he stipulated that the

5.4. Plaza San Juan, Eagle Pass, Texas, around 1920.

land should not be used for any other purpose (FIG. 5.4). The plaza was named after St. John because it was dedicated on June 24, the saint's day, and to commemorate John Twohig. Because the land for the plaza was never formally deeded to the city, there were several attempts to convert the space to other uses. When the Eagle Pass School Board expressed an interest in building a high school on Plaza San Juan around 1910, a local judge advised against it, claiming that the land was held in trust for the people of Eagle Pass as a plaza.

Five of the twenty plaza towns had multiple plazas in 1997 (TABLE 5.1). This situation is not unusual; the tradition of several large plazas and smaller *placitas* is common throughout Mexico. Multiple plazas in a town may be related to its age and population, but neither alone or in combination necessarily predicts multiple plazas. Brownsville, one of the largest cities of the region, has had two plazas since the end of the nineteenth century; Roma, a small town of comparable age, also has two plazas, although one was added more recently.

Only San Antonio and Laredo have more than two plazas. At Laredo, however, the town had been in existence for more than a century when the second plaza was added. Then, less than two decades later, at the close of the nineteenth century, Laredo was connected by railroad to San Antonio and Monterrey, the population jumped from 3,521 to 13,429, and

Laredo witnessed the construction of six plazas.[30] Three of these plazas—Market, Jarvis, and School Block—were public spaces. Three others—Bruni, St. Peter's Church, and the Texas Mexican Railroad depot—were initially private plazas. Market Plaza became the site of the Laredo City Hall in 1883, yet the space has remained a plaza into the twentieth century, and buildings erected around and near it, like the Plaza Hotel in 1926 and the Plaza Theater in 1947, reflect this continuing designation. Of the three private plazas, two have been donated to the city and one no longer exists. For example, Bruni Plaza was built by the Sociedad Mutualista Hijos de Juárez (1891–1918), a benevolent organization that assisted newly arrived Mexican immigrants. During the 1920s, Antonio Mateo Bruni obtained the plaza land and embellished the space with arched gateways, a hemicycle, and a fountain. Bruni Plaza, as it was called, was donated to the city of Laredo during the 1960s, and today is the site of a park surrounding a branch of the public library. The space continues to be used as a plaza.[31]

Types of Plazas and Geographical Situation

The function of the plaza as a social space in part relates to its position or situation in the community. In the South Texas towns, plazas could be situated centrally or peripherally with respect to the central business district and street grid. A plaza might be situated in a segregated manner, usually on the opposite side of a railroad corridor or disamenity barrier. Finally, a plaza could be a mall that was centrally positioned but attenuated in relationship to the street grid and surrounding blocks (FIG. 5.5).

Only five of the plazas in the towns had what might be termed a central focus (TABLE 5.1). These plazas were early organized as the focal points of their respective communities, much as in the so-called classical plaza model common throughout Latin America.[32] In traditional Spanish American towns, the plaza was the primary social node of a community, and the most prominent families typically lived nearby. Moreover, the space was usually bordered by institutional structures, like a church, and government buildings. Each of the central-focus plazas in the South Texas towns originally included a church, governmental space such as city hall, county courthouse, or post office, commercial space such as grocery stores or other types of retail-service establishments, and residential land use.

The old plaza in the South Texas town of San Diego, for example, was created in 1876, when the town was sited immediately north of San Diego Creek (FIG. 5.5). The plaza, which is now called Padre Pedro Park

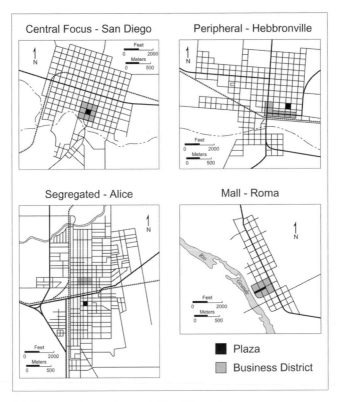

5.5. Plaza positions and types in South Texas towns.

in honor of Father J. Pedro Bard, who served the town from 1877–1920, was then little more than an open space with community gardens and jacales, bordered on two sides by substantial houses. The space is off-centered from the railroad and the principal highway that divides the town and links it with Alice and Corpus Christi. When the plaza was created, it was the central focus of the community. This is evident from the surrounding structures, which include several private residences, and from inspection of historic maps. The plaza measures 200 feet on each of four sides and is separated from abutting blocks by 70-foot-wide streets, 20 feet wider than the standard spacing elsewhere across the grid. Flanking the plaza today are the St. Francis de Pabla Church, the San Diego City Hall, and two abandoned merchant buildings that testify to former commercial functions for the plaza (see Chap. 6).

By far the most common plaza situation among the South Texas towns was a peripheral site relative to other community functions (TABLE

5.1). Although each of these plazas might contain one or two elements of institutional, commercial, and residential functions, the plazas were mostly on the margins of their respective central business districts. In Eagle Pass, Hidalgo, Benavides, Hebbronville, and Asherton, for example, the plazas are several blocks distant from the main commercial streets. Nevertheless, each plaza showed evidence of past and current commercial or institutional functions, such as neighborhood stores, churches, or a post office. In Zapata, the new plaza built in 1953, when the town was relocated, is on the periphery of the courthouse square, facing the main commercial artery that bisects the community. However, the plaza is not well integrated to either space and consequently looks neglected and little used.

Six plazas—in Alice, Cotulla, Del Rio, Carrizo Springs, Weslaco, and Donna—are set apart in the predominantly Mexican quarter of the town. Significantly, each of these towns was less than 90 percent Hispanic in 1990, whereas all other towns except Zapata and San Antonio were greater than 90 percent Hispanic (TABLE 5.1). In Alice, Cotulla, and Weslaco, the historical Mexican neighborhoods were literally across the railroad tracks. These plazas chiefly bordered residential land use areas, but in each case they included neighborhood businesses like grocery stores and other retail outlets and, in Cotulla, a church and a public school (see Chap. 6). In Del Rio, the Mexican quarter of San Felipe lies southwest of the Southern Pacific Railroad tracks that bisect the city and below San Felipe Creek, which has a history of flooding. Brown Plaza, named after the donor of the land, had various commercial establishments surrounding it in the early 1920s, for example, a theater, a hotel, restaurants, and a cleaners, as well as residential land use.[33] Many of these functions persist and largely serve residents of the surrounding community. In Carrizo Springs, Plaza Cinco de Mayo is situated in the Vera Addition on a rise at the northeast edge of town west of the Missouri Pacific Railroad. A 1914 map shows that the irregularly shaped properties surrounding the plaza were chiefly owned by Mexicans, and several street names like Martínez, Seco, and Plaza reinforce the character of the location as a barrio.[34] The plaza is positioned behind Our Lady of Guadalupe, a Catholic church built in 1949, suggesting that the space predates the church. Today, the plaza is flanked by private residences on three sides and is in poor repair, with broken glass, graffiti, and an unkempt lawn. Nearby streets contain neighborhood businesses including grocery and convenience stores, gas station and garage, *panadería* (bakery), barbershop, and an old movie theater that now rents videos.

The fourth type of plaza in South Texas towns is the mall (FIG. 5.5). In this layout, the open space of the plaza is an attenuated rectangle surrounded by commercial, residential, and institutional functions. Roma, a river port site on the Rio Grande, was founded by Charles Stillman, a Brownsville merchant who platted the townsite in 1848.[35] The plaza in Roma is 120 feet by almost 1,000 feet stretching two blocks from the river to a church sited on a facing block. In 1894 when the town had only seven hundred people, five commercial buildings fronted this plaza, including a substantial two-story warehouse, testifying to the commercial prominence of the town.[36]

An 1894 map of Rio Grande City, the only other town with a mall plaza, shows an elongated space enclosed by Britton Avenue, which runs perpendicular to the Rio Grande, uphill toward the county courthouse. The mall plaza, however, is a recent modification here, because an early twentieth-century map and a photo show the plaza with its *kiosco* or bandstand situated in the middle of Britton Avenue between first and Second Streets. Henry Clay Davis, the town founder, was said to have designed Rio Grande City after Austin, and thus Britton Avenue and the county courthouse five blocks beyond the river were meant to mirror Congress Avenue, the state capitol, and the Colorado River. Britton Avenue linked the courthouse and the plaza to a steamboat landing on the riverbank, and for fifty years after the town was platted, it was known only as Davis Landing.[37]

Plaza Landscapes

South Texas town plazas can be differentiated by landscape elements as well as by type and situation. Elements that might distinguish a plaza include a church, a traditional *kiosco*, and walkways, benches, fountains, and ornamental plantings. Although a church was not consistently a feature of Spanish plazas, in Mexico it became a principal signature of the *plaza mayor*. Currently twelve of twenty South Texas towns have what might be called church plazas (TABLE 5.1). At San Antonio's Plaza del Las Islas and Laredo's San Agustín Plaza, the first churches were erected shortly after the plazas were decreed, but for the other towns, mostly founded in the nineteenth century under Anglo Texan political authority, the churches were built considerably after the plazas were platted. For example, in Eagle Pass the plaza was built in 1850, but the first church not until 1887. In San Ygnacio the church on the plaza was built in 1875, almost forty-five years after the founding of the town. Furthermore, the position and orientation of churches to their respective plazas show little consistency or pattern. In a sample of seven church plazas, two had churches positioned east of the plaza, two northwest, one west, one south, and one northeast. Five of the seven churches fronted their plazas directly; three were in the middle of the facing block, and two in corners. Our Lady of Guadalupe Church in Hebbronville is immediately off the plaza, and Our Lady of Guadalupe Church in Carrizo Springs turns its back to the square.

In Mexico, the earliest plazas were often open and lacked ornamentation, except perhaps a well or fountain.[38] The open space had several purposes, including use by the military for drills, which is the source of the generic name *plazas de armas*, for horse-and-carriage racing and for trading.[39] The appearance of the *kiosco* and its gardenlike setting are associated with the French occupation during the mid-nineteenth century, and became a standard element of Mexican townscapes during the prosperous era of the Porfirio Díaz regime.[40] The *kiosco* appears to be oriental in origin. An early twentieth-century Spanish source lists a "quiosco" as "an oriental temple or pavilion, generally open on all sides, that is constructed on a platform in a garden for the purpose of relaxation or music."[41]

Sixteen of the plazas in South Texas towns included at least one plaza with a *kiosco* (TABLE 5.1). Zapata, the town relocated in 1953 when the original site was inundated by the creation of Falcon Lake on the Rio Grande, lacks a *kiosco*, yet the old town had one (FIG. 5.6).[42] Inadequate documentation makes dating *kioscos* in the South Texas towns difficult. Examination of fire-insurance maps for several towns, however, suggests that most *kioscos* in plazas were built during the late nineteenth or early twentieth century. For example, early photographs of Laredo show no *kiosco* in San Agustín Plaza.[43] The same is true for an 1894 map, but one from 1905 does indicate improvements there and what seems to be a platform for a structure.[44] In San Ygnacio, founded in 1830, there was no *kiosco* at Plaza Blas María Uribe as late as 1950, when it was a barren, open space typical of the early Mexican plazas (see Chap. 6).

All plazas with *kioscos* in 1997 positioned the bandstand in the center of the space except Washington Plaza in Brownsville and Bicentennial Plaza in Roma, where the *kioscos* were to one side, and at Rio Grande City, where the *kiosco* is at one end of the mall plaza (FIG. 5.7). Most plazas included concrete walkways that extended to the corners of the rectangle from the *kiosco*. Several plazas added perpendicular paths at the

5.6. *Kiosco* and plaza in Old Zapata, currently submerged by Falcon Lake.

cardinal points or concentric walkways around the *kiosco*. Fountains decorated contemporary plazas in Del Rio, Cotulla, Brownsville, Laredo, and San Antonio. The decoration of plazas to accentuate walkways and circular arrangements like the *kiosco*, fountains, flowerbeds, and arboreal groupings is an inheritance of the Renaissance French garden, where small spaces were intended as either social gathering places or focal points.[45] Most plazas included facilities for lighting, trees, lawns, and benches, often with commemorative plaques or messages honoring individuals in the community. Plazas in San Antonio, Laredo, Zapata, Rio Grande City, Brownsville, Hidalgo, Del Rio, San Diego, and Hebbronville contained other monuments and historical markers. At Laredo's San Agustín Plaza, a statue of General Ignacio Zaragoza, a native Tejano and hero of the 1862 Battle of Puebla that is the basis for the Mexican celebration of the Cinco de Mayo, stands in front of the *kiosco* facing the Rio Grande and Mexico. The monument was donated to the city of Laredo by the Mexican government in 1980. Washington Plaza in Brownsville contains a monument to Miguel Hidalgo y Costilla, the Mexican priest who ignited the wars for independence from Spain.

Activities on Plazas

A traditional social purpose of a plaza was the paseo or promenade, an activity inherited from Spain and practiced in Mexico especially by the

5.7. *Kiosco* on the mall plaza and Starr County Courthouse, Rio Grande City, Texas, 1948.

upper classes that lived close to the plaza.[46] The paseo usually involved males strolling around a plaza in one direction and females circulating around it in the opposite direction. Although the promenade was sometimes a daily ritual, more often it occurred on Sunday afternoons or, perhaps, several evenings a week. It was at its most flamboyant when a plaza accommodated a special celebration like a fiesta or religious occasion, or when a band played music from the *kiosco*.[47] In the South Texas plaza towns, the paseo has effectively been discontinued, as it has also in much of urban Mexico, in spite of its popularity historically. At Jarvis Plaza in Laredo, a paseo was held twice each week, on Thursday and Sunday evenings from eight to ten.[48] In Hebbronville, the paseo was a regular part of plaza activities.[49] At Brown Plaza in Del Rio, whole families were said to promenade in the Spanish fashion on Sunday evenings during June, July, and August.[50] The disappearance of the paseo can be attributed to changed patterns of courtship and also to the growing popularity of other entertainment outlets since the end of World War II.

In South Texas towns, fiestas or ferias were common during the last decades of the nineteenth century. Often held in the fall after harvest, they allegedly attracted ranch families from across the region, usually to a nearby plaza town where celebrations might continue for several days.[51] *Fiestas patrias*, patriotic celebrations, were commonly held at plazas. The most celebrated of these were the Diez y Seis de Septiembre (September 16), which commemorates Mexican independence, and the Cinco de Mayo (May 5), which commemorates the Mexican defeat of the French army at Puebla in 1862. The expanded reporting of these celebrations in local newspapers during the 1870s and 1880s may have resulted from increased migration from Mexico and from augmented awareness of Mexican cultural traditions by Texas Mexicans.[52]

An important element of festivities on the plaza was the participation of musical ensembles. The regular appearance of bands helps explain the *kiosco* as an architectural signature of the plaza. Several towns were known to have maintained local musical groups—Del Rio with its International Band, Eagle Pass with its Military Band, and the Orquesta Aguilar that performed regularly in Old Zapata.[53] At the turn of the century, musicians from Matamoros, Mexico, were hired to perform at La Feria de San Diego, emphasizing the continued link between the South Texas plaza towns and the homeland across the Rio Grande.[54]

Today, fiestas and special occasions are still celebrated on the plazas of some South Texas towns, but the function of these spaces as social nodes has changed decidedly. Festivals commemorating Mexican American themes have been retained by only seven of the towns: Benavides, Brownsville, Del Rio, Eagle Pass, Laredo, San Antonio, and San Diego.[55] Only in Benavides and San Diego are the activities for these festivals performed in plazas. Events in other towns are staged in city parks, where large crowds can be more easily accommodated than in plazas.

Nevertheless, San Diego and Benavides are the exception rather than the rule, because in most of the towns the plazas are largely ignored as special event spaces today. In several towns, however, including Laredo, San Ygnacio, Roma, Rio Grande City, Del Rio, and Hidalgo, local historical societies and chambers of commerce have spotlighted plazas in self-guided brochures that circulate to the public. Laredo, one of the largest communities and an important gateway to Mexico from Texas, has the most elaborate guide, which includes a map and walking tour of the historic downtown with the San Agustín, Market, and Jarvis Plazas briefly described.[56] Both Roma and San Ygnacio have several National Register Historic Structures on their plazas.[57] In 1983 the Zapata County Historical Society held a celebration at the *kiosco* on the plaza of Old Zapata that had become exposed when the waters of Falcon Lake receded temporarily. These examples illustrate the contemporary attachment to historic plaza spaces and suggest something of the importance of cultural identity symbols to Mexican peoples in some communities, but in the majority of South Texas towns the plazas are presently more like relics than vital conduits to a living past. Although the spaces are maintained, they do not attract pedestrian traffic in the manner of the traditional Mexican plaza.

Even in Laredo, San Agustín Plaza—nearly two and a half centuries old—does not function in its former capacity as a social node to many residents of the community. In part, this is because few people today reside near the plaza, so that its chief attraction is to tourists who lodge at the upscale La Posada Hotel on the southwest corner of the square. Although the plaza is city property, it is maintained by the hotel to fit a tidy tourist image. Moreover, even if city residents wished to use the plaza on a regular basis, the difficulty of parking on adjacent streets in the downtown would make the option problematic. As populations grow and the larger cities like Brownsville and Laredo expand, the old centers where plazas are situated become congested and thereby fail to easily accommodate the private automobile. The exception to this occurs when a plaza serves as a public transportation node, like Jarvis Plaza in Laredo or Market Plaza in Brownsville, where city buses rendezvous before departing for peripheral neighborhoods.

In Laredo, the "new plaza" is a regional shopping space, Mall del Norte, some 10 miles distant from San Agustín Plaza. During the 1980s, St. John Neumann Catholic Church occupied the east side of the mall and had free parking and its own access. Its exterior was ornate sandstone, in Spanish colonial revival style. Masses on Saturday and Sunday regularly drew a thousand worshipers, according to Father Marcos Martínez. Although St. John Neumann was forced to relocate, Mall del Norte incorporates various Mexican motifs in the interior decoration of the shopping space, such as pre-Columbian statuary and a Moorish fountain. The absence of the *kiosco* notwithstanding, mall space, it might be argued, is a contemporary version of transformed plaza space for Texas Mexicans in Laredo; it continues traditional ways in a modern setting.

Like the rancho, the plaza town survives chiefly as symbolic space in South Texas. Because most Tejanos reside in cities, the barrio and colonia have become the most recent lived spaces.

BARRIO AND COLONIA

In Mexico and Latin America, residential space in towns and cities is typically defined as a barrio, meaning neighborhood, or a colonia, referring to a subdivision or district. These terms spread into the borderlands, and today each is used in cities and suburbs where Mexican American populations have been present historically, although the term *barrio* appears to be more common than *colonia*, except in South Texas. While barrios are found in many southwestern cities, the process of barrio formation has not been modeled because its spatial evolution is sensitive to varied local conditions.[58] Furthermore, not every Mexican American barrio is the equivalent of a ghetto, with attendant negative images of ethnic isolation and degradation.

In South Texas, these terms can have specific reference. A barrio is an inner city neighborhood, often bearing a colorful name. Barrios are typically compact spaces, smaller than a modern suburb, with older housing on small lots. The boundaries of a barrio are recognized by its residents and sometimes by outsiders familiar with the central city. The term *colonia*, like *barrio*, refers to a city district, but in South Texas *colonia* has acquired a pejorative meaning. Here, colonias are chiefly rural and exurban, unincorporated, and sometimes impoverished habitations often lacking services and amenities such as piped water, treated sewage, and street maintenance.

Barrio

In South Texas towns and cities the barrio is typically spatially segregated from newer or Anglo parts of the cityscape. In many towns of the region, such as Eagle Pass, Del Rio, and Alice, barrios were historically segregated from Anglo neighborhoods; often they were on the opposite side of a railroad track, highway, or irrigation canal. Town segregation was popular in the Lower Rio Grande Valley, where land development companies actively subdivided places in the early twentieth century (FIG. 5.8). Until World War II most of these communities were dual towns, neatly separated into Mexican and Anglo (see the case study of Cotulla in Chapter 6).[59] The Mexican town was distinctive in many ways from its Anglo complement. Lot sizes were usually smaller in the Mexican town, and a plaza and colonia as well as Spanish language street names were often featured.

In dual towns, Mexican American residents referred to their barrio as "el pueblo mexicano" (Mexican town) or "nuestro lado" (our side).[60]

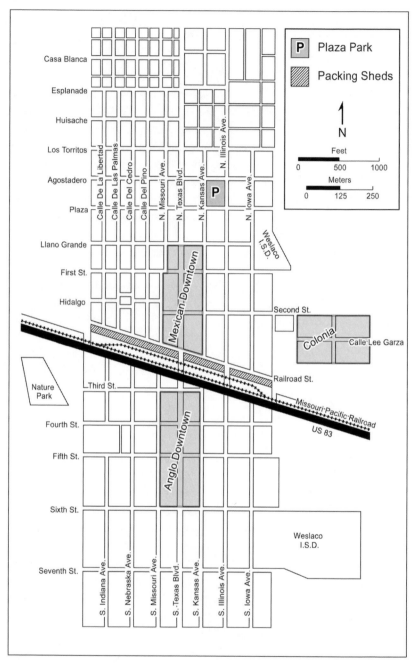

5.8. Dual towns in Weslaco, Hidalgo County, 1965.

As the Mexican American community grew and expanded, the incipient barrio was added to spatially create many barrios. In some towns, spatial divides still exist to separate the Mexican American barrios from newer Anglo and mixed Anglo–Mexican American neighborhoods. In Brownsville, for example, Boca Chica Boulevard cuts an east-west swath across the urban fabric. South of this divide is mostly a series of nonintegrated street grids reflecting several eras of early twentieth-century residential development, chiefly older Mexican American barrios with names like Villa Verde and La Buena Vida. To the north of Boca Chica are curving streets aligned with numerous old oxbow lakes and detached river meanders known locally as "resacas," around which are newer Anglo and Mexican American subdivisions largely developed in the 1960s and later and bearing names like Land O'Lakes and Honeydale.

The landscapes of older barrios blend distinctive housescapes with small, typically family-run commercial enterprises that pepper the neighborhood. In 1966, Arthur Rubel described the living landscape—both residential and commercial—of a barrio in Weslaco, a Lower Rio Grande Valley town in Hidalgo County. At the time, Weslaco had approximately 9,000 Mexican Americans and 6,000 Anglos. Anglos lived south of the Missouri Pacific Railroad and U.S. Highway 83. The Mexican American barrio was north of the track and highway and known locally as Mexiquito (Little Mexico) (see FIG. 5.8).

> If one strays from the main Boulevard [North Texas Blvd.] the dust of the unpaved side streets clings to face, hands, and clothing during the hot, humid spring and summer months. In autumn and winter the passage of pedestrian or automobile along these side streets is made difficult, or sometimes, impossible by mud and standing water. Homes are generally impoverished and unpainted, with here and there a brightly painted building surrounded by a high wire fence. The residences of the north side range from one-room shacks, consisting of corrugated paper stretched around four posts and covered with a roof of planks, to multi-room structures of wood or plaster, handsomely maintained and painted in bright colors of blue, green, orange, pink, or white.[61]

The commercial landscapes of Mexiquito were separate from the downtown main street (South Texas Boulevard), which chiefly served the Anglo community (see FIG. 5.8). Typical of businesses in Mexican American neighborhoods of the era, most stores were small, family-operated, and served almost exclusively the barrio residents. Mexiquito, like many barrios across the borderland, is situated next to an industrial quarter along a railroad alignment.

> Ten grocery stores front the Boulevard on the north side, and more than fifty small neighborhood grocery stores are distributed in the residential areas. Although they are conveniently located, their stock is small; most of the smaller groceries cannot sell either fresh meat or milk products, for example, because they lack refrigeration facilities . . . Three of the largest stores fronting on the main street sell work clothing . . . Four of the shops along the north Boulevard specialize in lending money to Mexican Americans at usurious interest rates . . . A number of retail outlets sell used furniture and household appliances. In fact, more stores sell used articles of clothing and furniture than sell those goods new. Although one of the three drug stores of the north side boasts a licensed pharmacist, all three are heavily stocked with well-advertised patent medicines, which are supplemented by an inventory of brightly packaged *medicinas caseras*—home cures . . . The remaining frontage on North Boulevard is occupied by a movie house dedicated to the showing of Spanish-language films, by seven restaurants, seven gasoline service stations, three bakeries, a tortilla factory, two photographic studios, a window-glass shop, a shoe repair store, a beauty shop, and a dry-cleaning establishment . . . As one walks across the tracks along the main thoroughfare of the city, he leaves one kind of scene and enters another. North of the tracks the whirring sounds of the mechanical belts, which bring the crates of packed vegetables and fruits from packing shed to motor truck and railroad car, are heard throughout the day and often until midnight. Interspersed with this north-side sound is the raucousness of the *ranchero* tunes from the juke boxes of the thirteen *cantinas* of that side of the tracks. These bars along the thoroughfare form the most popular type of commercial enterprise owned by Mexican Americans, with the exception of food markets.[62]

Three decades after Rubel cataloged these scenes, barrios in towns of the Lower Rio Grande Valley have witnessed tremendous growth and change. Paved streets, refrigeration, chain supermarkets, and fast-food fran-

TABLE 5.2 Retail Properties by Type in McAllen's Mexican American Downtown

TYPE	N	PERCENT[a]
Clothing	33	22
Jewelry	19	13
Discount variety	16	11
Electronics	16	11
Miscellaneous	15	10
Vacant	15	10
Beauty supply/perfume	10	7
Finance	7	5
Medical supply	7	5
Optical	4	3
Floral supply	4	3
Eatery	3	2
TOTAL	149	

SOURCE: Field survey by author, 1997.
[a]Percentages are rounded.

chises have permeated even the poorest barrio spaces and their peripheries. Yet, enclosed house properties, colorful building exteriors, small groceries, and neighborhood bars persist in their modern incarnations. Because the growth of the Texas Mexican population has generally exceeded that of Anglo Texans in Valley towns, even what were once restricted Anglo commercial landscapes have transformed to almost exclusively Mexican American shopping districts. In McAllen, regarded as the retail center of the Lower Rio Grande Valley, the traditional Anglo main street shopping district has been converted to a Mexican American downtown as upscale retail has been lured to suburban malls. In January 1997, some 149 commercial properties existed in this district, a six-block-long area bounded by South Main Street and South Broadway. Nearly half of the establishments were clothing and jewelry retailers. Another 22 percent were discount variety stores that marketed inexpensive goods and electronics stores (TABLE 5.2). These retail types have been found to be especially diagnostic of Mexican American shopping districts in South Texas.[63]

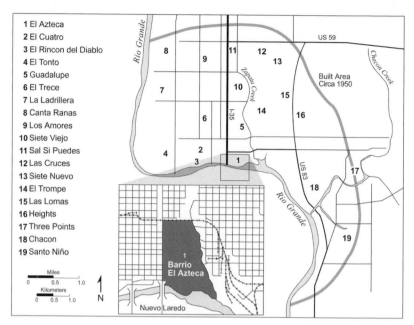

1 El Azteca
2 El Cuatro
3 El Rincon del Diablo
4 El Tonto
5 Guadalupe
6 El Trece
7 La Ladrillera
8 Canta Ranas
9 Los Amores
10 Siete Viejo
11 Sal Si Puedes
12 Las Cruces
13 Siete Nuevo
14 El Trompe
15 Las Lomas
16 Heights
17 Three Points
18 Chacon
19 Santo Niño

5.9. Laredo's barrios.

Today, in South Texas communities like Laredo where greater than 90 percent of the residents are Mexican American, most barrios are restricted to the oldest residential areas of the city developed before World War II. In 1980, Laredo officially recognized nineteen neighborhoods or barrios and their respective boundaries (FIG. 5.9). Several central city barrios built in the late nineteenth century, including El Cuatro, El Tonto, El Azteca, and Guadalupe, are historically significant because of the rich stock of vernacular housing styles that blend Mexican and Anglo American designs.[64]

A Laredo barrio destroyed for a freeway approach to the Juárez-Lincoln Bridge connecting the city to Nuevo Laredo across the Rio Grande was studied by historical archaeologists. The study, based on resident interviews as well as archival research, reveals important findings about the culture history of Texas Mexican barrios in the city. For example, an assessment of immigrant residents in the barrio reinforces Laredo's early connections to towns and cities in the Mexican states of Tamaulipas and Nuevo León, as described in Chapter 4 (TABLE 5.3).

In the built environment, it became clear that the general types of

TABLE 5.3 Selected Immigrant Residents from a Laredo Barrio

NAME	ADDRESS	OCCUPATION	PLACE OF BIRTH	DATE OF ARRIVAL
Santiago Martínez	411 Zaragoza	Rancher	Ciudad Guerrero, Tamaulipas	1880
Maria Ana Salazar de Flores	817 Santa Ursula	Homemaker	Villaldama, Nuevo León	1894
Juana C. de Viseaya Sierra	707 Victoria	Housekeeper	Nuevo Laredo, Tamaulipas	1909
Pedro Cabrera Jr.	1520 Washington	Lumber worker	Nuevo Laredo, Tamaulipas	1911
Teodora Martínez	409 Grant	Rancher	Ciudad Guerrero, Tamaulipas	1913
José Martínez	411 Zaragoza	Rancher	Ciudad Guerrero, Tamaulipas	1913
Dolores Martínez	411 Zaragoza	Housekeeper	Ciudad Guerrero, Tamaulipas	1913
Ninfa Martínez	411 Zaragoza	Housekeeper	Ciudad Guerrero, Tamaulipas	1913
Espiridion Gonzalez	408 Hidalgo	Merchant	Villaldama, Nuevo Léon	1914
Joaquín Gonzales Cigarroa	708 Matamoros	Physician	Mapimi, Durango	1923

SOURCE: John W. Clark Jr. and Maria Juárez, *Urban Archaeology: A Culture History of a Mexican-American Barrio in Laredo, Webb County, Texas,* 112.

5.10. Jacal dwellings were the dominant building forms in South Texas barrios before the arrival of railroads.

structures erected in the barrio according to the building materials used and the popularity of each by era were first jacal (prerailroad), then frame (railroad), followed by brick (postrailroad). Most extant dwellings in the blocks surveyed were of frame construction, but jacales were common in the early years of many barrios (FIG. 5.10). The Plaza de la Noria in Laredo is remembered by all residents interviewed as the social center of the barrio—where children would play, where social gatherings would be staged, where couples would *dar la vuelta* (stroll), and *serenatas* (serenades) were performed. One of the most important factors in barrio history is the familial role in land use and stability. Public records showed that many lot properties remained owned by one family over several generations and in some instances for nearly a century. This supports the theory that Mexican American kinship networks were an important part of urban development in South Texas towns and cities. In addition, marriage records show that upper-income Texas Mexican families in this barrio tended toward intermarriage within the same socioeconomic class, facilitating the redistribution of land and property through surviving kinship networks.[65]

Colonia

The colonia is a settlement form particularly associated with the Texas borderland, appearing only infrequently in New Mexico, Arizona, and California.[66] Along the Texas border, some 1,471 colonias are a response to inadequate housing supply. They are home almost exclusively to Mexicans and Mexican Americans. In the Lower Rio Grande Valley, encompassing the tri-county Cameron, Hidalgo, and Willacy area, there were 987 colonias counted in 1994, with 37,658 housing units sheltering 172,261 residents. The colonias in the Lower Rio Grande Valley represent 67 percent of all Texas colonias.[67]

Colonias developed through two means. A very few, perhaps less than ten percent, began as small communities of farm laborers employed by a single rancher or farmer. The overwhelming majority of these settlements started as subdivision speculations, some as early as 1908, but most since 1948.[68] In 1977, only 65 colonias existed in the Lower Rio Grande Valley with two-thirds of this total in Hidalgo County alone. Seventeen years later, the number of colonias in the area had exploded to nearly 2,000, again with the largest concentration in Hidalgo County.

While some colonias, like those that sprang from farms and ranches, were once rural dispersed settlements, most are now truly exurban subdivisions on the fringes of municipalities. This becomes clear when the colonias are mapped and found clustered especially in the southern portions of Hidalgo and Cameron Counties nearest the towns and cities of the Lower Valley, not in the open northern reaches of these counties.[69] In 1946, for example, four such colonias—Guadalupe and Hermosa on the south side, Norte and Independencia on the north side—straddled the city limits of McAllen. These communities became annexed to the city as McAllen expanded during the 1950s and 1960s.[70]

Most colonias today, however, are still outside the political limits of Lower Valley municipalities on unincorporated land. Colonias are created by speculative developers who acquire unproductive agricultural land, subdivide into small lots of about 50 × 120 feet, and sell these to individuals with the promise of forthcoming services. Mexican Americans and Mexican nationals, often but not exclusively recent immigrants to the Valley, purchase the plots through a contract known as sweat equity, in which the developer retains ownership of the land until the last payment is made.[71] The purchaser builds a home on the lot, often with assistance from family and friends, and then "sweats" each monthly payment until final ownership, knowing that a single missed payment can result in the loss of land and dwelling.[72] Surveys conducted suggest that low-income Mexican American families opt for this method because pride of home ownership is a powerful goal that can only be achieved by taking this risk, given the otherwise prohibitively high cost of conventional housing in cities. Many colonia families have responded to surveys that they chose residence in particular colonias to be near family, and sacrifices were regularly made to ensure the monthly rent. As a consequence, instances where lots and houses reverted back to the developer are not commonplace.[73] The price colonia residents pay for this type of housing is that services like treated water, sewage, paved streets, and police and fire services are either lacking or marginally available; most colonia residents do have electricity connections and propane service.[74]

Colonia settlement is not unlike squatter settlement housing surrounding many Mexican border cities, except that in Texas colonias residents enter into legal contracts to own rather than illegally squatting on land.[75] The material conditions of colonia housing are sometimes superior to those found in Mexican squatter villages, but vary with the age of the colonia. For example, Davies and Holtz found that younger colonias in Cameron County were in poorer physical repair than older, more established ones. Of 421 colonias surveyed in the Lower Valley, 45 percent of the house units were of frame construction in good condition, 20 percent were of frame construction in poor condition, 15 percent were of brick or cement block composition, 15 percent were mobile homes, and 5 percent were ramshackle dwellings.[76]

Building conditions notwithstanding, a recent critical assessment of the Texas colonia problem concluded that physical infrastructure is not the fundamental issue. "Colonias are a structural problem compounded by developers' greed, official neglect, ignorance, poor policy-making and weak administrative capacity, inadequate laws, and enfeebled leadership."[77]

EPILOGUE

Ranchos, plazas, barrios, and colonias are enduring signatures of Mexican lived spaces in South Texas. Ranchos were an early frontier settlement form brought from northern Mexico. They marked the region with a pastoral economy and lifestyle for over a century. By 1900, however, Texas Mexican ranchos were giving way to Anglo Texan farms, and today there are few ranches owned and operated by persons of Texan Mexican ancestry.

Plazas have been part of South Texas since the earliest towns developed. These spaces in towns are a distinctive community form, more common in South Texas than in any other Hispanic-settled region of the borderlands. The nature of the plazas in the South Texas towns varies by type and landscape character. Plazas in most towns are situated away from the center of the community, and not all of the spaces are oriented to a church. The *kiosco* or bandstand as well as lawns, trees, sidewalks, and benches are the most consistently observed physical signatures of the plaza landscape. The plazas in South Texas towns served as traditional social nodes during the nineteenth and early twentieth centuries especially as staging areas for the promenade, harvest fairs, and Mexican patriotic celebrations. Today, the traditional paseo has disappeared from these plazas, yet the spaces remain important symbolic landscapes for Texas Mexican communities.

Barrios and colonias are the consequence of Anglo American invasion of what had been primarily a region settled by Texas Mexicans. Spatial segregation became commonplace in towns that were typically divided by railroad corridors. This separation created dual towns within a single community, resulting in separate businesses, institutions, and services as well as residences. Barrios survive in many towns of the region, but residential mixing of Texas Mexicans and Anglo Texans is accelerating as the former group is growing faster than the latter and Texas Mexicans are becoming an increasing component of the burgeoning middle class. Segregation persists, however, in unincorporated colonias on the periphery of many South Texas cities. This is especially so in the Lower Rio Grande Valley, where Mexican nationals as well as Mexican Americans strive to become homeowners—part of a dream that has motivated the settlement of South Texas for some two and one-half centuries.

In South Texas each town is two towns—American and Mexican.

—PAUL S. TAYLOR, *MEXICAN LABOR IN THE UNITED STATES: DIMMIT COUNTY,*
WINTER GARDEN DISTRICT, SOUTH TEXAS, 1930

Texas Mexican Small Towns

Small-town life has been part of the human geography of South Texas from the earliest days of colonial settlement. This tradition is rooted in northern Spain, where settlements have historically been smaller than those in the south and where the concept of one's natal *pueblo* or village implies a spiritual tie to place that is equally as strong as community residence.[1] In many towns of the South Texas region, the heritage of small-town life derives from both Mexican and Anglo traditions, because even Mexican-founded towns have been populated and influenced by Anglo residents and customs.

In this chapter, I use three separate case studies to illustrate the Mexican ancestry and cultural landscape of South Texas small towns.

San Ygnacio in Zapata County has survived as a Mexican American village for more than 170 years. It is a town where Anglo American influence has been slight and where today more than eight of every ten residents are of Mexican ancestry. San Diego in Duval County is 95 percent Mexican today, yet the community has a long history of Anglo and European immigrant residents who have melded as a single Anglo American group. San Diego is, in some ways, an Anglo American–Mexican town. Cotulla in La Salle County was not founded as a Mexican town yet today is 79 percent Mexican. Cotulla thus typifies many towns of South Texas that have evolved from a segregated community to a predominantly Texas Mexican town.

Geographical studies of small towns in Mexico provide certain guidelines that have been modified and applied to the examination of Texas Mexican small towns. Geographer Dan Stanislawski, for example, asserted that the towns of Michoacán have distinct personalities, whether Hispanic or Indian, and he devised a method for assessing this difference by analysis of townscape.[2] Geographers Samuel Dicken and Leslie Hewes each studied a different northern Mexican small town, one in Nuevo León and the other in Sonora, and their separate investigations yielded common findings about the structure, function, and landscape of traditional communities.[3] I borrow from and add to these perspectives to paint a portrait of the variability yet compelling similarity of small-town geography so common to Mexican South Texas.

There is no consensus among researchers about the population threshold for small towns in the United States. The Census Bureau, however, does distinguish among places with fewer than 10,000 people as well as among places with fewer than 2,500. Using these criteria, I plotted the distribution of small towns in South Texas counties in which more than half the population in 1990 was of Mexican ancestry (FIG. 6.1). I excluded the small towns of metropolitan counties (Webb, Hidalgo, Cameron, Nueces), because those small places exist in the shadow of larger cities like Laredo, McAllen–Edinburg, Brownsville–Harlingen–San Benito, and Corpus Christi, making some of them more like suburbs than independent towns. Significantly, nevertheless, 36 percent of all people who reside in these nonmetropolitan counties live in places with less than 10,000 people. Three of these small towns are San Ygnacio, San Diego, and Cotulla.

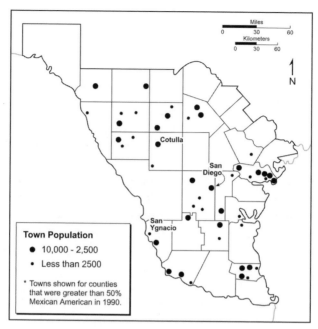

6.1. Texas Mexican small towns outside metropolitan areas, 1990.

SAN YGNACIO

San Ygnacio, the oldest town in Zapata County, was founded as a subdivision of the José Vásquez de Borrego land grant in 1830. Under the leadership of Don Jesús Treviño, residents from Revilla (Guerrero Viejo), Tamaulipas, first settled the town.[4] San Ygnacio was the patron saint of the town of Revilla, now Old Guerrero, which lies under Falcon Lake some miles south of San Ygnacio on the Mexican side of the Rio Grande (FIG. 6.2).[5]

Treviño selected a site on a sandy, level plain south of the Arroyo Grullo along the east bank of the Rio Grande, where he constructed a stone house that was added to over the years and that still stands as the oldest built structure in town. This site gave San Ygnacio protection by water on its west—the Rio Grande—and north—the Arroyo Grullo, an important location consideration, because Comanche raiding was a very real threat during the second half of the nineteenth century (FIG. 6.3). In fact, before U.S. 83 was constructed in the 1930s, Hidalgo Street extended from the center of town south across old river floodplain (presently cultivated land), and this road was the main entrance to San Ygnacio. This is evidenced as well by the ruins of an old outpost that is marked on a 1942 topographic map. Today, San Ygnacio is situated some 35 miles south of Laredo and 35 miles north of Zapata (FIG. 6.2).

The early population of San Ygnacio was almost exclusively composed of transplanted residents of Revilla. In addition to the Treviño family, there were the families of Vicente Gutiérrez and Manuel Benavides García. Within a single generation, a Treviño married an Uribe, another Revilla-descended family that lived on the Uribeño ranch near Zapata. Don Blas María Uribe became a town patriarch and a successful businessman, establishing a train of pack mules that hauled goods between Corpus Christi and San Ygnacio, as well as a line of freight boats that

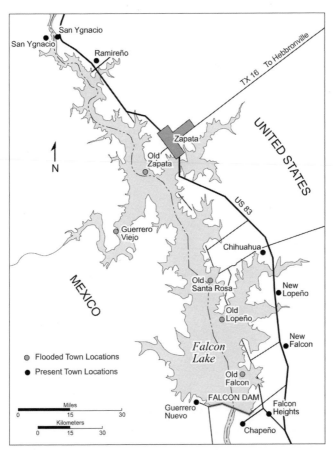

6.2. San Ygnacio and other towns in the Falcon Lake area.

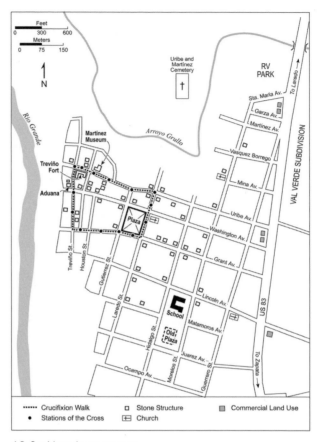

6.3. San Ygnacio townscape.

seasonally navigated the Rio Grande between San Ygnacio and Browns-ville.[6] Another family that became identified with San Ygnacio was the Martínez lineage, started by Cosme Damián Martínez who hailed from Revilla but lived in Laredo before moving in 1869 to San Ygnacio, where he also married into the Uribe clan. Cosme's son Don Proceso Martínez became a successful merchant, running a general store and managing farming and ranching lands, and served as a Zapata County official from 1869 to 1894.[7]

Before the railroad era in the late nineteenth century, San Ygnacio served as a pivot in trade between South Texas and Mexican markets in Monterrey, Monclova, and Saltillo. A primitive yet efficient ferry service across the Rio Grande at San Ygnacio allowed Texas cattle to be moved west and south into Mexico, while beans, flour, corn, *piloncillo* (raw sugar), and other staples were traded east and north across the river. A stone building on the west edge of town near the river served as an *aduana* (customhouse) when San Ygnacio was an official port of entry. On Fridays and Saturdays, custom agents from Laredo would visit San Ygnacio, then the only legal crossing along the Rio Grande between Laredo and the Lower Valley. A ferry service connected San Ygnacio, Texas, to San Ygnacio, Tamaulipas. During Prohibition, tequila smuggled from Mexico to Texas was reputed to enter through this port. The *aduana* was closed in 1967 when construction of a paved road on the Mexican side linked Nuevo Guerrero to Nuevo Laredo, thus bypassing San Ygnacio.[8]

The connections between the San Ygnacios in Texas and Tamaulipas were common until the *aduana* closed and ferry service halted. Adrián Martínez recalls regular crossings to shop in San Ygnacio, Tamaulipas, during the 1940s when he was growing up in San Ygnacio, Texas.

> The crossing was done only on Mondays and Tuesdays from 8 a.m. until 4 p.m. We went over on Mondays because that was the day the slaughtering of the animals took place and the meat was nice and fresh. I remember the ferry trip was 25 cents per person one-way. Other staples we would purchase besides the meat were sugar, piloncillo, table wine, Mexican candies, fruits and some vegetables.[9]

San Ygnacio's population was 198 in 1908 and reportedly reached 500 by 1917.[10] Decline set in during the Great Depression years, as the town's population fell to 400 in 1931 and 225 on the eve of the Second World War.[11] The postwar years saw San Ygnacio grow to a town of 1,000 by 1951.[12] In 1990 the town counted 871 residents. San Ygnacio's demographic profile mirrors the age distribution of Texas statewide, with 36 percent of the population less than 19 years old, 51 percent between the ages of 19 and 64, and 13 percent older than 64. The median age is 27.6 years, and males (455) slightly outnumber females (416). The town's Hispanic-origin population is 87.6 percent, mostly of Mexican ancestry, but with 42 residents claiming "other Hispanic" and 6 declaring Puerto Rican heritage. Some 752 San Ygnacians representing 92 percent of those 5 years old or older speak Spanish in the home. Almost 90 percent of the town residents were born in Texas, and about 10 percent are foreign-born. A remarkable 80 percent of residents surveyed in 1990 lived in the same house in the town in 1985, testifying to the deep-rootedness of the population.[13]

San Ygnacio's employed numbered 222 in 1990, with the largest single occupational category being craft and repair, followed by operators and laborers. Farming, service occupations, administrative support, and professional specialty positions were the remaining occupational categories in rank order. Approximately 79 percent of the town's employed population worked in Zapata County, with 21 percent working outside of the county in nearby centers like Laredo in Webb County. Some 36 percent of the town population was officially declared of poverty status in 1989, and almost three-quarters of this group were residents older than 65.[14]

San Ygnacio has largely remained a quiet village in the second half of the twentieth century. In 1951, however, the town was used in the filming of *Viva Zapata*. Also in 1951, the town was to be inundated by the reservoir that would result from the construction of Falcon Dam. Residents petitioned to have the condemnation of their town overturned on the grounds that the townsite was sufficiently above the anticipated high-water line of the reservoir to be safe from floods, and the community had escaped flood damage in years past. The petition was granted, but ironically San Ygnacio was partially inundated by the great river flood of 1953.

Legacy of the Built Environment
Hector Silva is a native San Ygnacian living in Laredo, but he visits his hometown because there is a quality of life there that is unique.

> I occasionally come here from Laredo when I desire tranquillity. There is a blend of history and solitude that transports me. When I stroll past some of the landmarks I feel they are mediums through which I can communicate with my past … All these buildings are testimonies to our pasts. For us to lose them, is to lose our roots.[15]

Dwellings have the power to evoke memory, a mnemonic important to many cultures. In small towns particularly, where residents become familiar with neighbors and knowledgeable about their surroundings, this quality is accentuated. Home is a repository of memory highly valued by San Ygnacians. In the past some residents of the community were able to range far and wide through business enterprises, yet most residents were circumscribed in their direct experience with the outside world, at least during their early years before adulthood broadened their horizons. This parochial nature was reinforced by an environmental sense of permanence, since much of the built landscape in San Ygnacio is constructed of stone, a material that did not readily change or disappear. Thus, residents developed strong attachments to the rock-wall, stuccoed buildings that give character to the town. Few realized the rare treasure of this landscape until recent years. Over the last two decades, San Ygnacio has been called "the most Mexican of all Texas border villages."[16] Without doubt, the inspiration for that declaration is the unusual quality of the historic built environment.

Until the 1870s, San Ygnacio remained a small settlement consisting of a few sandstone buildings arranged in a cluster around Treviño's fort near the present intersection of Treviño and Uribe Streets. In 1872 Don Blas María Uribe donated land for a church, Nuestra Señora del Refugio, and a town plaza. The town was platted in 1874. The community, labeled "Rancho de San Ignacio" on the plat, was arranged in a grid of some 20 blocks centered on the plaza, known first as Plaza Blas María and today as Plaza del Pueblo. By 1917 the town expanded south to Ocampo Street, and a second plaza called Uribe was constructed between Hidalgo, Morelos, Juárez, and Matamoros Streets.[17] Today, this lot is a little league baseball field and abuts the Benavides Elementary School (FIG. 6.3).

Until the 1950s San Ygnacio's main plaza—Blas María—was an open, unadorned space typical of early Mexican plazas (FIG. 6.4). Four stone buildings that presently surround the plaza were first constructed in the 1870s and 1880s. These include Nuestra Señora del Refugio Church, Amador Vela General Merchandise (abandoned; also known as the Manuel Sánchez house), the Trinidad Uribe house (present post office), and the M. B. Treviño house (also known as the Oscar Gutiérrez house) (FIG. 6.5). A program to beautify the plaza was initiated by the Delfino Lozano family during the 1960s. A covered *kiosco* was erected at the center of the plaza. Four diagonal walkways lead from the corners of the square to the *kiosco*, and trees and grass carpet the interstices. Like most plazas in South Texas towns, benches and light standards surround the space. A separate short walkway perpendicular to Laredo Street leads to a flagpole. In addition to the historic structures above, there is an abandoned grocery store (Lozano's) and seven other residences that mark the perimeter of the plaza.

As early as 1919, the stone buildings of San Ygnacio have intrigued outsiders, who have found them reminiscent of Spain and Mexico. Writing in *Architectural Record*, I. T. Frary commented: "The houses are built

6.4. Plaza Blas María Uribe around 1950.

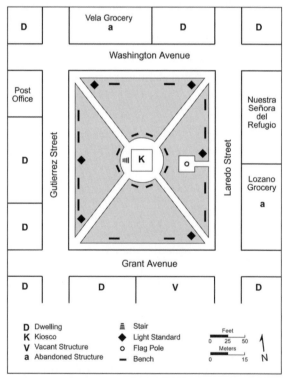

6.5. Plaza Blas María Uribe land use.

6.6. Stone house in San Ygnacio.

mostly of stone, plastered over and whitewashed, and against their white walls are contrasted the painted doors and window casings, which are invariably a bright blue in color."[18] In 1936, the Historic American Building Survey for Zapata County photographed many of the historic structures in San Ygnacio, a town that was yet to have a single paved street.[19]

Since at least 1964 when the Treviño fort-house—built in 1830 by the town founder and added to by later owners—was designated a Recorded Texas Historic Landmark, the stone buildings of San Ygnacio have attracted increasing regional, national, and international attention. In 1973, thirty-six stone buildings scattered throughout the town became a part of the San Ygnacio Historic District and were listed in the National Register of Historic Places.[20] According to architectural historian William Barbee, workers quarried sandstone, known as *piedra de arena*, east of town from hillsides where it is near the surface. Masons assembled the building pieces with mortar mud called *zoquete*. A plaster made from white sand from the Arroyo Grullo and lime-kilned locally sealed the stone (FIG. 6.6).[21] Most of these stone structures are located in the oldest section of town, north of Grant Avenue and west of Hidalgo Street (FIG. 6.3). In 1919, wattle-walled and thatch-roofed jacales were common in the town, housing the less well-to-do residents. Today, there are only a handful of surviving jacales and none are permanently occupied.

The Proceso Martínez house stands as one of the oldest and best-

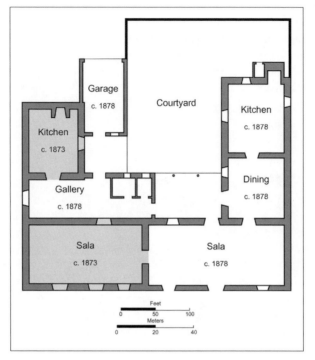

6.7. Proceso Martínez house, San Ygnacio.

preserved stone buildings in San Ygnacio. Proceso Martínez (1841–1937) was a prosperous merchant who opened the first general store in the town in 1868 and expanded his enterprise to become a successful importer-exporter through the 1920s. The oldest rooms of the Martínez house, the *sala* and kitchen, were constructed in 1873, but four additional rooms were built over the following decade, including a large *sala* that served as the general store (FIG. 6.7). Unlike the kitchens and gallery, the *salas* are airy rooms with high ceilings and with doors and windows that open directly to the street in typical Spanish and Mexican fashion. Because the exterior walls of the building adjoin the street line, sidewalks are absent. The rooms enclose a large courtyard that once functioned as a corral and storage area, with gates that opened wide to the street to accommodate teams of animals pulling wagons. Today, the Proceso Martínez house is owned by Adrián Martínez, Acela Martínez, and Adelfa Martínez, nephews of Don Proceso, and is operated as a museum and to some extent a family shrine. Many historic photos of the Martínez family grace the walls, and period furniture and artifacts decorate the rooms.

In the courtyard, several interior walls are painted with murals of the Martínez clan as well as a historic landscape view of a wagon train moving between Hacienda Dolores and Rancho San Ygnacio.

Ties that Bind

Reflecting on his life in San Ygnacio and his roots in Mexico, Adrián Martínez writes:

> Even before King Phillip sent that great fleet of battleships against the British, a man by the name of Juan Martínez Guajardo had already set foot somewhere in Mexico. He is the first of a long line of Martínezes on my father's side to be mentioned in Mexican archives. He is the patriarch of at least 16,000 descendants, most of whom live in Laredo and nearby towns.[22]

San Ygnacio remains a villagelike place, proud of its Texas Mexican heritage that it nurtures in several ways. Reverence for ancestors and *la familia* is fundamental to this outlook. Several San Ygnacian families can trace their ancestry to the colonial era, and remain tightly knit through ties that are reinforced by daily contact and occasional reunions. Religion helps to cement family to community. San Ygnacio celebrates several Catholic religious festivities, including one that has been practiced for almost the entire life of the town.

Two families, the Martínezes and the Uribes, have been intertwined with the history of San Ygnacio, and their legacies continue to influence the town. The Martínez lineage has been researched and described by Adrián Martínez, who grew up in San Ygnacio but now resides in Laredo. The Martínez family tree reaches to central Mexico in the sixteenth century, but it is more immediately rooted in nineteenth-century Revilla, from whence Cosme Damián Martínez hailed. Cosme's son Don Proceso Martínez, as described above, became a prominent entrepreneur and citizen of San Ygancio. Alberto Martínez Martínez, Don Preceso's son, fathered Adrián Martínez and his sisters, Acela and Adelfa (FIG. 6.8). The story of this line of the Martínez family is a bittersweet tale involving the early death of both parents and two other siblings and the orphan upbringing of Adrián, Acela, and Adelfa by aunts and uncles. The discovery and production of natural gas from family-inherited ranchlands transformed Adrián from a struggling restaurant manager into a wealthy philanthropist and investor in 1978.[23] Adrián's endowments to San Ygnacio

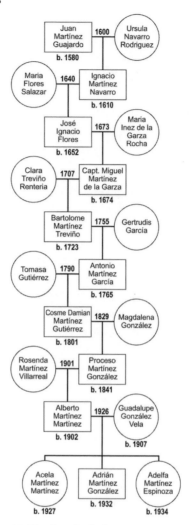

6.8. Martínez family line.

have included the renovation of several historic homes, as well as contributions to the restoration and appointments of San Ygnacio's Catholic church.

Mercurio Martínez (1876–1966), son of Don Proceso Martínez, worked in the "big swing" cotton harvest through East Texas. He later completed bachelor's and master's degrees at St. Edward's University in Austin, taught public school, and became a principal in Zapata. He was appointed Zapata County treasurer and sanitary inspector, worked as an accountant for a Laredo law firm, and coauthored a history of Zapata County. Mercurio's son, Mercurio Martínez Jr., taught at Laredo Junior College, runs a ranching and natural gas production business, and currently sits as a Webb County judge in Laredo.

The Uribe family, like the Martínez clan, is descended from Guerrero (formerly Revilla). In 1822, Doña Ygnacia Gutiérrez de Lara de Uribe and her sons Blas María and Juan Martín established residence north of Zapata at a place that became known as Uribeño Ranch. Blas María married into the Treviño family and thus became a resident of San Ygnacio. In 1842, upon the death of Don Jesús Treviño, founder of San Ygnacio, Blas María became a town patriarch. His interests included ranch livestock and a mercantile and freighting company that traded goods through Mexico. By his death in 1895, Don Blas had acquired more than half of the San Ygnacio division of the Borrego land grant, a total of some 100,000 acres.[24]

In 1983, some seven hundred descendants of the Uribe clan met at Rancho La Selva east of San Ygnacio for a reunion. Ten generations of the San Ygnacio Uribe clan attended the event, including Uribes from Laredo, Brownsville, Corpus Christi, San Antonio, Houston, and Dallas in Texas; Los Angeles, San Diego, North Hollywood, and Sacramento in California; Nuevo Laredo, Reynosa, Matamoros, and Mexico City in Mexico; and Detroit, Washington D.C., and Baltimore.[25]

The importance of the Uribe and Martínez lines to San Ygnacio is imprinted into the landscape beyond houses and plazas. Immediately north of the Arroyo Grullo on a high point of land is the private cemetery of the Uribe and Martínez families (FIG. 6.3). Here are interred the family patriarchs, Blas María Uribe and Proceso Martínez, as well as dozens of descendants. The graveyard is surrounded by a chain-link fence with cypress trees on the perimeter. Graves face west toward Mexico, and many are colorfully decorated with plastic flowers. A testimony to the powerful attachment to place exhibited by the Uribe and Martínez families was the 1978 disinterment of Trinidad Uribe, who died in Laredo in 1909. Although Trinidad was born in San Ygnacio, his family was unable to transport his body to San Ygnacio for its final resting place. Instead, he was buried in Laredo's Catholic Cemetery. Sixty-nine years after his death, the remains of Trinidad Uribe were unearthed and reburied in San Ygancio's Uribe-Martínez Cemetery. Trinidad is said to have left a legacy of 9 children, 26 grandchildren, 76 great-grandchildren, 196 great-great grandchildren, and 12 great-great-great grandchildren.[26]

South of San Ygnacio is the Cementerio del Pueblo or public cemetery, positioned on an open floodplain and surrounded by agricultural land. Early town founders like Vicente Gutiérrez and descendants of the Treviño clan are buried here. Because several grave markers are constructed of stone in crypt fashion, and because there are greater numbers of and larger trees around the site, it is likely that this cemetery predates the Uribe-Martínez graveyard. In Cementerio del Pueblo, graves also face west toward Mexico.

Like family, religion is a source of social cohesion that binds members of San Ygnacio to place. Catholicism has been part of the town at least since the church Nuestra Señora del Refugio was constructed on Plaza Blas María in 1874.[27] The church is a simple gothic structure with a single nave and belfry (see FIG. 6.4). There is no resident priest; instead, one visits from Zapata on Sundays and for special celebrations. In 1991, a fire severely damaged the structure, but the community rallied to raise money for its restoration. Repairs allowed the restored building to show off its original sandstone walls and vaulted ceiling and the mesquite lintels over windows. Local artisans recrafted mahogany doors, windows, and shutters, and forged metal hinges to lend historical accuracy to the restoration.[28]

The Catholic church is also the showcase of community spirit in its display of and veneration for the recently donated icon of the Virgin of San Juan de los Lagos, commissioned and presented by Adrián Martínez, who had an exact replica of the original icon crafted in Mexico. The icon is gilded with fourteen-karat gold and wears a blue gown given to Martínez by a bishop in San Juan, Mexico, where the original Virgin is resident. The hair of the Virgin is a gift of a twelve-year-old Mirando City, Texas, girl who, after making a *promesa* to the Virgin of San Juan, was healed of her paralyzed condition by the Virgin. The icon is part of the pantheon of religious figures in San Ygnacio's church that includes Nuestra Señora del Refugio, the Virgin of Guadalupe, Juan Bosco, and an image of Christ. The donation of the Virgin of San Juan spurred the celebration of San Juan Day, June 24, in which Mexican entertainment highlights a daylong fiesta.[29]

The most celebrated religious event in San Ygnacio is the Good Friday *procesión*. On every Good Friday since 1851, the town's residents have celebrated through procession the Via Dolorosa or Painful Walk, Christ's crucifixion walk.[30] To commemorate this event, fourteen stations of the cross are set up at specific points linked to San Ygnacio's

6.9. Good Friday procession in San Ygnacio.

prominent families. Each family is responsible for adorning a small table at the station stop in the middle of the street. The procession begins at Nuestra Señora del Refugio Church on the plaza and winds through the town, pausing at each station's table, where the celebrants place the statue of Nuestra Señora del Refugio and a liturgy is read (FIG. 6.3). A life-sized mesquite cross is carried in the parade, and participants sing homilies along the walk between the station stops (FIG. 6.9).

SAN DIEGO

San Diego, Texas, unlike its older and larger namesake in Southern California, is not immediately recognizable as a Mexican American place. Nevertheless, San Diego is a predominantly Texas Mexican community, typical of other small towns in the ranching, farming, and oil-producing region of South Texas.

San Diego remains special in at least two respects, however. Although it was founded in the nineteenth century under Anglo Texan political authority, its space arrangement conformed in principle to the classic Spanish colonial tradition, in which the plaza was the focus of the community. In fact, San Diego has two plazas, an unusual situation for such a small, villagelike place. The creation and use of these spaces distinguishes San Diego as one of the twenty plaza towns in South Texas, and the plazas have persisted into this century as symbolic social nodes for the local residents as well as others of this ethnic group in the region. The plazas of San Diego, like those in other towns of South Texas, are adaptations of the small-town public space heritage found in much of Latin America. Plaza creation and persistence reveal how public space in the Latin tradition has survived at this settlement scale and how it is being rediscovered and preserved in the South Texas region. San Diego is also one of several Duval County small towns that stage Mexican festivals or fiestas. This is an old tradition in the region that has been revived in Duval County with marked success; such fiestas typically attract more visitors to these small towns than the entire town population.

Founding, Growth, and Present Townscape

San Diego is located in central South Texas, about 100 miles south of San Antonio and roughly between Corpus Christi, a port city on the Gulf of Mexico, and Laredo, the Rio Grande town with a crossing into Mexico (FIG. 6.10). San Diego is situated on the Rio Grande plain, an undulating landscape of mesquite and woody scrub vegetation that stretches across

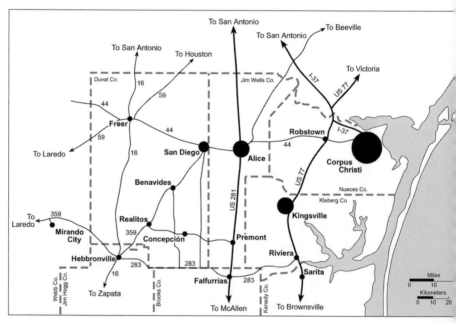

6.10. San Diego and vicinity.

much of the interior of South Texas. The site of San Diego reportedly was known to eighteenth-century travelers between La Bahía, Texas, and Mier, Tamaulipas, because of a nearby spring that contributes to San Diego Creek, which crosses the southern edge of the community.

Around 1800, Julian and Ventura Flores were granted by the Spanish Crown eight leagues (39,680 acres) of land consisting of two grants, San Diego Arriba and San Diego Abajo, in present-day Duval and Jim Wells Counties.[31] The first settlers to the area may have been herdsmen working for Flores, who founded a ranch here in 1815. The Flores family is said to have sold some of its grant land along the north bank of San Diego Creek to Pablo Pérez in 1848. Pérez brought a small group of settlers from Mier, erected several stone buildings, and called the settlement Perezville.[32] Perezville is reputed to have been renamed San Diego in 1852, when the town's first post office was established at the Casa Blanca, a stone house erected on the banks of San Diego Creek that still stands today and may well be the oldest surviving structure at the site. San Diego was little more than a trading center for mustang and wild cattle herders at this time.[33]

An early settler of Perezville/San Diego, Encarnación García is reported to have divided San Diego into parcels and lots, designating a plaza (present Padre Pedro Park) and a church. The Oblate Father Claude Jaillet was assigned to the parish and erected a wooden church, which became the only Catholic congregation between Corpus Christi and the Rio Grande.[34] Mexican families came to San Diego especially from Tamaulipas. Of thirty-three gravestones surveyed in the town cemetery that include information about place of birth, twenty show the deceased residents were born in Mier, Tamaulipas (FIG. 6.11). Other early families included García, Salinas, Pérez, and Soliz. Two early residents interviewed in 1954 were Señorita Maclovia García (eighty-seven) and her sisters, Refugio (ninety-three) and María (sixty-one), descendants of Encarnación García, who died in 1921. This family moved to San Diego from Mier, Tamaulipas, in 1864 and returned to Monterrey, Nuevo León, in 1896. They returned again to San Diego in 1915 to escape civil war in Mexico.[35]

Sheep ranching first dominated the local economy, and San Diego became a service center for surrounding ranches and a distribution point for the export of wool. This economy attracted several Anglo and European settlers, including Norman G. Collins, Frank C. Gravis, E. N. Gray, Walter W. Meek, James O. Luby, Frank W. Shaeffer, and William Hubberd. There was a notably cosmopolitan flavor to the town, with French families

6.11. Grave markers in San Diego cemetery showing birthplace as Mier, Tamaulipas.

including Gueydan, Bodets, Labbe, Tiblier, and Martinet; Germans like Brandt, Heldenfelt, Moos; and Jews such as Cohen, Levy, Henry, and Beta.[36]

From the beginning of settlement, San Diego's Mexican population was composed of prominent ranchers and merchants as well as working-class folk. Texas Mexicans have also been part of the entrepreneurial and political elite of San Diego and Duval County. Early on, Mexicans like Jacinto Guerra, García Saenz, and Bruno Ríos were represented in many businesses, from the wool trade to hat manufacturing, lodging, and retail. Later, after the decline of the Parr political machine in the county during the twentieth century, Texas Mexicans came to hold such political positions as county commissioner, judge, assessor, deputy sheriff and justice of the peace, and mayor.

In 1860, San Diego counted 38 people, only three of whom were not Mexican. By 1875, the town reportedly counted "about 500 Mexicans and 50 Americans," and the next year when Duval County was organized San Diego became the county seat.[37] In 1880 the town counted 1,000 residents and included a bank, three churches, and a Spanish-English weekly newspaper. San Diego claimed almost 2,000 people by 1910, and the population rose to 3,500 after oil was discovered in the region two decades later.[38] The town's population slipped to 2,674 in 1940 but rebounded to 4,394 in 1950. San Diego steadied at around 4,400 people until 1980, when it grew to

5,236.[39] In 1990 the town was home to nearly 5,000 residents, and 95 percent of the population was of Mexican ancestry.[40]

San Diego is a town organized by a grid of streets that are platted close to magnetic north, so that the checkerboard pattern is tipped slightly east of true north (FIG. 6.12). Two conditions have cut across this grid and

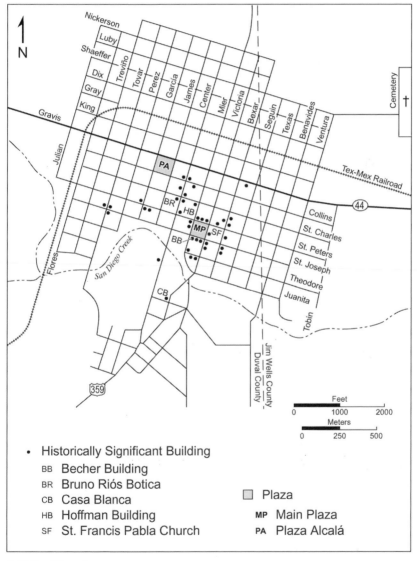

- Historically Significant Building
  - BB Becher Building
  - BR Bruno Riós Botica
  - CB Casa Blanca
  - HB Hoffman Building
  - SF St. Francis Pabla Church

- ☐ Plaza
  - MP Main Plaza
  - PA Plaza Alcalá

6.12. San Diego townscape.

impact the present townscape: a railroad and a county boundary. The San Diego, Rio Grande and Narrow Gauge Railroad was initiated by Uriah Lott, a New Yorker who resided in Corpus Christi. The line extended from that port town in 1876 and, after several interruptions, arrived in San Diego in 1879. San Diego remained the terminus of this railroad until 1881 when the line, renamed the Texas-Mexican Railway, was extended via Benavides and Hebbronville to Laredo.[41] This access proved valuable to the wool industry of the region, because Duval County claimed to be the nation's largest producer of wool between 1873–1883, and San Diego was the inland collecting point for transshipment to Corpus Christi for export. The railroad enters the town grid from the east, north of Texas Highway 44 along the Gray Street alignment, then turns south to exit San Diego along Flores Street on the western edge of town. Historically, several industrial land uses flanked this corridor, including a mill, a petroleum depot, and some warehousing.[42] While the railroad continues to operate, its role and importance to San Diego have diminished considerably from its past function, and at present there are no industrial activities along the line that benefit the town.

Political rule and competition with the town of Alice to the immediate east of San Diego created an unusual jurisdictional divide through the town that persists to the present. The powerful Parr family that kept a close rein on San Diego political affairs resisted attempts to encourage economic growth in the early twentieth century for fear of destabilizing their control of the town. As a consequence, nearby Alice became a hub city for the region and oil service center. When Jim Wells County was carved out of Duval and Nueces Counties, Alice became its county seat in 1911.[43] The western boundary of Jim Wells County bisects the eastern third of San Diego, so that a portion of the residential and commercial district of the town lies in a separate county (FIG. 6.12). When Jim Wells County officials were successful in routing U.S. 281, a major north-south corridor across South Texas, through Alice, San Diego lost a critical opportunity to position itself as a transportation node linking San Antonio with the Lower Rio Grande Valley (see FIG. 6.10).[44]

San Diego remains a socially and sometimes politically divided town still, despite the dominant Mexican-origin population. Different quarters of the city are given vernacular names that mirror these associations. The generally poorer residential district north and east of Gravis Street (Texas 44) is sometimes called Barrio de los Perros. By contrast, the old upper-income quarter southwest of Gravis Street and west of Center (Texas 359) has been known as El Clavelito (The Gavel) because so many of its former residents worked for the county and thus wielded economic clout.[45]

A Legacy of Plazas

San Diego's first plaza was created in 1876, when the town was platted at its present site.[46] The multicultural nature of the town was evident in an early photograph of the plaza that shows Mexican jacales mixed with European-inspired stonewalled houses with pitched roofs surrounding a palisade-fenced commons (FIG. 6.13). Today, the plaza is called Padre Pedro Park, in honor of Father J. Pedro Bard who served the town from 1877–1920. When the plaza was created, it was the central focus of the community and surrounded by institutional, commercial, and residential land uses (see FIG. 5.5).

Flanking Padre Pedro Plaza today are St. Francis de Pabla Church, on the east end of the square along Victoria Street, and the San Diego City Hall, opposite the church and facing Mier Street on the west end of the plaza (FIG. 6.14). These institutional anchors give the plaza its traditional authority, typical of such spaces throughout Mexico. Two abandoned merchant houses, the Becher Building, a limestone masonry structure built in 1891 on the southwest corner, and the Levy Building (now a church), a wood frame structure on the northwest perimeter, testify to

6.13. Main Plaza (Padre Pedro Park), San Diego, 1876.

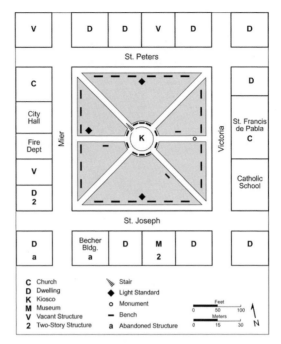

6.14. Padre Pedro Park (Main Plaza) land use.

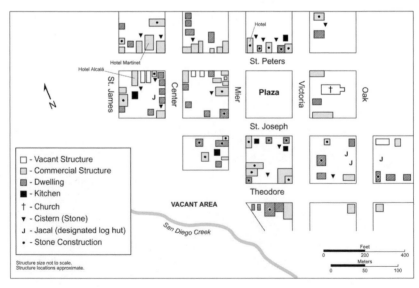

6.15. San Diego townscape, 1885.

former commercial enterprises on the plaza. The plaza measures 200 feet on each side and is separated from surrounding blocks by 70-foot-wide streets, 20 feet wider than standard street widths.

A comparison of fire insurance maps for San Diego in 1885, 1922, and 1932 illustrates changes in the evolution of the land uses around the plaza. In 1885, when the town counted 1,500 inhabitants, the square was surrounded by the town's first Catholic church, seven dwellings, and numerous businesses, including a hotel, boardinghouse, restaurant, barbershop, tailor's, tin shop, two grocery and dry goods stores, a notions store, a general store, and two billiard halls (FIG. 6.15).[47]

The plaza was the stage for the ritual promenade or paseo, an activity inherited from Mexico and practiced especially by the upper classes that lived close to the plaza. However, the activities that drew the entire community to the plaza were the *fiestas patrias* or Mexican patriotic celebrations, especially the Cinco de Mayo, which celebrates the Mexican victory over French forces in the Battle of Puebla, and the 16th of September, Mexican independence day. Hundreds of Mexican seasonal workers during the sheep-shearing season from April to June and again between August and September would crowd the plaza for these patriotic celebrations, providing a visible link between the culture of the homeland across the Rio Grande and the Mexican American town.

Like many plazas in Mexican towns, San Diego's plaza was without ornament or landscaping when first organized. Louis de Planque's remarkable photograph taken in 1876 shows the open space filled with jacales that were typical rural dwellings in northeastern Mexico during this era (FIG. 6.13). Arranged within the space were several *palizadas* or fenced enclosures, which suggests that the plaza may have been used as a commons to hold livestock such as sheep and goats. The first evidence that the plaza was more than an open space to accommodate animals appeared in an 1886 report of a celebration on the square organized to raise funds to improve and adorn the plaza. This account related how town folk walked around the brilliantly lighted space, patronizing numerous food stands, dancing to live music, and crowding around lottery stands from early in the evening until midnight.

Today, Padre Pedro Park includes an elevated, red-tile-roofed *kiosco* encircled by a concrete walkway that intercepts diagonal paths from the four corners of the space and receives two additional perpendicular walkways from the Victoria and Mier Street sides of the plaza (FIG. 6.14). In San Diego, Anna Hoffman Collins, a local benefactor, provided for the construction of the present church on the plaza and for the beautifica-tion of the plaza and its *kiosco* in 1904.[48] Presently, Padre Pedro Park is shrouded in live oak and elm trees that give a canopy effect to the space while ground cover consists of grass that is mowed and trimmed regu-larly by city workers. Three light standards give illumination to the plaza and no less than thirty-eight benches border the perimeter and walk-ways, many bearing the inscriptions of benefactors (FIG. 6.14).

Early in the twentieth century, a second plaza was built. Plaza Alcalá, as it became known, is situated approximately six blocks northwest of Padre Pedro Park (FIG. 6.12). It is not certain why a second plaza was created in such a small town. Changes in the fortunes of the local elite may have been a factor in the appearance of a new plaza. After 1910, the South Texas regional economy shifted from the export of wool to cotton. Several prominent Texas Mexican farmers and merchants benefited from this economic transformation, and it is likely that they saw the new plaza as symbolic of their particular stamp on the town's landscape.

This shift in the regional economy was mirrored by a shift of the business districts in San Diego. The old plaza, Padre Pedro Park, had been the focus of the late nineteenth-century wool export business. By 1932 the town's population neared 3,500, yet the number of businesses sur-rounding the old plaza had dwindled from twelve to six. When cotton became king in San Diego, a new commercial focus emerged on Center Street (Texas 359) between St. Peter's and Collins Streets. Today, this core has largely been abandoned in favor of a newer automobile commercial strip, but the derelict two-story brick storefronts that line Center Street testify to an earlier commercial prosperity.

Plaza Alcalá is located on Collins Street one block west of Center. It occupies a large city block and measures some 250 feet on each of its four sides, a larger space than the old plaza at Padre Pedro Park. In 1932, nine dwellings and three businesses including a hotel surrounded the plaza on three sides; the western flank across García Street was an open field. There is no church on the plaza. At the center of the square stood a high *kiosco* (since removed and replaced by a rectangular platform) where musical ensembles performed, both local bands and several orchestras that toured from Mexico. Surrounding the *kiosco* were wooden benches arranged for sitting; later this seating was covered, in part to shield the audience from the sun when the plaza became used for other celebrations. Unlike Padre Pedro Park, Plaza Alcalá is a strictly special event space, so that the gardenlike ambiance of shade trees, walkways, and commemorative benches is absent. It is more reminiscent of an athletic field or play-ground than a traditional Mexican plaza.

The special event that marked the Plaza Alcalá from early in the twentieth century was the Feria de San Diego. Fairs were common in South Texas towns during the early twentieth century, often held in the fall after the cotton harvest (see Chap. 8). These celebrations, like the *fiestas patrias*, were said to have attracted ranch families from across the region, usually to a nearby plaza town where festivities might go on for several days. One account of the feria at Plaza Alcalá recalled that food stands, lottery booths, and a roulette table defined the perimeter of the space, in addition to the requisite musical ensemble stationed in the central *kiosco*.

Today, fiestas and special occasions are still celebrated on the plazas in San Diego, but the traditional function of these spaces as social nodes has changed. Not surprisingly, the formal paseo has largely disappeared from Padre Pedro Park as a result of changes in attitudes about courting and the substitution of modern entertainment outlets like television and videos. The traditional plaza was the place to see and be seen, but that purpose has been replaced by other social activities. A significant contributor to this change has likely been the embracing of the automobile and enhanced mobility.

Nevertheless, Padre Pedro Park plaza remains a symbolic space, reinforcing the heritage of an earlier era. Perhaps because the town has remained small, the old plaza with its garden landscape is still used, if less frequently than in the past, as a social node by the local residents. Importantly, it persists as a formal plaza, with the parish church and city hall on two sides. These institutions bring town residents to the plaza weekly if not daily (FIG. 6.16).

Furthermore, Plaza Alcalá remains the site of San Diego's Pan de Campo Fiesta, the modern-day version of its early-twentieth-century feria which thereby may represent one of the longest-lived celebrations carried out in a plaza in the region.[49] Several towns in South Texas today stage these and other festivals in new city parks that are larger and more accommodating to crowds than the historic plazas. Yet in San Diego the Pan de Campo Fiesta, celebrated on the first weekend in August, attracts some 15,000 visitors over three days, swelling the town by a greater number of people than its total resident population. Changing social awareness enhanced by such special events in plazas may signal the rediscovery of the Mexican plaza as a social space in towns across South Texas. San

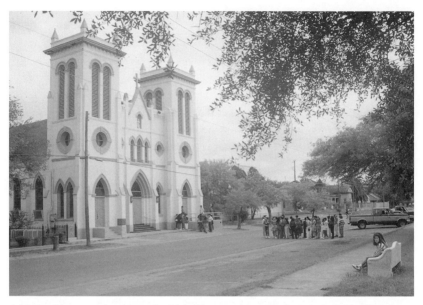

6.16. San Diego youth prepare for Holy Communion at St. Francis de Pabla Church on Main Plaza.

Diego has commissioned a study to incorporate Padre Pedro Park into a historic district focused on the plaza and adjacent historic buildings like the Becher Building.[50] These preservation efforts may be a vehicle for the revitalization of these traditional spaces. That plazas are being restored and rejuvenated here suggests the recognized importance of this symbolic space to Mexican-ancestry people in the region and the need to formalize and give visible expression to a pride of place.

COTULLA

In a recent survey of small town living in the United States, only two communities in South Texas qualified as "decent" places by complex criteria of size, relative location, and function.[51] One of these places is Cotulla, a nineteenth-century railroad town of 3,694 people and the county seat of La Salle County. Cotulla is roughly equidistant from San Antonio and Laredo on I-35, on the eastern edge of the Texas Winter Garden District (see FIG. 6.1). Founded immediately north of the Nueces River, the small town evolved as a classic dual town in which the railroad corridor divided the Anglo Texan from the Texas Mexican community. At the end of

World War II, the town was still mostly Anglo, but by the mid-1970s Cotulla was 65 percent Mexican American. Today, 79 percent of the town is of Mexican ancestry. Cotulla thus serves as an example of the transformation process in South Texas towns, where Texas Mexicans have come to dominate the landscape of a place as well as its population.

Cotulla was created on land donated by Polish-born settler Joseph Cotulla to induce the International and Great Northern Railroad to extend through La Salle County in 1881. In the same year, a local postmaster, Jesse Laxton, surveyed and created a townsite adjacent to Cotulla on the east side of the railroad corridor that now bisects the town. In a spirit of competition and rivalry that has highlighted many frontier towns, Laxton followed an obscure Texas law that called for county seats to be named after the county name, and in 1881 he was granted a post office for his fledgling settlement named, appropriately, La Salle.[52] These two place names persisted on some maps into the twentieth century, although La Salle was formally incorporated into Cotulla in 1883 when the county seat was also moved to Cotulla.

This early dual founding persists in a double street grid, in which the Cotulla portion is oriented northwest-southeast and positioned west of the railroad corridor, while the portion that was La Salle is chiefly aligned northeast-southwest and east of the track that is now the Missouri Pacific Railroad (FIG. 6.17). Until recently, this railroad divide was also a social barrier, because the Texas Mexican population was historically segregated to the east of the track and Anglo Texan residents to the west.[53]

Over the years, the commercial focus of Cotulla has gradually slid west with changes in transportation and access. Front Street was the town's first main drag, and the two-story brick storefronts that face the railroad track testify to that early location. When the auto era appeared, Cotulla's new commercial drag shifted one block west to Main Street (also Business U.S. 81), evident today by the concentration of old service stations and motels, some abandoned, that line this strip, along with eateries, grocery stores, a pharmacy, and a liquor store among others. The most recent slide has been further to the west, where the I-35 bypass has witnessed the collection of newer service stations, motels, and eateries clustered where FM 468 crosses the interstate. Front Street is not completely abandoned, however, as a western clothing store, hardware store, video store, and city offices are in place there. Main Street as well contains a dozen or so viable businesses amidst a pallor of decay.

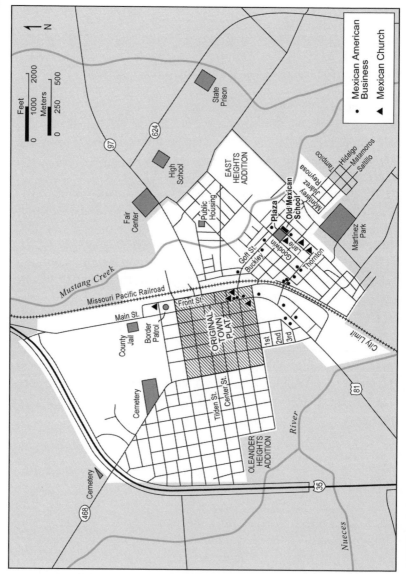

6.17. Cotulla townscape.

Mexican Barrio

True to disamenity location theory, Cotulla's Mexican American barrio, sometimes referred to as La Colonia, is largely situated on low ground and wedged between the railroad track and Mustang Creek, a precarious location that makes the district subject to flooding when waters rise in the creek (FIG. 6.17). An elevated area or heights east of the creek extends the barrio to the city limits. Although most streets in the quarter do not have Spanish names, others like Sánchez, Juárez, Hidalgo, Garza, Reynosa, Matamoros, Saltillo, and Tampico belie the Anglo Texan character of the neighborhood.

An eastside landmark is Plaza Florita, built in 1925 on donated land and dedicated to Mrs. J. T. Maltsberger. Although it is off-center relative to the grid, the plaza may have been centrally focused when first built, because it is surrounded on three sides by a Protestant church (originally Our Lady of Guadalupe), two grocery stores, and a preschool and kindergarten that was built as a "Mexican school." As is typical of plazas in other South Texas towns, Plaza Florita is square with diagonal walkways leading to a central *kiosco,* surrounded by a fountain, seating areas, palms and deciduous trees, grass, and no less than thirty-three commemorative stone and concrete benches (FIG. 6.18). A platform and a basketball court are positioned at one end, and light standards exist at the corners. The plaza appears little used except for the occasional pickup basketball game, but the space is not in disrepair and is maintained as a signature of community pride. Special events staged at the plaza include a high school seniors dance in the spring, and the church *jamaica* or social in the fall. In the past, the 16th of September and Cinco de Mayo were celebrated on Plaza Florita, but are irregularly held at the square in recent times according to local informants.

Like barrios all across South Texas, Cotulla's Mexican quarter has businesses separate from those of the town's Main Street. The primary artery is Thornton Street, which includes a grocer, barbershop, furniture store, and butane service center, feedstore, and two houses converted to bars (FIG. 6.17). A few other businesses including a beauty salon operated out of a home, a record store, and some abandoned enterprises like the Ramirez Meat Market are scattered throughout the district. Typical of many small towns in the region, zoning ordinances do not exist, so that a backyard auto garage business can thrive in the middle of a residential neighborhood.

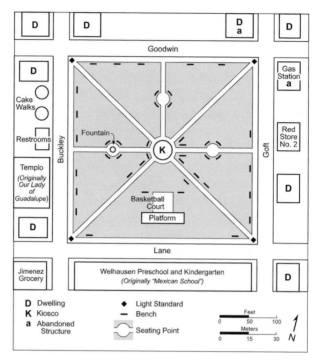

6.18. Plaza Florita land use.

Three active churches, all Protestant, exist in the barrio. In addition to the plaza church, originally Our Lady of Guadalupe, there is the Iglesia Metodista and Primer Iglesia Bautista on Lane Street, each of which offers services in Spanish. Three additional fundamentalist churches with Texas Mexican congregations are found immediately west of the railroad track along and near Front Street; one is a River of Life Outreach church and two are storefront churches, a Liberty Christian Ministry and a Foursquare Gospel church. The Sacred Heart Catholic Church is located on Main Street at Rio Grande, outside of the barrio proper. The explanation for this may lie in the fact that the church has always served several populations, both Mexican Catholics and Catholic Poles and Czechs that have been part of Cotulla from its founding. Sacred Heart advertises a Spanish-only Sunday mass at eight in the morning and an English mass at ten. The Anglo Texan population in Cotulla is served by a First Baptist, a First Methodist, and a First Presbyterian Church, located on the west side of town.

Cotulla's barrio housescapes, a house and its immediate surroundings, are typical of those seen in other Texas Mexican towns (FIG. 6.19).[54]

Fenced-front properties, usually a four-foot-high chain-link enclosure, bright exterior house colors of aquamarine, hot pink, and canary yellow, and eclectic yard art including religious shrines are each evident in the residential landscape. An especially common embellishment is the family nameplate that graces the most humble abode. Houses range widely in style: simple clapboard as well as board-and-batten jacales, traditional mass-planned small houses with pitched roofs common from the 1920s to the 1940s, many mobile homes both old and new, and a very few newly constructed conventional houses of neoeclectic styles. Near Mustang Creek, house properties are more expansive *ranchitos* with livestock, including horses, bulls, and chickens. Two homes included extensive housing for fighting-cocks in the backyards. A small compound of duplexes that pass for public housing is located on Pecos Street facing Texas Highway 97.

From Dual Town to Texas Mexican Town
Inherent in the concept of a dual town is the recognition that two separate social groups occupy different spaces in a community. In the Mexican American borderlands the divide between the two groups has more often than not been a railroad track.[55] The map reveals the geometry of

6.19. Housescapes in Cotulla's barrio. Mexican American houses are frequently painted in bright exterior hues. The house on the left is aquamarine; the one on the right is lavender.

spatial inequality that results from this division. Historically, Cotulla's Texas Mexicans have occupied a smaller segment of town space, but that is changing rapidly as the Anglo Texan population of the community shrinks and the Mexican-descent population expands.

Some Texas Mexicans in Cotulla have long resided west of the railroad corridor, especially below Rio Grande Street, the city limit in 1933; it is a zone where the river terrace that supports most of the Anglo Texan neighborhoods of the west side of town falls off toward the Nueces bottom (FIG. 6.17). Besides this hollow along 1st, 2nd, and 3rd Streets there are now scattered Texas Mexican households all across the southern part of the old town grid up to Center and Tilden Streets. To determine the spatial spread of the Texas Mexican households, I plotted the locations by addresses for Hispanic surnames given in the 1996 Cotulla telephone directory, a total of 368 households. Eighty percent (295) of the Hispanic-surname households are located in the east side barrio and on streets of the west side below Tilden Street. An area in the north and west of the town—part of the original town plat and an addition called Oleander Heights—contains the remaining 20 percent (73) of Hispanic-surname households. Field inspection of every street in this quarter, with particular attention to Mexican American housescape elements including family nameplates, suggests that this district is still predominantly Anglo Texan but is beginning to exhibit a succession of Texas Mexicans in houses on some streets. Unlike the Mexican quarter, this Anglo residential district shows few signs of a young or middle-aged population. Few children's toys or children playing outside are evident. Homes are clear of much yard clutter, but some appear unkempt, suggesting aging residents perhaps unable to maintain the exterior. The telling signature of the Anglo American housescape here remains the front lawn, something largely absent from the Mexican American housescape. Front yard fencing, another Mexican American housescape diagnostic, is almost entirely absent from this west side district, except in those properties along the southern edge of the quarter.

The transformation of the southern portion of Main Street to predominantly Texas Mexican owned and operated businesses is yet another signal of the decline of Anglo Texan influence in Cotulla. Mexican enterprises along Main Street include, for example, Riverside Mini-Mart (with *barbacoa* available on Saturdays and Sundays), Carta Blanca Bar, Uncle Moe's Country Kitchen and Comida Mexicana (owned by the Ruiz family since 1973), Valdez Bakery and Panadería, García's Cash and Carry Grocery, Montemayor Service Station, and others (FIG. 6.17).

Cotulla still survives economically as a dual town. Like many county seat towns of the South Texas region, government at all levels is the largest single employer.[56] School districts and city and county offices have historically shared the majority of this workforce, and Mexican Americans here as elsewhere hold a large percentage of these bureaucratic positions. Cotulla also has a regional U.S. Border Patrol office and field station, as well as a new state correctional facility that alone employs 110 persons. But reminiscent of the railroad speculation that gave birth to the community, modern Cotulla, which is equidistant from San Antonio and Laredo, hopes to profit from increased highway trade along I-35.

EPILOGUE

While San Ygnacio, San Diego, and Cotulla typify Mexican American small towns in the South Texas region, each of these places also represents a cultural quality that is being revived, preserved, and reshaped. With expanding urbanism across the country, small town life has seen a resurgence of popularity. How might South Texas Mexican small towns capitalize on their cultural-historical heritage?

In San Diego, a recent study declared that the single most significant asset for the town is the richness of its cultural resources, especially its existing historical structures and the town's vaquero legacy, one of the first effective economic activities of the area. San Diego can capitalize on this cultural heritage in two ways. One avenue, the Pan de Campo Fiesta, is already being promoted with marked success. This event brings historic visibility to the town and highlights the nineteenth-century ferias and vaquero legacy, while bringing critical revenue that is used to beautify the community. The festival also functions as an inspiration for family reunions, bringing San Diegans that are scattered all across Texas and the nation to their hometown for several days in August. Mayor Alfredo Cardenas, who is also publisher of the *Duval County Picture*, notes that newspaper circulation outside the county is substantial and that this publication allows expatriate San Diegans to keep up with local happenings. A second effort that has yet to be fully implemented is the historic restoration of buildings around Padre Pedro Park and along Center Street, in order to create an historic district. A museum presently exists in a restored building on Main Plaza, but the reconstruction of the historic built environment might stimulate further investment and tourist activity. Millions of tourists are drawn to the Rio Grande Valley each year, and

San Diego is in a strategic position nearby; it is accessible to U.S. 281, one of the primary transportation corridors connecting central Texas to the Valley, which would seem to give it great advantage over other, less historically significant stopovers.

San Ygnacio, perhaps even more than San Diego, is poised to benefit from the cultural tourism that is being promoted as part of Los Caminos del Río Heritage Project, which highlights historic places on either side of the Lower Rio Grande between Brownsville–Matamoros and Laredo–Nuevo Laredo.[57] San Ygnacio's cultural significance is already recognized by its national historic district status, but the State of Texas has also proposed a preservation strategy.[58] Major interpretive themes might include San Ygnacio's rich architectural fabric, a subject for guided and self-guided tours, and the town's cultural continuity, since many town residents are descended from early-nineteenth-century founding families. These themes might be promoted to Texans and Mexican nationals alike, because San Ygnacio is one of only a handful of settlements in the United States effectively founded as Mexican towns before 1848.

Finally, Cotulla is most directly poised to benefit from the increased motor traffic between San Antonio and Laredo. This is clear from the recent developments along the I-35 bypass. But Cotulla can be more than a convenience stop. Given its historic importance as a railroad distribution node for both ranching and irrigated onion farming, the town could add to an already interesting county museum by expanding displays that accentuate the role of Texas Mexicans in its local history and economy. Like San Diego, Cotulla is a county seat and thus has the greatest likelihood of designing and directing its own future as a cultural center in the Winter Garden District.

It [San Antonio] is the first American city of any importance which the Mexican merchant visits when he comes to the States, and to her commercial interests he applies when in need of goods.

—BUSINESS MEN'S CLUB OF SAN ANTONIO, 1899

We Know Mexico. Mexico Knows Us. Serving Two Nations Since 1892.

—ADVERTISEMENT FOR LAREDO NATIONAL BANK, 1998

Texas Mexican Cities

In 2000 Texas counted nine of the top twenty cities in the United States with the largest Mexican American populations. In three of these Texas cities Mexican Americans were a majority of the population: San Antonio, El Paso, and Laredo. In the South Texas towns of San Juan, Eagle Pass, Laredo, Robstown, Brownsville, Mercedes, and Pharr, Mexican Americans comprised 90 percent or more of the population (TABLE 7.1). Yet, demographic dominance alone fails to communicate the symbolic significance of place. In South Texas, San Antonio and Laredo are emblematic cities with historic reputations as cultural and economic centers for Texas Mexicans.

One of the strongest measures of urban identity is the association of a city with a particular ethnic group and its landscape. The

TABLE 7.1 Places with the Largest Absolute and Relative Mexican American
Populations, 2000

LARGEST NUMBER OF MEXICAN AMERICANS		HIGHEST PERCENTAGE OF MEXICAN AMERICANS	
City	Population	City	Population
Los Angeles, Calif.	1,719,073	Coachella, Calif.	97.3
Chicago, Ill.	750,644	E. Los Angeles, Calif.	96.8
Houston, Tex.	730,865	Socorro, Tex.	96.4
San Antonio, Tex.	671,394	Maywood, Calif.	96.3
Phoenix, Ariz.	449,972	Calexico, Calif.	95.2
El Paso, Tex.	431,875	San Juan, Tex.	95.1
Dallas, Tex.	422,587	Eagle Pass, Tex.	94.8
San Diego, Calif.	310,752	Laredo, Tex.	94.1
San Jose, Calif.	269,969	Commerce, Calif.	93.6
Santa Ana, Calif.	257,097	Nogales, Ariz.	93.5
Austin, Tex.	200,579	Robstown, Tex.	93.0
Denver, Colo.	175,704	Brownsville, Tex.	91.2
Tucson, Ariz.	173,868	Pharr, Tex.	90.6
Fresno, Calif.	170,520	Mercedes, Tex.	90.0
Laredo, Tex.	166,216	Edinburg, Tex.	88.6
Long Beach, Calif.	165,092	Donna, Tex.	87.1
Ft. Worth, Tex.	159,368	San Benito, Tex.	86.9
Corpus Christi, Tex.	150,737	S. El Monte, Calif.	86.0
Brownsville, Tex.	139,722	Douglas, Ariz.	85.9
E. Los Angeles, Calif.	120,307	Mission, Tex.	81.0

SOURCE: U.S. Bureau of the Census, *2000 Census of Population and Housing.*

NOTE: Places with the largest number of Mexican Americans have greater than 100,000 population, and places with the highest percentage of Mexican Americans have greater than 10,000.
Population totals given as Hispanic or Latino in preliminary 2000 census. Based on 1990 census,
places given were the most Mexican American places.

Chinese in San Francisco and the French Creoles in New Orleans are
examples, but there are many others. This pattern of urban ethnic association has persisted in this century, although today many of the United
States' older urban immigrant centers are less diverse than newer immigrant destinations.[1] For example, immigrants are significant in Los Angeles where Hispanic subgroups combined count as 46 percent of the city
population, in New York where they measure 27 percent of the total city
population, and in Chicago where Hispanics are 26 percent of the city

residents.[2] These examples of demographic concentration alone do not ensure a Hispanic identity for these megapolitan places, because a Hispanic plurality exists in each. Even Los Angeles, where Hispanic has long been equated with Mexican, is now diversified by the presence of Cubans, Central Americans, and South Americans in different quarters.[3]

In 1920, San Antonio was the city with the most Mexican Americans. Today, among large cities, San Antonio is the urban area with the highest proportion of Mexican Americans in the country; the Hispanic subgroup was 59 percent of the city in 2000. San Antonio's claim as the premier ethnic capital for the Mexican subgroup still has significant currency because, unlike other big cities with numerically large Mexican-descent populations, in San Antonio Mexicans are unchallenged as *the* Hispanic group of the city demographically, socially, and historically.

By 1930, Laredo was the fourth-largest Mexican American city in the United States, after Los Angeles, San Antonio, and El Paso.[4] This meant then that Laredo had more Mexican Americans than Chicago, Houston, or Tucson. Today, among South Texas cities with greater than 100,000 population, Laredo has the largest proportion of Mexican Americans in the region, counting more than nine of every ten residents as members of this ethnic group. Laredo's ancestry—it is one of the oldest Hispanic-founded towns in the United States—and its continuous social and economic association with Mexico, especially as a gateway, have served to create a unique bond between Texas and Mexico.

This chapter describes how and explains why San Antonio and Laredo are the most symbolic Texas Mexican cities.

SAN ANTONIO: THE TEJANO CAPITAL

Early boosters bestowed on San Antonio a series of epithets, including the City of Missions (there are five), the Metropolis of Texas (it was the state's largest city until 1930), and the City of the Alamo (certainly the most famous of the five missions). San Antonio was recognized as a predominantly Mexican place as well. References to the city such as "the old capital of Mexican life and influence" and "the capital of the Mexico that lies within the United States" were declarations made by some of the city's more celebrated observers.[5]

The association of Mexicanness with San Antonio has evolved over the city's life of almost three centuries. During the colonial era and into the nineteenth century, the city center, especially its plazas, embodied much of the spirit of the place. By the twentieth century, the largely segregated West Side business district and surrounding barrios became the Mexican quarter. Today, residues of these Mexican landscapes and others survive in the modern city, yet San Antonio's Mexicanness is not captured easily by a single landscape or place. Rather, the city has emerged as a sort of cultural mosaic of things Mexican but with a twist that incorporates a plural or mixed heritage. Emblematic to that end, San Antonio seems to have reinvented itself as the Tejano capital, a symbolic proclamation of its Mexican roots grafted to a Texan spirit that seeks national attention.

San Antonio de Béxar

San Antonio was founded early in the eighteenth century on the northeastern frontier of New Spain. Between 1718 and 1731, five missions, a presidio, and a *villa* (civilian colony) evolved as the nucleus of the settlement.[6] This concentration of varied institutions at one general location made San Antonio unique among settlements in the Spanish borderlands. The missions were scattered along the San Antonio River, and the presidio and *villa* were situated between San Pedro Creek and the river where it makes an ax-shaped eastward meander.

The *villa* was known as San Fernando after 1731, but the presidio name, San Antonio de Béxar, usually shortened to Béxar, persisted throughout the Spanish period.[7] San Antonio served as the capital of the province of Texas and was granted city status in 1811, making it the equal of Durango, Saltillo, and Monterrey. Positioned on the far northeastern edge of the Spanish colonial domain, San Antonio remained a border town with a population that hovered around 2,000.[8]

From its founding early in the eighteenth century, San Antonio was a presidial settlement, and the present Military Plaza or Plaza de Armas was technically the community's first open place, although it was not used as public space until the nineteenth century. In 1731, colonists from the Canary Islands organized the Villa de San Fernando immediately east of the presidio and created a second public place, known in early days as Plaza de las Islas (after the Canary Islands) and today simply called Main Plaza (FIG. 7.1).[9] Joseph de Urrutia's *Plano de la Villa y Presidio de S. Antonio de Vejar* in 1767 showed these two plazas as distinctive open areas amid the few scattered blocks of the fledgling settlement.[10] More than a half century later, the two plazas were still the chief public places of the built landscape of San Antonio, visible in Ygnacio de Labastida's 1836 map of the city.[11]

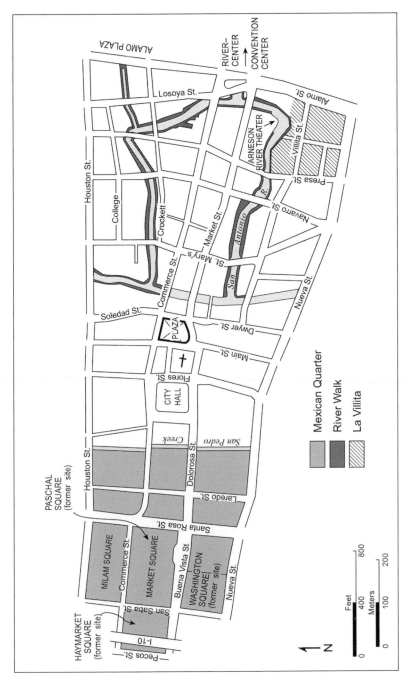

7.1. Downtown San Antonio.

Sovereignty of San Antonio changed three times between 1820 and 1850: from Spain to the Republic of Mexico in 1821, from Mexico to the Republic of Texas in 1836, and then to statehood in the United States in 1845. The population almost doubled, rising to 3,500, and Mexicans became an increasingly significant part of this total. The settlement continued to comprise three distinctive, partly integrated communities: the secularized missions, a military garrison at the Alamo, and the civil colony at San Fernando that consisted of four separate barrios.[12]

As San Antonio accommodated a more cosmopolitan—especially European—population in the middle to late nineteenth century, the town's principal plazas became the social centers of the local community, as well as the chief attractions visited by outsiders. The "plazas filled a unique role by serving as combination bazaar, amusement park, and thoroughfare for townspeople, soldiers, visiting cattlemen, health-seekers, and often astonished tourists."[13] The remarkable glass slides and stereograph photos made by amateur and professional photographers capture the caravanesque atmosphere at San Antonio's plazas during this era.[14]

It was also during the last decades of the nineteenth century that San Antonio made the transition from a Hispanic to a Euro-Texican town. The townscape changes that appeared then marked the emerging dual landscape that would develop in the commercial center of the city. The city was still significantly Hispanic, but the cultural stamp of this group was beginning to fade as a more pluralistic imprint appeared. By the early twentieth century, this process led to the division of San Antonio, creating separate downtowns, one Mexican and one Anglo.

Plaza de Armas or Military Plaza was the open space surrounded by San Antonio's presidio (present City Hall) (FIG. 7.1). Urrutia's eighteenth-century map shows the presidio and plaza bounded by an *acequia* or irrigation ditch to its west (present San Pedro Creek) and by the back side of San Fernando Cathedral facing Main Plaza to the east. On its sides, the space was surrounded by adobe structures that made up the presidio, several of them small and scattered and others L-shaped dwellings or continuous long blocks.[15] It is doubtful that the plaza space was ever completely enclosed by the presidio. Maps published between 1836 and 1855 show remnants of the old presidio, essentially pieces of the north and south blocks of barracks and dwellings.[16] William Corner, whose map of 1890 shows the dwellings and ramparts as they once existed, states these structures had been removed by 1850.[17] Before that time, the Plaza de Armas was not a public space but rather a military post for soldiers, families, and animals. Corner's map gives early property owners on surrounding blocks as Pérez, Rodríguez, Bustillos, and Flores, but also indicates elsewhere that the city had acquired several parcels on this periphery from private holders.

In 1892, a stylish French Second Empire city hall designed by Otto Kramer and built of native Texas limestone and polished granite was built on Military Plaza (FIG. 7.1). Because the hall was positioned in the center of the plaza, it disrupted permanently the decades-long tradition of the plaza as open space market, social center, and general gathering place. One contemporary observer lamented:

> It [the hall] will prove an ornament to the city and a credit to the administration under which it is being built, though it will doubtless be viewed with a sigh by many who see in its erection the obliteration of the most picturesque sights of our city—viz; the Mexican chili con carne stands and markets.[18]

The transformation of Military Plaza from an open informal gathering spot to the site of a formal municipal government seat was a process that would nearly repeat itself at San Antonio's other major plaza. When the Villa de San Fernando was created in 1731, the *casa real* or municipal office was erected on the east side of Plaza de las Islas, directly across from San Fernando Cathedral, then the dominant landmark in the open space (FIG. 7.1).[19] When Bexar County built its first modern courthouse in 1882—in French Second Empire style designed by Alfred Giles— it was positioned one block north of Plaza de las Islas on Soledad Street, thus preserving at least temporarily the church's dominance over the plaza. In 1896, however, a new courthouse in dazzling Romanesque style designed by James Riely Gordon and built with native Texas red sandstone and granite was completed on a south corner of the plaza. This courthouse, which still stands, is a massive building flanked by towers— one seven stories tall with a beehive spire—and sits prominently on the better part of the entire north-facing block of the plaza between the San Pedro Ditch and old Quinta (presently Dwyer) Street (FIG. 7.1). This encroachment on Main Plaza capped several decades of private property conversions that had been slowly transforming plaza-front parcels originally owned by families with Hispanic names like Treviño, Flores, Salinas, Yturri, Grenados, and Montes to non-Hispanic ones like Maverick, Lewis, Callaghan, Groesbeeck, Dwyer, and Frost.[20] The flat-roofed adobe, single-story buildings that once surrounded this plaza were replaced mostly by stone structures, as well as by some brick and frame structures, by 1892. Residences gave way to hotels, mercantiles, saddle and harness shops, and especially the saloons that were plentiful on the perimeter of almost every block.[21]

At the turn of the century, then, the two major public places of San Antonio had been encroached upon and each converted from its previous Hispanic authority to a newly dominant Anglo Texan cultural imprint. This landscape change mirrored the demographic shift that occurred in the city between the Spanish colonial and the early Mexican era, when the population was chiefly Hispanic. By the late nineteenth century, multiethnic migration from Europe, the upper and lower South, the North, and other parts of Texas remade the city. In 1850 San Antonio's Hispanic—largely Mexican—population was some 47 percent of the total number of residents, but in 1900 that percentage dropped to 22 percent.[22] The percentage of San Antonio's population counted as Mexican would not exceed the 1850 percentage for many decades. Nevertheless, the absolute number of Mexicans in the city changed dramatically, from 14,000 to 84,000 during the first three decades of the twentieth century, as Mexican immigrants flooded San Antonio and it became the central pivot of Mexican influence in the United States.[23] That process would again produce a genuine Hispanic landscape, but one that was segregated and alien for almost all but the Mexicans of the city.

The Mexican Quarter

By early twentieth century, observers of the local scene in San Antonio repeatedly remarked upon the distinctive geographic situation of the Mexican population in the city. For many, crossing the San Pedro Creek to the west of Military Plaza was the equivalent of fording the Rio Grande. "You might imagine yourself in Mexico as you cross to the west-side of San Pedro Creek and proceed in the direction of the West Side Squares."[24] In 1938 one of the guidebooks to the city declared that San Pedro Creek, long a line of demarcation, was westward from the old plazas of the Spaniards yet within sound of the cathedral bells of San Fernando, and the point at which the Mexican quarter of San Antonio begins.[25] In the years following the Second World War, this segregated geography of the central city was still very much evident to residents and outsiders. "The Mexican district of San Antonio is a city all to itself, existing side by side with the gringo city across San Pedro Creek. It stretches away south and west of Milam Square, toward the stockyards and beyond the Missouri Pacific Railroad. Into this area of about four square miles—comprising perhaps six hundred city blocks—the vast majority of San Antonio's Mexicans are crowded."[26] The heart of this trans–San Pedro quarter was a ten-block core of commercial land and open squares west of the creek between Houston Street on the north, Monterey Street (presently Nueva) to the south, and extending west to Pecos Street (presently west of the Interstate 10 loop) (FIG. 7.1).

During the 1920s and 1930s, this district was focused on the city market, originally a three-block-long parcel between Santa Rosa and Leona Streets (beyond Pecos Street). Once designated as Presidio Square, this land became city property in the 1890s, when the market function of Military Plaza relocated here after the city hall came to occupy that space. A new brick and iron market house, in modified Queen Anne style designed by Alfred Giles, was positioned on the eastern third of the block between the old Produce Row (a pedestrian mall today) and Commerce Street and included a refrigeration plant with a large meat-processing capacity.[27] This new market was strategically flanked by open squares on all four sides. Washington Square to the south and Haymarket Square to the west were open-air spaces that came to be the principal produce markets for the city; Milam Square to the north and Paschal Square to the east of the city market were essentially pedestrian plazas (FIG. 7.1). At Haymarket Square, the chili stands that once gave Military Plaza much of its pungent character continued to operate in the evenings until 1937, when city ordinances prohibiting street vending of food were enforced. Nevertheless, the square continued to perform as the social center for wandering bands of Mexican minstrels. At Milam Square, men seeking day or seasonal labor would gather routinely. Also, in the summer the square hosted the civic event known as "Night in Mexico," in which local organizations sponsored Mexican folk dances and other traditional celebrations.[28]

East of Santa Rosa across from the market squares was a six-block area that contained the highest concentration of Mexican-operated and -patronized businesses in the city, perhaps in all of the United States (FIG. 7.1). Because San Antonio was recognized in Mexico and across the southwestern states as a major commercial node for a vast agricultural hinterland and a collecting point for migrant labor, its Mexican business district ranked second to none.[29] In addition, since the Mexican Revolution in 1910, a substantial Mexican entrepreneurial class had become es-

TABLE 7.2 Texas Mexican–Operated Businesses in San Antonio's Mexican Downtown, 1924

BUSINESS	N
Barbería (barbershop)	14
Restaurante (restaurant)	9
Sastrería (tailor shop)	9
Abarrote (grocery store)	7
Calzado (shoe store)	6
Joyería (jewelry store)	6
Droguería (drugstore)	5
Hotel (hotel)	5
Librería (bookstore)	3
Música (musician's store)	2
Imprenta (print shop)	2
Panadería (bakery)	1
Carpintería (carpenter's shop)	1
Segunda mano (second-hand store)	1
Quiropráctico (chiropractor)	1
Club (social club)	1
TOTAL	73

SOURCE: Sologaistoa, *Guía general y directorio mexicano de San Antonio, Texas*, 211–222.

tablished in the city. A 1924 directory (TABLE 7.2) indicated seventy-three Mexican businesses on these six blocks alone, with the greatest number of establishments (forty-nine) located along Laredo Street between Houston and Nueva.[30] Here were hotels, restaurants, drugstores, shoe stores, bookstores, general stores, jewelry stores, tailors, barbers, and more (FIG. 7.2).

Approximately 25,000 of the emigrants who left Mexico for San Antonio between 1900 and 1910 were political refugees.[31] Because San Antonio nurtured varied Mexican political ideologies in the early decades of the twentieth century, Mexican elites typically took up residence in the city and became prominent in the business community. One of the most notable exiles was Ignacio E. Lozano, a native of Nuevo León, who came to San Antonio in 1908. He worked for a local newspaper until 1913, when he founded the influential Spanish-language *La Prensa*, which until 1954 remained the leading Spanish-language newspa-

7.2. Acosta Music Company, 608 West Houston Street, was typical of Texas Mexican businesses in downtown San Antonio around 1930.

per circulating in Texas. It was also the most widely circulated Spanish-language newspaper in the United States for many years and had an international readership.[32] *La Prensa* operated out of a building on Santa Rosa, across from Milam Square in the Mexican quarter.

Another celebrated exile was Xochimilco-born Dr. Aureliano Urrutia, who had been a successful surgeon in Mexico City, Mexican Ministro de Gobernación (Interior), and confidant to President Victoriano Huerta. Urrutia became an outcast from the Huerta regime in 1914, and fled with his family to Galveston and then San Antonio. Urrutia was a prominent figure in San Antonio circles, establishing a clinic and pharmacy near Santa Rosa Hospital in the Mexican quarter (FIG. 7.3). His Spanish-Moorish-style home, Quinta Urrutia, located near Brackenridge Park on five acres was, before its demolition, a distinctive landmark of the city, with an elaborate sculpture garden that survives today as a private park.[33]

7.3. The Urrutia *farmacia* or pharmacy, at the corner of North Laredo and West Houston Streets, served San Antonio's Mexican downtown until it was razed in the 1960s.

7.4. Teatro Nacional was San Antonio's premier Mexican theater during the 1930s.

At the corner of Commerce and Santa Rosa stood the most important theaters serving the city's Mexican community: the Teatro Nacional and Teatro Zaragoza.[34] The Nacional, a 1,200-seat auditorium, opened in 1917 and featured *revistas* (variety shows), *zarzuelas* (musical comedies), and *variedades* (vaudeville). After 1929, *cines* (motion pictures with sound) were a regular feature (FIG. 7.4).

The heart of the Mexican quarter of San Antonio was a commercial landscape chiefly operated by Mexicans and mostly for the benefit of Mexicans. Before its redevelopment as a tourist district in the 1970s, this business district served almost exclusively the Mexican residents of the city. This community remains the soul of Mexican San Antonio. It was known in its early days as Laredito (Little Laredo) and is today a complex of subbarrios known collectively as the West Side.

The West Side

The geographical roots of the West Side are evident in the divisions of San Fernando de Béxar made when Canary Island settlers appeared in the eighteenth century. In 1809, the civil community was divided into four quarters that included Barrios Norte and Sur, as well as Valero and Laredo.[35] Laredo was designated on the western periphery beyond San Pedro Creek, but little is known about its character. Canary Islanders positioned themselves between the San Antonio River and San Pedro Creek on the best lands north and south of the Plaza de las Islas (Barrios Norte and Sur), and immigrants who arrived in the late 1700s received land grants on the less desirable West Side. Residences here were not enclosed by watercourses and were distant from the military camp at Valero, so Indian raiding was more frequent.[36]

The origin of the West Side barrio named Laredo or Laredito is uncertain. Possibly the barrio was named after the road that exited this area of Béxar in the direction of Laredo on the Rio Grande. Between 1847 and 1881, both cart and stage roads linked San Antonio south to Laredo, as well as west to Chihuahua.[37] Yet, three of the most popular mid-nineteenth-century accounts of Texas that included visits to San Antonio failed to make reference to Laredo or Laredito as a distinctive barrio of the city.[38] Even resident Alsatian artist Theodore Gentilz, who drew and painted many scenes of the Mexican community between the 1840s and 1860s, seems not to have referenced the west side of San Pedro Creek by a specific name.[39] Finally, in 1877, a visitor to the city by railroad made reference to the Mexican barrios of San Antonio: Chihuahua and Laredo.[40]

Typical Mexican Home
and Family,
San Antonio, Texas.

7.5. Jacales were common residences for Texas Mexicans in the West Side barrios of San Antonio during the early twentieth century.

Although the names of the early West Side barrios may not have been commonly expressed, the distinctive Mexican house types of Béxar were a continual point of curiosity to travelers. As early as 1826, it was observed that most residences in the city were jacales or thatched huts.[41] By the last quarter of the century, one traveler commented:

> Every where about the outskirts of the town are innumerable low huts built of sticks and mud and straw and any old drift, roofed with thatch coming almost to the ground, and presenting an appearance of utmost squalor. These are the Mexican jacals . . . If you should glance into one of these jacals, you would find earthen floor cleanly swept, a bed neatly made and brightly covered . . . to the casual eye it seems clean and orderly, but poor to the last degree of poverty.[42]

In the early twentieth century, the Mexican jacal, its residents, and its ramshackle condition became institutionalized tourist scenes of San Antonio, especially as postcard views (FIG. 7.5).

By the 1880s, the West Side was a clearly segregated district of San Antonio. San Pedro Creek was the eastern border of the barrio by now known as Laredito, and which stretched westward approximately ten blocks

to Comal Street, just beyond the International and Great Northern rail-
road tracks, and nine or ten blocks north-south between Chavez and San
Luis Streets (FIG. 7.6). By 1900, this district had expanded north to Delgado
Street and south to Tampico Street. In fact, street names that typically
followed the names of Mexican states and towns were signatures of the
Mexican part of town, for example, Matamoros, Durango, Colima, and
Veracruz Streets.

On Sanborn fire insurance maps published during this era, neighborhoods on the West Side were sometimes stamped "Mexican Dwellings" across each block (FIG. 7.7). The low density and irregular arrange-

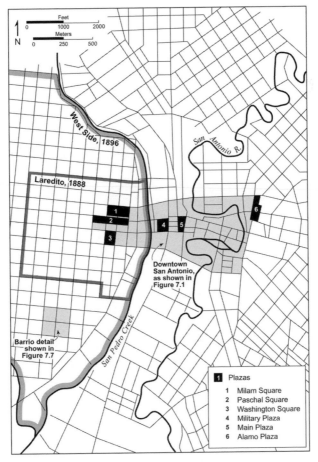

7.6. Laredito, San Antonio's oldest West Side barrio, in 1888 and
the expanded West Side in 1896.

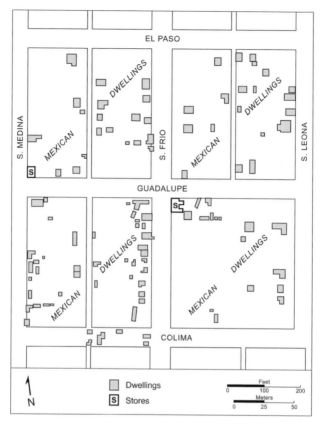

7.7. West Side Mexican dwellings labeled on San Antonio fire insurance maps, 1904.

ment of dwellings on the blocks suggests that housing was unstandardized
and not typical of suburban developments. Close inspection of a detailed
map shows barrio stores or *tienditas* evident along Guadalupe at the corners of South Medina and South Frio, foreshadowing the commercial
functions that would evolve along this street in subsequent decades. Road
surfaces are unpaved, alleys run north-south between the blocks, and
structures sometimes appear in the middle of a street, reinforcing the
irregular housing pattern.

Between 1900 and 1940, San Antonio added 200,000 people and
the Mexican population of the city increased more than seven times
(TABLE 7.3). A large part of the growth resulted from the immigration of
Mexican nationals during that country's revolution. San Antonio was a

destination for thousands of immigrants who were attracted by the city's economic opportunities, but also by its Mexican ways. Fernando Sánchez, a native of Saltillo, Coahuila, remarked in 1918, "I haven't been able to learn English, for I haven't made an effort to do it, and because I don't need it for anything as in San Antonio Spanish is spoken everywhere."[43] Two decades later, the commonness of Spanish was still reported:

> The bulk of nearly 40 percent of San Antonio's population that is Mexican lives in the area west and a little south of the business section. A visitor walking westward along West Commerce or Dolorosa Street will gradually feel more like a foreign tourist unless he reads and speaks Spanish.[44]

While Anglo San Antonio began to suburbanize during this period, the Mexican population remained chiefly in the expanding West Side barrios, which by 1924 extended some 3 to 4 miles west of the city center.[45] These neighborhoods coincided with the Second Ward of the city and quickly developed an unenviable reputation as the poorest resi-

TABLE 7.3 San Antonio's Mexican Population, 1900–2000

YEAR	MEXICAN POPULATION	TOTAL POPULATION	PERCENT MEXICAN
1900	13,722	53,321	25.7
1910	29,480	96,614	30.5
1920	59,970	161,379	37.2
1930	82,373	231,542	35.6
1940	103,000	253,854	40.6
1950	160,410	408,442	39.3
1960	243,627	587,718	41.5
1970	341,333	654,153	52.1
1980	421,774	785,410	53.7
1990	520,282	935,933	55.6
2000	671,394	1,144,646	58.6

SOURCES: Robert Garland Landolt, *The Mexican-American Workers of San Antonio, Texas*; U.S. Bureau of the Census, *Census of Population: 1960, Subject Reports, Persons of Spanish Surname*; U.S. Bureau of the Census, *Census of Population: 1970, Subject Reports, Persons of Spanish Origin*; U.S. Bureau of the Census, *Census of Population: 1980, General Population Characteristics, Texas*; U.S. Bureau of the Census, *1990 Census of Population, General Population Characteristics, Texas*; U.S. Bureau of the Census, *2000 Census of Population and Housing*.

7.8. Housing on San Antonio's West Side consisted chiefly of simple frame dwellings into the 1960s.

dential sections of San Antonio.[46] Eighty-five percent of San Antonio residents living at or below bare subsistence in 1938 were Mexican, and an estimated half of some 20,000 Mexican families were dependent, wholly or in part, upon government assistance.[47] Mexicans had the lowest rate (30 percent) of homeownership compared to Anglos (50 percent) and Blacks (40 percent) in the city in 1930. Housing conditions have been described as primitive huts and shacks (FIG. 7.8), some built in small court-yard arrangements called corrals, named after horse stalls.[48] Houses were also arranged in alleys less than 20 feet wide, which did not conform to the city code. Not surprisingly, the first public housing project in San Antonio—the Alazan-Apache Courts, completed in 1941—was built on the West Side to house exclusively Mexican residents.[49]

From the end of the Second World War to the 1960s, the West Side was transformed as some families moved up and out of the barrio. An especially popular path was northwest toward the Woodlawn area between Culebra Avenue and Fredericksburg Road. Prospect Hill, an early-twentieth-century middle-class barrio, was situated near here, and its location likely influenced movement northwest.[50] Several motivations spurred Mexican Americans to the middle-class Woodlawn district, including larger affordable homes and proximity to better schools like Thomas Jefferson High.[51] Nevertheless, the West Side continues to function as a distinctive barrio and immigrant neighborhood, and local institutions and organizations reinforce this identity. These include Communities Organized for Public Service (COPS), a Catholic church–based West Side advocacy group, Mexican American Unity Council, an empowerment organization formed in 1967 to promote economic development on the West Side, and the West Side Chamber of Commerce.

During the decade from 1960 to 1970, San Antonio returned to a demographic condition it had not known for more than a century: Mexican dominance (TABLE 7.3). Still, San Antonio's Mexican population was spatially concentrated on the west and south sides of the city.[52] A district consisting of thirty-five census tracts, each of which counted a Mexican population greater than 70 percent, projected outward from the center to the west and south sides—a *barrio grande* that contained 55 percent of all Mexicans in San Antonio in 1970. The post-1950 spatial expansion of the barrio was shaped by the pre-1950 enforcement of racial and ethnic deed restrictions in residential areas, especially on the northwest side of the city.[53] This district was further cordoned when the Interstate 410 loop and I-35 were constructed in the 1980s. Contemporary San Antonio has become more integrated ethnically and racially than perhaps at any time in its past, but the residue of Mexican spatial concentration from earlier eras is evident on the map of the city, with the most Mexican areas encircled by freeways on the West Side.[54]

Symbolic Identity and Architecture

Mexicans are once again the overwhelming majority of residents in San Antonio, and the city's ethnic identity has evolved along with this demographic shift. True, there remain institutional signatures of the city's Spanish past, whether real like the missions or fantasized like the Paseo del Río or River Walk.[55] Political empowerment, however, has further expanded Mexican ethnic identity in the city, and the word *mestizaje* or racial blending is being applied in a cultural sense as never before.[56] One of the most visible forms of this new cultural expression has been the city's evolving architecture.

Hispanic architectural themes have been part of San Antonio's modern evolution. During the 1920s and 1930s when Spanish Revival flowed from California, Hispanic themes proved irresistible to designers intent on exposing the city's indigenous vernacular.[57] Despite the 1968

7.9. Plaza Guadalupe and La Parroquia de Nuestra Señora de Guadalupe.

HemisFair extravaganza, San Antonio's Hispanic architecture retreated until the 1980s, when city-sponsored projects like the Avenida Guadalupe urban renewal effort began to remake commercial and institutional spaces in Guadalupe, a historic West Side barrio. Plaza Guadalupe was completed in 1984 as a series of open-air spaces with brilliant colored-tile facades to complement the 1921 parish church Nuestra Señora de Guadalupe (FIG. 7.9). On the same block, the former Progreso Theater from 1941 was remodeled as the Guadalupe Theater in 1984, emphasizing the same colorful tile exterior of the plaza. Today, the Guadalupe Theater is home to San Antonio's International Mexican Cinema Festival as well as other cultural celebrations.[58]

By the mid-1990s, the merging of a new group of successful Hispanic business people with traditional non–Hispanic business interests, as well with the city government, resulted in the approval of Mexican modernist Ricardo Legorreta's design for the new San Antonio Main Public Library. This vibrant colorful building, called the "red enchilada" by locals, was a symbolic break with all previous architectural styles in San Antonio's downtown. In the wake of that watershed construction, one prominent architectural firm has begun to articulate what it calls "*Mestizo* Regionalism," inspired by Virgil Elizondo, a professor of theology at the Oblate School in San Antonio who has written about *mestizaje* in frontier cultures of the modern world. The firm of Kell-Muñoz-Wigodsky argues that "San Antonio, with its unique multicultural mix of heritages and its rich legacy of well conserved buildings, has claim to being considered the cradle of *Mestizo* Regionalism."[59] The future outcome of this asserted regional style is uncertain, and although Kell-Muñoz-Wigodsky has incorporated its mestizo vision in several projects in the city and across South Texas, critics have stayed on the sidelines.[60]

The experience of Sandra Cisneros, a MacArthur Fellow, successful writer, and recent resident of San Antonio, captures the changing mood about Mexican architectural identity in the city. Cisneros grew up shuttling back and forth between Chicago, her home, and Mexico City, her father's home. In San Antonio, she declares, "The light changed the language, the landscape, the colors."[61] Cisneros moved to San Antonio in 1992 and chose as her home a fixer-upper Victorian house on the south side of the oldest historic neighborhood in the city, the King William District. The house had been a rental property for most of its ninety-four years, but Cisneros began to transform the modest cottage into her vision of a Mexican house. For the exterior, she selected a periwinkle hue that was technically Corsican purple. Also technically, the house color did not meet code according to the San Antonio Historic and Design Review Commission (HDRC), which argued that purple was not a legitimate historic color for the neighborhood. The issue sparked a flurry of local debate and national attention.[62] Armed with cultural ammunition about Mexican color traditions, Cisneros argued for what she called "colores fuertes." "I want to clarify here that I am not simply picking colors because I am Mexican, I am picking Mexican colors because this was Mexico."[63] After more than a year of contention, the HDRC caved in and allowed the purple house on Guenther Street, in part because time had faded the original bright hue to a mellow violet. Nevertheless, Cisneros had achieved an important symbolic victory, not only asserting her right to demonstrate a personal vision of Mexicanness, but shedding bright light on the issue of Mexican cultural identity and its resilience in San Antonio, the Tejano cultural capital.

LAREDO: GATEWAY TO MEXICO AND MEXICO-AMERICA

In 1997, some two million trucks crossed to and from Mexico at eight different South Texas ports of entry. Over one million truck crossings alone—56 percent—were recorded at Laredo. After Detroit, Laredo is the largest U.S. inland port and considered the dominant port in U.S. export trade with Mexico.[64] This gateway condition has been part of Laredo's identity for more than a century. The South Texas border town's connection to Mexico is as both trade outlet and tourist portal. The geographical advantage of a border location has shaped Laredo's past and still today imparts a fundamental importance to the character of the city.

Laredo is also overwhelmingly a Texas Mexican city, more so even than San Antonio. Among medium-sized cities, Laredo may be the most Mexican place in the United States, with 94 percent of its residents claiming Mexican ancestry (TABLE 7.1). For more than two centuries, the Texas border town has survived as a chiefly Mexican place, and today Anglos and other non-Hispanics remain minorities socially as well as demographically.

A Place of Transit and Trade

Laredo was founded as a ranching center and part of the larger mid-eighteenth-century Rio Grande colonization scheme of José de Escandón (see Chap. 3). Its early isolation and specialized livestock production—first cattle, then sheep—restricted commercial development. When commerce did emerge, it was Laredo's geographical situation between San Antonio and Monterrey that gave it strategic advantage, a quality it maintains to the present.

Tomás Sánchez, awarded land concessions at Laredo by Escandón, selected an area of elevated terrain overlooking the Rio Grande and originally named the town Pass of Jacinto de León. It was later renamed San Agustín de Laredo by Escandón to honor a Bay of Biscay town in his native province of Santander.[65] Laredo was organized as a classic Law of the Indies settlement around a plaza, but the community very early spilled across the river, where a commons and later a smaller settlement emerged. Until 1848, however, the two settlements were known collectively as Laredo, and only after the creation of the international boundary did Nuevo Laredo, Tamaulipas, assume a separate identity.[66]

Although elevated to a *villa* in 1767, Laredo was a small ranching center during the colonial era, hardly a town in the common conception. The population was 708 in 1789, yet the character of the place was chiefly one-room jacales with a few stone and adobe structures. The ranching specialization of the residents meant they traded and bartered for almost all manufactured goods, including food, largely supplied by *carreteros* (wagon drivers) from Saltillo, where an annual fair and market were staged.[67] By the time Laredo ranchers turned to the sheep and wool trade in 1820, some wine, soap, and *piloncillo* (dried cane sugar) were produced locally, but Laredo's dependence on imported goods continued. Not until 1833 did the census report resident merchants. Laredo's single asset, by the accounts of travelers, was its location on the Rio Grande on the road to Béxar.[68]

When Laredo became part of Texas after the Treaty of Guadalupe Hidalgo and the Mexican War in 1848, the town evolved a resident commercial base. Mexican Americans moved into merchandising from their homes, first around the plaza and eventually all across town. With Fort McIntosh on the immediate outskirts of the city, one of a series of United States installations along the Rio Grande frontier, Laredo became a trade and hinterland service center. Anglo Americans and Europeans became part of the town, mixing socially with upper-class Mexican Americans, even intermarrying, but Laredo Mexicanized its foreigners more than Mexicanos became Americanized.[69]

Mexican freighters from Laredo began to shape the border trade with Mexico before the Civil War. The Mexican border trade connected Saltillo and Monterrey to San Antonio via Eagle Pass and Laredo.[70] This trade was based on mule- and ox-drawn wagons. Cargo to Mexico included hardware, machined cotton cloth, firearms, and ammunition, whereas return freight was bullion from mines in Nuevo León and Coahuila, flour, wool, liquors, handcrafted leather goods, and hand-woven cloth. Cattle, sheep, and horses were also major trade commodities. Buyers in Missouri, Kentucky, and Tennessee paid handsomely for tens of thousands of livestock annually. The Gil brothers, members of a longstanding Laredo Mexican family, built a freighting service with *carretas* or ox-drawn wagons, linking San Antonio and Corpus Christi to the border trade at Laredo. The largest *carretas* were pulled by five to six yoke of oxen and could haul five thousand pounds of freight.[71] Laredo later became a forwarding station for Confederate cotton produced in Texas and freighted along the river on the Mexican side via Mier and Camargo to Matamoros and Bagdad on the Gulf.[72]

Securing the Gateway

Laredo's position as a freighting center foreshadowed its emergence as a gateway to Mexico. No single event was more significant in creating this new identity than the arrival of railroads to the border. Before railroads, Matamoros as the hub of the cotton trade was the most economically vital and cosmopolitan place on the Texas–Mexico boundary. Once Laredo was linked by rail in 1881, it lurched ahead of Brownsville with its Matamoros link to become the premier access point connecting central Mexico to South Texas, the Midwest, and the East.

The windfall of railroads through Laredo had less to do with Laredo per se than with its geographic situation relative to the emerging port of Corpus Christi and the commercial dreams of Uriah Lott, who owned a forwarding business that handled shipments between Texas and New York. Lott envisioned a railroad that might service the South Texas ranching domain between the Nueces and Rio Grande, thereby diverting the Brownsville-Mexico trade to Corpus Christi, and Laredo would be its link to the border.[73] Before the railroad was completed, however, a Colorado Springs, Colorado, syndicate that had contracted with the Mexican government to link a railroad line from Laredo to Monterrey purchased Lott's Corpus Christi–Laredo line. The result was the Texas-Mexican Railway, a narrow-gauge line that opened in November 1881 between Corpus Christi and Laredo and reached Monterrey in 1882. One month after the Tex-Mex line was inaugurated, the International and Great Northern was completed between San Antonio and the border, extending Laredo's reach to St. Louis, Chicago, Philadelphia, and New York. This standard-gauge line ultimately linked to the Mexican National line that connected Laredo to Mexico City.[74] The Rio Grande and Eagle Pass Railroad—a small, narrow-gauge line designed to carry coal mined from fields north of Laredo to the city, where it was transferred to the Tex-Mex and International and Great Northern—made Laredo a junction of four railroads and the principal portal to Mexico on the South Texas border.

In 1889 a local directory heralded the city as "The Great International Gateway of the Two Republics."[75] Into the new century, Laredo continued to be promoted in private publications and chamber of commerce advertisements as the gateway city.[76] Chiefly, that identity was a function of commerce and railroad connections. A brochure published in 1926 captures the themes of this identity (FIG. 7.10). The larger rectangular image symbolizes the products of South Texas like oil and citrus enveloping an orderly farmstead highlighted by a single tractor in a field shaded by a tropical palm. Ironically, there were in fact few "family farms" in South Texas during this era, as suggested by this image, because most agriculture in the region was large-scale and corporate and dependent on Mexican labor to plant and harvest crops.[77] The gateway image is

7.10. Laredo, the Gateway to Mexico.

smaller and focused on the first railroad bridge and a smoking locomotive pulling boxcars, presumably filled with the products illustrated above. Laredo was thus a pivot point for this transport across the international divide, and the railroad was the vehicle and means that allowed that transfer. Indeed, a 1928 industrial survey of Laredo ranked the town as the most important exporting center on the Texas-Mexico border, with five trains crossing daily into Mexico. Laredo handled 60 percent of the 11,291 railroad cars that crossed the border from Texas into Mexico in that year, more than two times that handled by the nearest competing ports, Eagle Pass and El Paso.[78]

The inauguration of the Pan American Highway in 1935 reinforced Laredo's gateway identity. The 761-mile route from Laredo to Mexico City became the first paved highway from the United States border to the

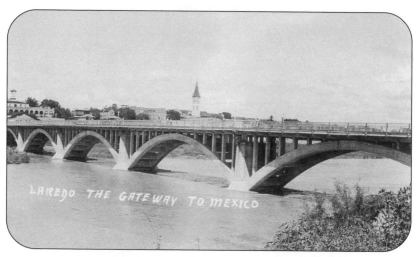

7.11. International Bridge connecting Laredo to Nuevo Laredo around 1930. View looks across the Rio Grande toward Laredo.

Mexican interior and the most direct automotive route from the Midwest or East to the heartland of Mexico.[79] Laredo was described in contemporary guidebooks and promotional magazines as a thriving, small city, the most important point of entry to Mexico and an accommodating town to visitors.[80] In 1921 Laredo constructed its second bridge, a stylish automotive and pedestrian concrete structure that came to be called the International Bridge or Inter-American Bridge (FIG. 7.11).[81] After following U.S. 81 from San Antonio to Laredo, motor travelers merged into C.N. (Camino Nacional) 1 at Nuevo Laredo across the river. This scenic paved roadway extended south to Monterrey, skirting the tropical coastal plain to Ciudad Victoria, the capital of Tamaulipas, before climbing through the Sierra Huasteca between Valles and Pachuca in the states of San Luis Potosí and Querétaro, respectively, and entering Mexico City.[82]

With a modern highway and railroad connection between Laredo and Mexico City, the Texas border town became a major tourist destination as well as gateway. A significant new import economy emerged with the development of the Mexican curio trade. Crafts and popular artworks are termed *artesanías* in Mexico. These materials have historically come from a cluster of chiefly southern states, where specific towns and villages are identified with particular craft products.[83] Because transportation from the Mexican interior to Laredo was well established, the Texas town became a principal gateway for the importation of these products for local sale, as well as for regional and national distribution (FIG. 7.12).

Purchasing tourist curios, along with other border town experiences, lured thousands of tourists to Laredo by 1940, and the international tone of the city was said to be manifest everywhere in display signs, placards, and window posters printed in Spanish more often than in English.[84] Between 1952 and 1962, the number of Mexico-bound tourists and autos crossing at Laredo exceeded by many times the same number at the next two most active ports of entry (FIG. 7.13). Laredo had become by almost every measure the foremost gateway to Mexico.

7.12. Laredo became the premier import destination for Mexican curio crafts along the South Texas portion of the Rio Grande.

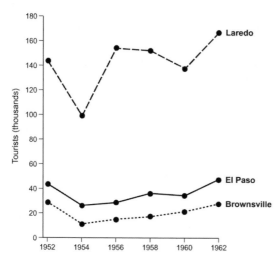

7.13. Mexico-bound tourists along the Texas border, 1952–1962.

Mexican American Laredo

While Laredo's external identity has certainly been shaped by its gateway position, the Texas town is also the most demographically Mexican medium-sized city in the United States. At no time in Laredo's past have Mexicans ever been less than a majority of the town's population, a statistic that may be unique for such a large city. Yet, the power of that fact has not seemed especially important to Laredoans. Perhaps because they are the majority, Mexican Americans in this city have argued less about discrimination and prejudice, choosing instead to see themselves as players in a continual process of becoming both Tejano and American yet holding to a Mexican past.[85] Laredo is not only the fastest-growing city in Texas, it is one of the fastest-growing in the nation. Since 1990, the border town has added more people than it ever counted in its first two centuries (TABLE 7.4).

Laredo exemplifies what geographer Terrence Haverluk terms a "continuous" Hispanic community.[86] A continuous community is one founded by Hispanics in which Hispanics have remained the majority population throughout the community's history. Continuous communities are unlike "discontinuous" Hispanic communities that were invaded by non-Hispanics, so that Hispanics lost demographic dominance and political control, or "new" communities that were originally founded by Anglos and only recently have experienced Hispanic immigration. Continuous Hispanic communities have experienced only limited non-Hispanic immigration and consequently have not fully assimilated to Anglo American norms. Haverluk identified 106 Hispanic communities in the American West, 60 new communities, 21 discontinuous communities, and 25 continuous communities.

Texas and New Mexico each counted 10 continuous communities, Arizona contained 4, and California had 1. Eight of the 10 Texas continuous communities are in South Texas. Laredo is the largest of all 25 continuous communities, being more than three times as populous as the next-largest place and the only one that is a metropolitan area. In 2000,

TABLE 7.4 Laredo's Population for Selected Years

YEAR	TOTAL POPULATION	PERCENT MEXICAN AMERICAN/NON-HISPANIC
1850	1,173	98/2
1870	2,043	79/21
1880	3,521	86/14
1890	11,319	—
1900	13,429	90/10
1910	14,855	—
1920	22,710	—
1930	32,618	72/28
1940	39,274	—
1950	51,910	86/14
1960	60,678	82/18
1970	69,024	81/19
1980	91,449	89/11
1990	109,796	89/11
2000	176,576	94/6

SOURCES: Gilberto Miguel Hinojosa, A Borderlands Town in Transition: Laredo, 1755–1870, Table 1, 123; Michael T. Kingston, ed., The Texas Almanac and State Industrial Guide, 1984–1985, 350; Arnoldo De León and Kenneth L. Stewart, Tejanos and the Numbers Game: A Socio-Historical Interpretation from the Federal Censuses, 1850–1900, Table 1.3, 12; U.S. Bureau of the Census, Fifteenth Census of the United States: 1930, Table 23; U.S. Bureau of the Census, Census of Population: 1950, Special Reports, Persons of Spanish Surname, Table 7; U.S. Bureau of the Census, Census of Population: 1960, Subject Reports, Persons of Spanish Surname, Table 15; U.S. Bureau of the Census, Census of Population: 1970, Subject Reports, Persons of Spanish Origin, Table 13; U.S. Bureau of the Census, Census of Population: 1980, General Population Characteristics, Texas, Table 16; U.S. Bureau of the Census, 1990 Census of Population and Housing, Summary Tape File 1C; U.S. Bureau of the Census, 2000 Census of Population and Housing.

NOTE: Data for 1870, 1880, 1900 include Webb County; those for 1950–1990 include metropolitan area; all others are for City of Laredo.

Laredo's population was 94 percent Hispanic, chiefly of Mexican ancestry. Some 95 percent of Laredoans spoke Spanish at home, there were four Spanish-language daily newspapers, and the evening television news was broadcast in Spanish and English. In addition, 83 percent of professionals in the community were Hispanic (in San Antonio, by comparison, only 30 percent were Hispanic). Further, Laredo had one of the highest number of Hispanic elected officials among all continuous communities.[87]

Because Laredoans have historically been chiefly of Mexican ancestry, Anglos and other non-Hispanic minorities have tended to become Mexicanized, a condition that evolved early in South Texas among Anglo and European ranchers and continued among merchant groups (TABLE 7.4). After the Mexican War in the mid-nineteenth century, the Texas legislature confirmed many land grant titles belonging to Laredo's Mexican elite, and this along with considerable intermarriage among old and new elites consolidated wealth and power for the Mexican population, so that ethnic divisions became secondary to those of class.[88] When the railroads brought an influx of Anglo merchants to Laredo in the late nineteenth century, they did not occupy a vacuum, because a Mexican merchant class was already in place.[89] By 1900 Anglos were more segregated residentially in Laredo than Mexican Americans, an unusual circumstance in the urban borderlands.[90]

After World War II, Laredo remained an exception among Southwest cities in that its index of residential dissimilarity, a key statistical measure of segregation, was among the lowest of all cities.[91] Not until the 1960s did Laredo sprawl much north of the present international airport, generally beyond U.S. 59 and Saunders Street, about 2 or 3 miles from downtown.[92] By 1970, when Laredo counted almost 70,000 people, the city consisted of seventeen census tracts, and all but two on the northeast and far north sides of town were overwhelmingly Mexican American. In fifteen of the tracts, Mexican Americans averaged 86 percent of the population, whereas in the two north side tracts they averaged 60 percent.[93] Clearly, Mexican Americans dominated the residential fabric of the city and even in neighborhoods where non-Hispanics were concentrated, Mexican Americans were still the majority population. As Laredo suburbanized north in the 1990s, non-Hispanic residents were mixed among their Hispanic neighbors in the city's newer affluent subdivisions.[94]

But how has Mexican American demographic dominance shaped ethnic identity in Laredo? Because the city is Mexican in its origin but also American since 1848, its character as a place is, not surprisingly, a cultural blend that sets it apart from other Mexican American border locales in South Texas. Three conditions are part of this hybrid identity. First, Laredo and Laredoans have been fashioned by an isolation that imprinted place and people. From colonial times Laredo was a frontier settlement, distant from even the older towns of the Mexican north like Saltillo and Monclova as well from the Tejas capital at Béxar. Its ranching families were tested by persistent, unforgiving Lipan Apache and Comanche raiding until the late nineteenth century.[95] Almost a decade before the Mexican War, Laredo was the declared capital of the short-lived Republic of the Rio Grande, a Mexican secessionist episode that joined Tamaulipas, Coahuila, Nuevo León, and the disputed lands of Tejas between the Nueces River and Rio Grande. These states and the disputed territory aligned themselves as defiant federalists against Santa Anna's centralist government.[96] After 285 days, the republic was crushed by Mexican troops, but the willingness to stand alone is emblematic of the separateness ingrained in Laredoans, who found themselves little served by a distant, controlling capital.

Second, beyond isolation, Laredo changed allegiance in 1848, an act that severed it from its colonial cross-river complement, Nuevo Laredo. What had been one town in two parts became two peoples in two towns in two nations, who would in time begin to display some antagonism, despite ancestral commonality.[97] While there has been and still is considerable cross-border cooperation between Los Dos Laredos—from civic celebrations to economic dependency—strains of autonationalism survive beneath a veneer of binationalism. Alan Weisman exposed the nerve when he interviewed a Laredo Mexican American council member in 1985 who said, "We came from there, but they're not us. They toss their garbage in the Rio Grande and want us to pay to clean it up. We may share a baseball team and a past, but we aren't one community."[98]

A third characteristic of Laredo's identity is the transgeographic posture that has been elaborated above and which dates from the earliest days of commercial development. Laredo and Laredoans have not turned their backs on Mexico. A large part of downtown Laredo's retail vitality still depends on shoppers from Nuevo Laredo, and community integration is still pursued.[99] Laredoans may not want to be part of Mexico, but they realize that proximity to Mexico is key to their continued economic prosperity. Laredo continues, therefore, to see itself as a gateway, but its sights are not set only on the cross-border industrial zones in Nuevo Laredo or Monterrey or on the old linkage at San Antonio. Laredo is now stretched deep into Mexico and extended even farther north and east in the United States. This is clear by the fact that 60 percent of the transborder truck commerce that passes through the city is not related to the maquiladora industry in Nuevo Laredo; rather, it is long-haul or corridor traffic that connects the interior of Mexico with Midwest and East Coast destinations.[100]

And so we come full circle. Laredoans are first and foremost Mexicans and Americans. They acknowledge and sometimes celebrate their Mexican heritage and realize that their future is tied to Mexico and its economy, yet they see the difference between the two. To wit, the baseball team that the two Laredos have shared for more than a half century is seen by both communities as "the cultural and economic property of Nuevo Laredo," despite the fact that games are played on both sides of the Rio Grande.[101] At the same time, Laredoans cannot dismiss the bonds, especially familial, that do exist between residents of Los Dos Laredos. In a fictionalized memoir of Laredo from the 1940s through the 1960s called an "autobioethnography," Norma Elia Cantú, born in Nuevo Laredo and raised in Laredo, re-creates the experiences of life that engaged her as a young girl—the people and places that are part of a dual yet singular world, the Texas-Mexico border.[102] Those experiences, found in the lives of many Laredoans, are what sets Laredo apart from other South Texas border cities and makes this place a gateway and bridge between Mexico and Mexico-America.

CHAPTER 8

Tex-Mex ... Despite the northern Mexico influence, it is not Mexican food ...
Neither is Tex-Mex the same as New Mexican or Californian Mexican foods,
although together these are all part of a Mexican-American system that can be
distinguished from the cooking of Mexico as a Southwestern North American
style. —HELEN SIMONS, "THE TEX-MEX MENU"

Frequently these South Texas ferias of the final decades of the nineteenth century
lasted three or four weeks. Held in the fall after the harvest season, they attracted
ranch families from miles around—usually to the regional villages with the largest
plazas. —ARNOLDO DE LEÓN, THE TEJANO COMMUNITY, 1836–1900

Texas Mexican Social Identities

Group identity can manifest through many cultural qualities. Language and religion are two of the most obvious diagnostics of identity. Spoken Spanish and adherence to Catholicism are often considered normative behaviors among Hispanic subgroups, yet there is significant variation in both Spanish language retention and religious affiliation among Mexican Americans.[1] Language especially has been studied as a signature of ethnic persistence, on the one hand, and a flag of ethnic erosion, on the other. In South Texas, sociolinguists and folklorists have asserted that regional variations are evident in vocabulary, dialect, and song and that these differences distinguish Texas Mexicans from other borderland Mexican Americans.[2]

Food and celebration, like language and religion, can be diagnostic of ethnic group identity. Foodways, or the practices of food preference, preparation, and consumption are regionally specific as well as ethnically distinctive. Public celebration also projects group identity through organized ritual festivity and display.

Foodways study has preoccupied American cultural geographers for several decades, but early efforts were mostly concerned with mapping distinctive patterns.[3] Zelinsky's study of regional ethnic restaurant associations expanded our understanding of pattern, including Mexican eateries, as well as process, particularly the role of ethnic foodways in transnationalism.[4] Zelinsky documented that Mexican eateries are the dominant ethnic restaurant cuisine in metropolitan areas in the southwestern United States, including all of Texas, New Mexico, Arizona and southern California. He then suggested that ethnic eating in the region is a signal of an emerging transnationalization of culture in North America.

Ethnic and regional foodways study has been extended and embraced by students of folklife, anthropology, and history, as well as of cultural geography. A leading concern among researchers is to unravel how ethnic cuisines are part of symbolic identity and how these food systems communicate for and about a subgroup.[5] Historian Jeffrey Pilcher has examined the cultural history of food in Mexico and how food preferences from pre-Columbian times to the present have shaped Mexican national identity.[6] Geographers Barbara and James Shortridge see this concern with identity and region as part of a larger phenomenon they term "neolocalism" in the United States. The ultimate blending of foodway and region occurs when a particular food assumes the role of an icon for a place.[7]

Celebration is yet another mainstay of group identity. Organized festivity that becomes ritualized is especially reinforcing of cultural memory and group solidarity. Pilgrimage to sacred space particularly commemorates religious beliefs, and community festivals celebrate national or local events. In Mexico, it has been reported that some 5,083 civil and religious celebrations are staged annually, and that no more than nine days pass without a fiesta somewhere.[8] The Mexican penchant for ritualized celebration is, like foodways, a cultural practice perpetuated by Mexican Americans in the borderland Southwest.

Mexican Americans celebrate a number of calendar customs, or events associated with particular holidays, both religious and political. Numerous Christmas celebrations, including Las Posadas and El Día de los Reyes, are common in Mexican American communities.[9] Political celebrations are equally popular and have been known in towns since the late nineteenth century. Mexican Americans, like their brethren in the homeland, celebrate a ritual of ethnic solidarity called *fiestas patrias*, which are typically focused on Mexican Independence Day (September 16) and Cinco de Mayo, which honors the victory of the Mexican forces over the invading French army at Puebla in 1862.[10]

Many Mexican American celebrations as well as foodways are pan-regional because activities are staged by or food preferences are common to ethnic Mexican communities across the country. Events and traditions can also be regionally specific or even unique to individual towns.[11] In this chapter, I examine foodways and public celebrations as case studies to reveal how Texas Mexican social identities are expressed geographically and how they are regionally distinctive.

FOODWAYS

In December 1985, the prestigious French Prix Vermeil, or golden prize, for the best foreign restaurant in Paris was awarded to a Mexican restaurant. Papa Maya was the brainchild of Mario Cantú, a San Antonio restaurateur whose Mexican and Tex-Mex fare gained enthusiastic diners in the capital of haute cuisine.[12] Cantú's success was part of a wave of Texas Mexican food popularity that swept the United States in the 1980s, when fajitas became the nouvelle grill food of the decade.[13] Approximately one century earlier, Texas Mexican food became equated across the southwestern frontier as Mexican food, thereby helping to shape and influence the popularity of Mexican food across the United States. Still, certain Texas Mexican foodways remain distinctive and are most closely associated with South Texas. Among South Texas Mexicans, these foodways are emblematic of the region and thereby part of Texas Mexican identity.

San Antonio Innovation Center
John G. Bourke, writing in the *Journal of American Folk-Lore* in 1895, may have been the first serious writer to distinguish the regional food types of the Mexican American borderland.[14] His lengthy treatise is based on travel throughout the border region from San Luis Potosí to San Antonio and from southern Arizona to South Texas. Bourke's description of public eating in the plazas of San Antonio extolled the availability of savory tamales, tortillas, *chiles rellenos* (stuffed peppers), *huevos revueltos* (scrambled

eggs), *lengua lampreada* (braised tongue), many kinds of *pucheros* (boiled dishes) and *ollas* (stews), along with leathery cheese, burning peppers, stewed tomatoes, and many items too numerous to mention.[15]

San Antonio's plaza may not have been too different from plazas in other north Mexican towns, except that here were Anglo Americans, Europeans, African Americans, and others shoulder to shoulder with Mexicans consuming Mexican food. Because San Antonio was the first Mexican community encountered by nineteenth-century travelers along the southwestern frontier, the city's cultural ways became the source of important impressions about Mexican Americans. From plaza vendors and established eateries to food production and distribution, the popularity of Mexican cuisine in U.S. food consumption originated in San Antonio.[16]

The most celebrated Mexican food attraction in the city was the chili stands in the plazas. The stands and the vendors, called chili queens, enjoyed enormous success and received comment from most nineteenth-century visitors.[17] The ritual was chiefly nocturnal, as food vendors replaced the daytime marketing function of the plazas. Although the basic foods such as tamales, tortillas, and even chile had an ancient Mexican Indian lineage, they gained notoriety in San Antonio's plazas. The chili stands were a tourist attraction by the 1890s, but they were moved from their original locale in Military Plaza to other plazas when a new city hall was erected (see Chap. 7). In 1900 chili vendors were still found on Milam Square at the western edge of downtown and on Alamo Plaza in front of the old Federal Building. Haymarket Square, adjoining the produce market west of Military Plaza, was the last plaza to accommodate the stands of benches and tables. By 1937 health officials discouraged chili vending unless glass-enclosed carts were used.[18]

The demise of the chili stands strengthened the role of both formal and informal dining.[19] Mexican families provided neighborhood dining, often outside on benches and tables but occasionally inside private homes. By the early twentieth century, Mexican restaurants were being advertised in tourist literature. The owners were sometimes Anglo, but the kitchen crews were Mexican. The Original Mexican Restaurant, owned and operated in 1910 by Otis M. Farnsworth, advertised a twenty-five cent supper. It consisted of tamales, chile con carne, enchiladas, frijoles, *tortillas de maiz* (corn tortillas), *sopa de arroz* (rice soup), and *café*; the dollar supper added *pescado* (fish), *mole poblano* (country-style mole), *huevos con chile* (eggs with peppers), *chiles rellenos* (stuffed peppers), *ensalada de aguacate* (avocado salad), *helados* (ice cream), *chocolate* (chocolate), and *cigarritos* (cigarettes). The interior of this establishment was decorated with Mexican serapes, flags, pottery, and baskets and served food daily from 11:30 a.m. until midnight.[20] A 1924 directory listed twenty-eight formal Mexican eateries in the city.[21]

From San Antonio plazas and eateries came a food type called Tex-Mex, a style that has been described as "native foreign food."[22] It is native, because it was invented in the United States, yet it is foreign in that its inspiration comes from Mexican cuisine. This does not mean necessarily that all Texas Mexicans would define Tex-Mex as "their" food, but it does suggest how Mexican food from Texas came to embody a food style for others. The emblematic Tex-Mex dish is the Mexican plate, a combination of "chili-covered enchiladas or tamales (or both), refried beans, and Spanish rice," typically smothered by melted cheese.[23] This plate, perhaps more than any single Mexican food dish, spread across the United States to become "Mexican food" in the minds and stomachs of several generations of Americans.[24] Whether served in dinner houses in Des Moines or truck stops in Tucumcari, as a frozen entree or cafeteria special, the Mexican plate is quintessentially Texas-Mex.

San Antonio was also at the forefront of commercial Mexican food production for local, regional, and countrywide markets. William Gebhardt, a German immigrant from New Braunfels, Texas, began to manufacture and sell chili powder in San Antonio in 1896. Gebhardt imported ancho peppers from Mexico, ground dried ones into a fine powder, and packaged the condiment in airtight containers. By 1911 Gebhardt was the first entrepreneur to produce canned Mexican foods like chili con carne and tamales (FIG. 8.1). The success of Gebhardt's Mexican foods meant that a non-Mexican public began to equate Mexican food with products from San Antonio. The firm now produces seventy-eight different items and markets them throughout the United States as well as in nineteen foreign countries.[25]

A further indication of San Antonio's significance as an innovation center for Mexican food products is the Pace Picante Company, which created the first commercial salsa or chili sauce in 1947. Picante sauce is a variation of a northern Mexico tomato-based sauce that includes vinegar and is sometimes called *salsa roja* (red sauce). Before Pace began to use the term, nobody commercially called this salsa picante sauce. Since Pace concocted his sauce, most competitors have used the same ingredients—tomatoes, water, onions, peppers, vinegar, salt and spices—although

8.1. Gebhardt's in San Antonio was the first company to package and export Mexican food products for national consumption.

variation exists in the percentage of ingredients and the use of additives like thickeners and preservatives. By the 1990s, salsa replaced catsup as the hottest-selling condiment in the United States, and conglomerate giants like Beatrice and Cheeseborough Ponds began producing picante sauces. It was no surprise, therefore, when in 1994 the Campbell Soup Company bought Pace Picante Sauce for $1.1 billion; only a decade earlier Pace's formula was assigned a market value of $1 million.[26] *Pico de gallo* (rooster's beak), a Tex-Mex condiment and accompaniment to fajitas (in Mexico it is simply *salsa mexicana*), is a fresh relish of diced tomatoes, serrano or jalapeño chiles, onions, and cilantro now being mass-marketed across the country as the latest addition to the burgeoning fresh Mexican food products industry. San Antonio was at the starting line when Mexican food was introduced to Americans, and it is still considerably ahead of other cities in its sensitivity to Mexican American foodways.

Persistence of Regional Foodways

Just as Mexican food was slow to become part of U.S. diet, Mexican specialty foods have gained acceptance slowly in the U.S. foodways. *Chicharrón* or fried pork rind is a popular snack food in Mexico and in the border Southwest.[27] In Mexican American communities, *chicharrones* may be sold on the street by vendors or in ethnic food markets, but they are also now widely available on supermarket and convenience store shelves, next to potato chips and corn chips.[28] These crispy, salty favorites have been appropriated into U.S. consuming habits. Yet, there are other Mexican foods that remain privileged and unappropriated, including specialty meats, offals, and breads.

Goats have been part of livestock herding in northeast Mexico, particularly Coahuila and Nuevo León, since colonial times, and the practice of keeping and eating goats became part of ranching in South Texas, especially among Texas Mexicans.[29] A consequence of goat culture is the regional delicacy *cabrito* or kid goat, also known as *cabrito al pastor* because the method of roasting is on a vertical spit. *Cabritos* are usually less than a month old and typically fed only milk until they are slaughtered. In South Texas, *chivos* or pastured goats are also eaten, but kids are the favored dish, served in restaurants and often identified in advertising by the flayed and split kid set on a metal skewer.[30] From *chivos* comes another delicacy called *machitos*, an offal food that includes the esophagus, lungs, heart, kidney, liver, and intestines, sautéed or stewed with condiments, then rolled into a gut lining and grilled or baked.[31]

Certainly the most popular Texas Mexican food specialty is *barbacoa* or barbecue, a delicacy that bears no resemblance to its U.S. namesake but a savory folk favorite in South Texas. While *barbacoa* is known and eaten in Mexico, as well as throughout the Mexican American Southwest, it has become peculiarly associated with the South Texas border region (TABLE 8.1). Folklorist Mario Montaño asserts that *barbacoa* is a folk food of the Texas Lower Rio Grande Valley border that has resisted appropriation by the dominant culture and thereby become indicative of a foodway identified almost exclusively with South Texas Mexicans.[32]

In San Antonio, Laredo, McAllen, and all across the South Texas region, *barbacoa* is chiefly a weekend ritual, especially on Sundays, *los domingos*.[33] Technically known as *barbacoa de cabeza de vaca* or cow's head barbecue, the folk behavior of eating this dish on Sundays has changed little since rancho days, but the method of preparing it has transformed with the urbanization of Texas Mexicans. On South Texas ranches, after slaughtering a cow, the head was cleaned but the tongue, brain, and eyes were left intact. Wrapped in burlap, the head was placed in a pit layered with mesquite wood embers and lined with *pencas de maguey* (agave leaves), and then covered with earth and cooked for ten to twelve hours, until

TABLE 8.1 *Barbacoa* Survey (N=67)

PLACE OF BIRTH		FREQUENCY OF EATING[a]				DEFINITION OF BARBACOA[a]	
	N	Regularly	Weekends	Special Occasion	Never	Cow Head	Any Pit-Cooked Me
Texas	38	2	19	18	1	33	3
Mexico	8		5	3		3	5
California	7			5		1	5
Arizona	6			5	1	1	5
Illinois, Indiana	4		2	2		3	
Other	4		1	2	1	3	2

SOURCE: Survey administered by author in Arizona and by Norma Cantú in Texas, 1997–1998.
[a]Totals do not compute because individuals sometimes answered more than once.

8.2. *Barbacoa*, a Mexican South Texas weekend eating tradition, is still prepared in pits in some small-town neighborhoods like this one in Roma, Texas.

tender. This procedure is rare in South Texas cities today because health ordinances prohibit cooking food in pits, but it is a tradition still adhered to in small towns like Eagle Pass and Roma (FIG. 8.2). In cities, *barbacoa* is typically prepared in stainless steel pressure cookers for six to eight hours. Sanitation laws and insurance regulations have strangled neighborhood stores that traditionally vended *barbacoa* that was pit-prepared in backyards. These stores cannot afford the capital investment of pressure cookers and gas plumbing that is now required, and as a consequence only a few wholesale producers and distributors of *barbacoa* now operate and supply consumers throughout South Texas.[34]

Still, consuming *barbacoa* is now an urban tradition that creates an even greater demand for the food (FIG. 8.3). It has been observed and reported that urban *barbacoa* eaters prefer the "meat" only, meaning the cheek meat as opposed to mixed meat, which includes tongue, eyes, brains, snout, and lips.[35] Consider these testimonials from Laredo natives:

> In Laredo, *barbacoa* is a Sunday morning tradition. It is sold in restaurants, grocery stores, and special *barbacoa* stands. It is eaten with corn or flour tortillas (I prefer the latter)—freshly made makes it even more delicious. Add a little *pico de gallo* and you've got yourself a real treat! LAURA RENDON, AGE 49

> The *barbacoa* I'm familiar with is cow's head meat cooked in a pit. My family has been buying it for generations, and when time permits *barbacoa* will be prepared the old-fashioned way in a pit. We eat *barbacoa* only on Sundays for breakfast, usually after church. SANDRA TREVIÑO, AGE 24

> Every part of the cow's head seems to be delicious. I prefer to eat the tongue. But when I think about what it actually is I get disgusted. My sister fights to claim the eyes. She says they taste great and she sucks on them with such delicacy. I have no idea why it is so popular on weekends only. It's almost tradition to eat this on Sundays. NANCY GARZA, AGE 28

Another South Texas Mexican food specialty is *panocha*, sometimes called *pan de campo*. This is country-baked bread that is largely restricted to preparation and consumption on special occasions, typically at festi-

8.3. In urban barrios in San Antonio's West Side, backyard household production of *barbacoa* has declined because of sanitation laws and insurance regulations.

vals. *Panocha* was invented on South Texas ranches by vaqueros, and it is prepared and eaten still by some deer hunters who camp out in the brushland. *Pan de campo* is made with wheat flour and baked in a Dutch oven covered with coals to produce thick, tortilla-shaped bread that has the consistency of a biscuit and is sometimes stuffed with chorizo, eggs, or chicken. Bread-baking cook-off contests are regular features of two South Texas festivals held each year, one in San Diego and one in Edinburg.[36]

THE FLOUR TORTILLA TACO AS REGIONAL ICON

Pearsall is the seat of Frio County, one hour south of San Antonio on the northern reach of South Texas. The town is situated one mile east of I-35 at the intersection of U.S. 83 and Texas 140. Taco huts dot the road into town, small frame buildings painted hot pink and aquamarine with drive-ups and hand-drawn signs advertising the daily fare. The eating options at these huts are typical of the South Texas region, where one can get almost anything from meats to vegetables served in a folded flour tortilla taco. Less than 50 miles farther along the road toward the border is Cotulla, seat of La Salle County and situated on the north bank of the Nueces River, the historic divide between Texas and Tamaulipas. At Uncle Moe's on U.S. 83 on the south side of town, the fare is Texas barbecue and Mexican food. The ranchero barbecue plate is tasty brisket with sides of coleslaw, potato salad, and beans and a choice of white bread or flour tortillas. Continuing south on I-35 to Laredo, some 65 miles from Cotulla, one finally arrives in taco heaven, where local fast-food franchises like Taco Palenque and Taco Tote serve thousands of flour tortilla tacos to hungry Laredoans twenty-four hours a day. Laredo has even invented its own version of the flour tortilla taco called a mariachi, a flour tortilla 8–10 inches in diameter filled with a single item like *guisado* (meat stew), fajita meat, or frijoles, folded in half and grilled slightly to give the exterior a hint of crispness. Mariachis are served exclusively in Laredo and are found nowhere else in South Texas.

The flour tortilla taco is the regional icon of South Texas Mexican food and more than any single item distinguishes this ethnic foodway from other Mexican American food traditions (FIG. 8.4). Other regional Mexican American cuisines in California and Arizona use flour tortillas, but only South Texas Mexican cuisine calls anything in a flour tortilla a taco. That distinction might seem minor, but it is a marked signature of regional difference. In California and Arizona, flour tortillas fold, roll, and

8.4. Flour tortilla tacos distinguish South Texas Mexican food from other regional Mexican American foodways. At La Esquina del Taco in McAllen, tacos are served with beef *pastor* (cooked on a vertical spit), or with tongue, brains, *barbacoa*, or *fajita* meat.

enclose any number of food products, but are called burritos and burros, not tacos.[37] One ethnographer who studied Tejano migrant farmworkers claims that "the tamale has no serious rival" in the array of artifacts with which these people identify themselves.[38] This is hard to imagine, not because tamales are insignificant—they are in fact a highly symbolic food for special occasions, particularly the Christmas season—but their very labor-intensive preparation means they are a specialty item, not typically consumed each and every day.[39] The flour tortilla is the equivalent of daily bread for many South Texas Mexicans. In the form of a taco it is consumed particularly for breakfast and lunch—sometimes even for dinner. Its presence is recent, yet its rapid popularity and emblematic nature are cause for declaring it the food icon of the region.

The word *tortilla*, which means omelet in Spain, was introduced to Mexico by clerics like Bernardino de Sahagún, whose Florentine Codex or *General History of the Things in New Spain* defined the numerous maize preparations of the Aztecs.[40] The corn tortilla of aboriginal Mexico became the daily bread of peasant classes in the Republic, but during the Porfiriato and Revolutionary eras, tortillas became associated with primitiveness and underdevelopment as well as being a barrier to modernization. Between 1900 and 1946, Mexico engaged a program to convince the lower classes to replace corn with wheat as part of the national diet.[41] This campaign succeeded chiefly in the north, where wheat cultivation was implemented and where *norteños* sought to modernize their regional culture.[42]

In Mexico today, corn tortillas are universally available in all regions, but flour tortillas (*tortillas de harina*) only are associated with Sonora, Chihuahua, Coahuila, and Nuevo León, all northern states. Furthermore, the flour tortillas of Coahuila and Nuevo León in northeastern Mexico and bordering South Texas are considered distinctive ("más pequeñas y gordas," smaller and fatter) than those of Sonora and Chihuahua.[43] Hispanic folklorist Arthur Campa asserts that wheat flour replaced corn in tortilla making in the home because it was more convenient and easier to manipulate.

> Wheat *tortillas* replaced the corn product in Hispanic homes in northern Mexico and most of the Southwest. It was considerably easier and faster for the housewife to prepare the biscuit like dough and roll it out than to go through the long process of making *nixtamal* by parboiling corn with lime and then washing it five times before grinding it over a backbreaking *metate* [stone grinder]. After the

masa or dough was prepared, she still had the laborious work of patting out each individual *tortilla* cake between her hands and baking them over the griddle. With wheat *tortillas* she could have bread on the table in a matter of minutes.[44]

By the early twentieth century, however, the first tortilla-making machines that had been pioneered in Mexico began to appear in Mexican American cities, and San Antonio boasts that it was the first to adopt this technology, in 1924.[45] Several sources interviewed suggested that it was during the 1930s that flour began to replace corn as the chief medium in tortilla manufacture in Texas.[46] During that time, every town and city in South Texas had one or more neighborhood *tortillería* where flour as well as corn tortillas were produced daily. In the 1990s, there were more than four hundred independent tortilla producers in the United States, mostly small family-owned operations in California and Texas, but consolidation has been predicted for the industry as the market expands and larger producers enter the competition. Between 1980 and 1990, nationwide tortilla sales quintupled, and in 1993 35 billion tortillas were consumed in the United States. Sixty percent of tortilla sales are of the wheat flour variety.[47]

In the Lower Rio Grande Valley, flour tortilla tacos are increasingly being called *patos* or ducks. The association of a food item like the white flour tortilla with an animal form is not an uncommon practice in Mexico, where chickens and pigs regularly endear food advertisements. Since 1974, El Pato Restaurants have grown to become a cherished institution among Valley taco aficionados. Founded by Lillie A. Gonzalez, who was born near San Antonio and raised in Chicago, El Pato eateries started in McAllen, where there are three establishments; six additional restaurants are located in Brownsville, Harlingen, Weslaco, Edinburg, Pharr, and Mission.[48] El Pato makes its own white flour tortillas, approximately six inches in diameter, and each taco is made to order, filled with any number of possible combinations (TABLE 8.2).

In South Texas, the flour tortilla taco is better known than the barbecue sandwich. Its familiarity is so taken for granted that most would not conceive of it as a geographical phenomenon. Yet, its range can be plotted like all items of material culture, and its perimeter geography is strongly coincident with two transition boundaries for contrasting subcultures and their foodways. Along the western flank of South Texas, above Del Rio, are two small towns in Terrell County, Dryden and

TABLE 8.2 Taco Possibilities at El Pato Restaurant in McAllen, 1997

REFRIED BEANS	POTATOES	BEEF GUISADO[a]	AVOCADO	CHICKEN GUISADO[a]	MIGAS[b]
Cheese	Beans	Beans	Jalapeños	Cheese	Chorizo
Chorizo	Cheese	Cheese	Beans	Rice	Tomato and Cheese
Eggs	Chorizo	Rice	Potatoes	Potatoes	Bacon
Bacon	Jalapeños	Potatoes	Cheese	Jalapeños	Ham
Potatoes	Eggs	Avocado	Rice	Lettuce and Tomato	Onion and Cheese
Rice		Lettuce and Tomato	Eggs	Onion	Beans
Onion			Onion	Avocado	
Jalapeños					

SOURCE: Field survey by author, 1997.
[a]*Guisado* is a stewlike meat sauce.
[b]*Migas* are a mixture of corn chips, eggs, and salsa.

Sanderson, strung out along U.S. 90 as it links South Texas with West Texas. In each of these communities Mexican food served in a flour tortilla is called a burrito. Northeast of these towns along I-10 in Crockett County is Ozona, and as in Dryden and Sanderson, Mexican food served here is folded into a flour tortilla referred to again as a burrito. This divide represents the geographical limit of the South Texas Mexican foodway region, because west of the line throughout West Texas one finds references to the "burrito" and the influence of Chihuahua in Mexican food,[49] while to the south and east of this line the dominant reference to this food is to the "taco" (see FIG. 8.5). Reinforcing the transitional nature of this cultural divide, in Del Rio two popular Mexican restaurants each feature tacos and burritos on their menus. At Don Marcelino's, burritos are available, but they are curiously served "taco-style," meaning the flour tortilla is folded in half like a taco rather than tucked and rolled like a burrito. At Memo's, a family Mexican restaurant founded in 1936, burritos again appear on the menu, but so too do flour tortilla tacos.

On the eastern flank of South Texas, U.S. 181 extends between Corpus Christi and San Antonio. In small towns from Sinton to Beeville to Karnes City to Floresville, Mexican food served in a flour tortilla is called a taco, as it is almost uniformly south and west of this divide (FIG. 8.5). North and east of this line, the taco yields to the barbecue sandwich as the preferred convenience food of the region, reflecting the strong presence of Germans, Czechs, and Scandinavians mixed with Southern Anglos and with African Americans to create the "shatter belt" culture area of Central Texas.[50]

The taco-burrito and the taco-barbecue lines coincide almost exactly with geographer Richard Pillsbury's "transition" zones between "Southwestern" and "Southern" cuisine regions in the United States.[51] Inside the borders of the South Texas Mexican foodway region, the flour tortilla taco is the premier ethnic food icon. The taco is not simply a food of convenience but an emblem of the Texas Mexican stamp on the culture of the region. In McAllen, in the Lower Rio Grande Valley, news is made when a San Antonio taco chain restaurant invades the turf of El Pato Restaurants.[52] In San Antonio, where some 362 Mexican restaurants vie for consumer loyalty and where 85 establishments include the word *taco* in their business name, there is the suggestion, not entirely in jest, that the Alamo City be renamed Taco Town.[53]

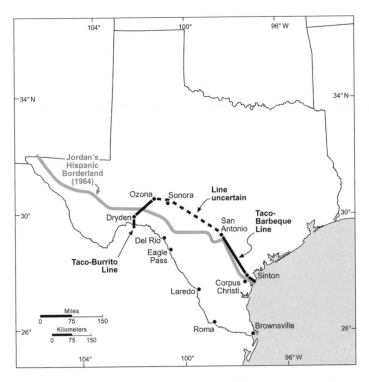

8.5. The Taco-Burrito and Taco-Barbecue lines define the western and eastern limits of the South Texas Mexican food region.

PUBLIC CELEBRATIONS

"The ethos of a culture is represented in its rituals, ceremonies, and cel-ebrations," writes sociologist Rosario Torres-Raines. Among South Texas Mexican Americans, Torres-Raines divides those rituals into categories of faith, family, and public ceremony.[54] Like rituals among their brethren across the borderland Southwest, many of these celebrations and ceremo-nies are nearly universal to Mexican Americans and therefore geographi-cally pan-ethnic. But what is distinctive about South Texas Mexican pub-lic celebration? And how do these distinctive forms reinforce group identity to symbolize Texas Mexican geographical personality? Using Torres-Raines' typology as a beginning, I define public celebration as selected sacred rituals, cultural displays, and ceremonies. Because my primary concern is to arrive at the role of place as part of group identity, I do not include individual or family rituals that may be distinctive among South Texas Mexican Americans.[55] My purpose is to explain group representations that are place-specific and especially how these have become institution-alized events and displays that are linked to Texas Mexicans.

Folk Catholicism, Pilgrimage, and Sacred Place

Mexican American religious symbolism is said to be "popular religiosity" that remains chiefly outside the structures of institutional Catholicism.[56] In South Texas, French Oblate priests were largely responsible for con-structing the early formal church hierarchy in Mexican American com-munities in the region, and this cultural religious intrusion was resisted by native Texas Mexicans when it sought to discredit traditional worldviews.[57] Important in the worldview of Mexican American Catho-lics is a folk Catholicism inherited from the homeland and based to a very great extent on what Anita Brenner calls "idols behind altars," a native tradition of beliefs in pre-Columbian gods that conveniently al-lowed a syncretism with the saints of Catholicism. That belief system as demonstrated by geographer Mary Lee Nolan is also one committed to pilgrimage and sacred place.[58]

Sacred places are found in many South Texas Mexican communi-ties. A frequent sight is a cross on a hill near a town, like the Loma de la Cruz (Hill of the Cross) near the barrio San Felipe in Del Rio, another of the same name downriver in Eagle Pass, or the unnamed cross on the hill outside Rio Grande City, still further downriver. In Laredo, there are community shrines that are specific to certain barrios, like the Capilla

Juan Bosco (Juan Bosco Chapel), erected in 1946 by María and Jesús Garza in answer to a prayer that their son return safely from World War II. These displays of devotion and commemoration are common as well throughout Mexico and the Mexican American Southwest. One sign of the popularity of pilgrimage to potential sacred sites in South Texas is the unusual number of apparitions recorded in the region that attract visitors, if only ephemerally.[59] Folklorist Mark Glazar, who maintains the Rio Grande Folklore Archive at the University of Texas–Pan American in Edinburg, asserts that most apparitions do not lead to the creation of a sacred place.[60] The archive contains close to 100,000 items, including approximately 1,000 religious folktales.

Nevertheless, in South Texas pilgrimage to sacred sites that are associated with particular charismatic saints is more entrenched as a folk tradition than in other parts of the Mexican American borderland. The most recognized Catholic pilgrimage sites in the border region are the sanctuary at Chimayó, New Mexico, which now celebrates the Santo Niño de Atocha, and the crypt of Jesuit missionary Eusebio Kino in Magdalena, Sonora, which is popular with Arizona Mexican Americans and others.[61] More recent but less popular pilgrimages are said to attract some Mexican Americans to Clifton, Arizona, to commemorate Teresita, the Saint of Cabora (Teresita Urea), and to Tijuana, Baja California, to honor the folk saint Juan Soldado.[62] In South Texas and nearby northeastern Mexico, there are only three major pilgrimage sites (FIG. 8.6). These include the grave of Don Pedrito Jaramillo in Falfurrias, Texas; the home and gravesite of El Niño de Fidencio in Espinazo, near Monclova, Coahuila; and the shrine of the Virgen de San Juan del Valle in San Juan, Texas. During sacred celebrations, each of these sites attracts tens of thousands of pilgrims or *peregrinos*, both Mexican American and Mexican national.

Don Pedrito Jaramillo is without argument the most celebrated *curandero* or folk healer in South Texas, and his grave in a small cemetery at the outskirts of Falfurrias, county seat of Brooks County and located between McAllen and Alice, has become a folk shrine. Little is known about Don Pedrito except that he was born in Guadalajara in 1829, he came to South Texas in 1881, and he took up residence at Los Olmos Creek in what was then Starr County; he died in 1907.[63] He first served as a healer for Mexican families at Los Olmos and other neighboring ranches.

Folklorist Ruth Dodson, who researched Don Pedrito in 1951, pub-

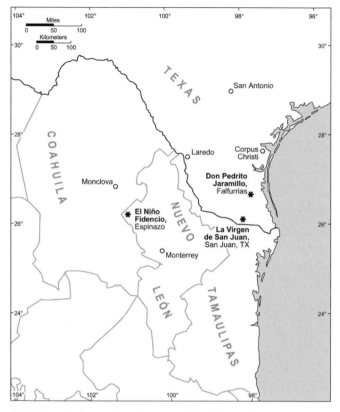

8.6. Major pilgrimage sites that attract South Texas Mexicans.

lished the locations of some 40 supplicants who were known to have used his services. Their geographic range was chiefly South Texas. These included persons from ranches in Duval (12), Jim Wells (5), Starr (4), San Patricio (3), and Live Oak (3) Counties, and one each from Bexar, Bee, DeWitt, Goliad, Hidalgo, Nueces, and Refugio Counties; the list also included 5 residents from towns in northern Mexico and 1 person from New Mexico.[64] Anthropologist Octavio Ignacio Romano, who researched Don Pedrito in 1959, reported a ledger of some 500 visitors for a six-month period. Their hometowns included fifty-nine different Texas cities, towns, and rural communities, mostly from the South Texas area stretching between Laredo and Brownsville.[65]

Among the devout, Don Pedrito Jaramillo has been elevated to folk saint status.[66] That the Texas State Historical Commission in 1971 erected a marker at the site recognizes the historic importance of the healer of

Los Olmos to the South Texas region, and may be evidence that he is now considered a popular icon as well. The shrine is featured in many guidebooks and has become an attraction for passers-by motoring between the Lower Rio Grande Valley and San Antonio along U.S. 281. At the curio store next to the cemetery outside Falfurrias, believers and tourists can purchase Don Pedrito prayer cards, candles, and statues, along with herbal remedies, literature, and assorted pilgrimage paraphernalia (FIG. 8.7).

Some 200 miles west of Falfurrias across the Mexican border in a dry mountain pass southeast of Monclova, Coahuila, in the state of Nuevo León, is the hamlet of Espinazo, sacred home and grave of Mexico's most revered *curandero*, El Niño Fidencio. The town is the site of three pilgrimage festivals, two in October that celebrate El Niño Fidencio's birth and death, and one that celebrates his saint day in March. The shrine is significant in this discussion because South Texas Mexican Americans are an important component to these celebrations.

José Fidencio Sintora Constantino was born in Guanajuato in 1898 and spent most of his adult life in Espinazo, where he died in 1938. His curing powers were known throughout northern Mexico and South Texas

8.7. The Don Pedrito Jaramillo shrine near Falfurrias includes a curio shop that vends prayer accessories like candles, cards, incense, and herbs.

during his life, and since his death Espinazo has witnessed pilgrimages to honor and celebrate the legendary healer. Supplicants are known as *fidencistas*, with the female *fidencistas* called *materias* and the males called *cajones*. These subjects, who act as mediums for El Niño, are visible at gatherings by their white shirts and red bandannas. *Materias* especially help attract followers by establishing *misiones*, usually at home. A *misión* devoted to El Niño Fidencio typically is an elaborately decorated room with an altar, photographs, other images, and statuary of El Niño and other saints, in which weekly gatherings and curing ceremonies are staged.[67]

Like other folk saints, El Niño Fidencio is not recognized by the Catholic Church. However, *fidencistas* have built temples and centers for cultural and spiritual studies of El Niño in cities across northern Mexico.[68] The director of the center at Monterrey, Nuevo León, declares that there are 300 registered *materias* and *cajones*, and that some 60 are residents of South Texas. In 1988, the fiftieth anniversary of El Niño's death, some 40,000 followers visited Espinazo over a four-day period. At the March 1990 festival, it was estimated that "hundreds of thousands of people" visited the site where there are no hotels and few restaurants. In a ritual similar to that known at other folk shrines around the world, *fidencistas* drag themselves barefoot and on their knees from the town to La Cerra de las Campañas outside of town where El Niño was said to hold healing ceremonies. *Fidencistas* also visit El Niño's tomb, *el pirulito* or sacred tree, and *el charquito* or sacred pool for additional activities. Merchants congregate at the town to hawk everything from Dallas Cowboys T-shirts to El Niño memorabilia.[69] Like Don Pedrito Jaramillo, El Niño Fidencio has become a popular icon as well as folk saint.

Halfway between Espinazo and Falfurrias, in the Lower Rio Grande Valley east of McAllen, is the town of San Juan, Texas, home to the shrine of La Virgen de San Juan del Valle, one of the most popular saints of South Texas and northern Mexico. The shrine was first a church in 1920. In 1949 Father Joseph Azpiazu, O.M.I., brought from Guadalajara a replica of the famous Virgin of San Juan de los Lagos, a popularly venerated saint in Jalisco, Mexico. His intention was to encourage Mexican Americans in the Lower Valley to bond with the saint of the same name as the Texas town. The replica introduction gained immediate acceptance in San Juan and across the Valley and quickly became a pilgrimage site. By 1954, the crowds were so great that a new shrine with convent and rectory was completed and dedicated to accommodate 800 worshipers, including services for pilgrims such as a cafeteria, retreat house, grade school, nursing home, and radio programs.[70]

On October 23, 1970, during assembled services, a plane crashed at the sanctuary site, destroying the church, but miraculously parishioners and pilgrims escaped injury. Furthermore, the icon of La Virgen was rescued, so that temporary services could continue until the shrine was rebuilt. On April 19, 1980, a massive new shrine with a seating capacity of 1,800 was dedicated amid an estimated crowd of 50,000 celebrants.[71]

Between 10,000 and 20,000 pilgrims gather weekly at the shrine, and some 80 percent are Mexican Americans from the Valley. Beyond this, in rank order, pilgrims travel from San Antonio, Laredo, Corpus Christi, and Houston, as well from Mexico.[72] A popular site at the shrine is the fountain next to the basilica, where blessed water is collected in plastic containers by the devout for transport home and ritual use. A gift store and housing for pilgrims are part of the extensive grounds. On the exterior wall of the cathedral is a massive color mural of the Virgen de San Juan, plainly visible to passers-by on U.S. 83, the east-west freeway that links Valley communities. According to folklife specialist Kay Turner, La Virgen de San Juan del Valle may be the most importantly venerated regional icon of South Texas.

> In Mexican–American and Mexican religious life, one lives with an important Icon very much on a day-to-day basis, the everyday and the festival day included . . . the Icon is not a single image located only in the church but an infinitely replicable code produced in several channels. The main function of replication is *visibility*. In all settings, the emphasis is on keeping the Icon *visible*—within the gaze of the believer.[73]

La Virgen de San Juan has been called a "triangular virgin" because her petite form is delta-like, an inheritance of diminutive virgins from Spain (FIG. 8.8). The San Juan icon is also distinctive because of its *paenula* or cape, which is sky blue: color coding is a common feature that distinguishes triangular virgins.[74]

As a consequence, La Virgen de San Juan is especially popular as the celebrated saint in *capillas* or yard shrines in towns and cities and on gravestones in cemeteries, and can also be found in Mexican American home *altares* or altars throughout South Texas.[75] She is known as the patroness of journeys and is therefore extremely popular among migrant

8.8. La Virgen de San Juan del Valle may be the most venerated regional icon among South Texas Mexicans. Her image is seen throughout the region, as here at Casiano Homes Housing Projects in San Antonio.

workers from Texas and newly arrived immigrants. Immigration and Naturalization Service officers claim that more than half of the Mexican nationals who cross the border into Texas carry photographs of the Virgin of San Juan.[76]

The shrines of Don Pedrito Jaramillo, El Niño Fidencio, and La Virgen de San Juan del Valle are clearly sacred spaces, as important to Texas Mexicans as to other Mexicans and Mexican Americans who visit these sites. Each holds a special place in the history and hearts of devout Texas Mexicans, emphasizing their identity with particular folk Catholic personalities and the importance of making a pilgrimage to these sites.

Ferias to Festivals

Like sacred place and pilgrimage, there are a host of public celebratory events that are part of South Texas Mexican culture, yet these customs are practiced in other Mexican American communities as well. The *pelea de gallo* or cockfight and the *charreada* or Mexican rodeo represent two examples of celebration that are traditional in Mexican culture. Their Mexican American counterparts are well known in South Texas, as they are in Southern Arizona.[77] Similarly, Mexican Americans reenact medieval Catholic dramas like *Los Pastores* (The Shepherds) and *Danzas de los Matachines* (Dances of the Matachines), which celebrate the birth of Christ and the contest of Christians and Moors, respectively.[78] In San Antonio, *Los Pastores* has been a traditional staged event during the Christmas season since the eighteenth century. The present version of the drama has been performed since 1913 in the backyards of West Side barrios, as well as in neighborhood churches like Our Lady of Guadalupe. A popular tourist adaptation is given at the historic Mission San José, sponsored by the San Antonio Conservation Society.[79]

When customs become celebrated annually by a Mexican American community, they become a fiesta or festival.[80] While many places in Texas hold Mexican festivals, the greatest concentration is in South Texas (FIG. 8.9). San Antonio, a city especially famous for its lively fiestas, is host to some eighteen regular Hispanic celebrations annually, making the city the recognized capital of such festivities, not only in Texas but also in the United States.[81]

Brownsville, in the Lower Rio Grande Valley, has celebrated Charro Days every February since 1938. The festival was first organized to educate local residents and visitors to the Mexican culture of the Brownsville-

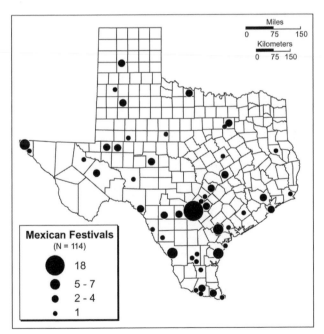

8.9. South Texas towns celebrate Mexican festivals more than towns in any other region of the state.

8.10. Charro Days, first organized in Brownsville in 1938, is one of the oldest continuously celebrated Mexican festivals of South Texas.

Matamoros area (FIG. 8.10). Typically, the festival occurs over several days at multiple locations and features music, food, and folk-art displays of the South Texas border area. Major attractions include a parade, a *charreada*, and a costume review of traditional Pan American dress styles. In the past, Charro Days even created artificial environments to mimic Mexican scenes, such as a generic Mexican village built by the Missouri Pacific Railroad or the re-creation of Mexico City's famous floating gardens of Xochimilco in a local *resaca* or river meander. Charro Days attracts more than 150,000 participants yearly.[82]

Two Mexican South Texas celebrations that are symbolic of the role of festivals to the ethnic subgroup are the Duval County ferias or fairs and San Antonio's Tejano Conjunto Festival. The ferias are a revival of a nineteenth century celebration common in the ranchlands of South Texas, while the conjunto festival is a modern urban incarnation that highlights a working-class musical tradition invented in the South Texas–northeastern Mexico borderlands.

The tradition of annual celebration on ranchos in South Texas dates to the nineteenth century in Webb County, and in the Lower Rio Grande Valley the town of La Feria got its name from the ritual of fairs held on a nearby ranch.[83] In Duval County, in central South Texas, the cotton fiesta replaced the old rancho celebrations in small towns like San Diego, Benavides, and Concepción by the early twentieth century. These fiestas persisted up to the period of the Second World War before losing their popular appeal. Writer Lionel García, who was raised in San Diego, recalls the ambiance and activities of these annual events.

> The Cotton Fiesta was the busiest during the four weekends in August. That was when the farmers came to town to buy groceries, clothes, and other supplies. The fiesta occupied an empty city lot that took the appearance of an old-world town plaza with all kinds of attractions around the perimeter and the people walking around and around inside its confines kicking up dust. Indeed, from afar one could spot the location of the fiesta by the cloud of dust suspended over the square block it occupied. More pronounced at night, the cloud of dust, illuminated by the many lights, was an eerie sight. In the center of the grounds was a kiosk where the band played, the mayor gave his annual speech, and the queen was crowned. It was possible for a few couples, the ones who didn't care who stared at them, to dance in the kiosk. Around the kiosk were wooden benches where one could rest and enjoy the music after going around and around for so many hours . . . People from all over the region rented spaces around the old square and set up their stands—tents, temporary wooden buildings and carnival games. Little food stands were set up where families could eat out in the open. There were some that made their entire living off the fiesta . . . Smaller games of chance at the fiesta were the *manita*, similar to the wheel of fortune . . . The *Lotería* was very popular with the older people. It was run by the church . . . The *Lotería* is a Spanish form of bingo using a board with vertical columns filled with squares with both numbers and drawings, the drawings for the people who could not read . . . My grandmother and mother loved to play *Lotería*. They so looked forward to it as they dressed and walked to the fiesta to sit down for the night to play. It was more of a ritual than anything else.[84]

Interrupted for several decades, Duval County fiestas were resurrected by two Benavides residents, Poncho Hernandez Jr. and Ernesto Gonzales.[85] They consulted with fiesta organizers in San Antonio and coordinated with local officials in the county and in the towns. In 1978 they staged the first revival of the Duval County fairs, calling them "ferias" in honor of the original ranch celebrations.[86] Three towns—San Diego, Benavides, and Concepción—each stage a fiesta one month apart in the fall. San Diego's celebration is called the Pan de Campo Fiesta and launches the season in early August, followed by the September Fiesta de Benavides and the Fiesta del Rancho in Concepción in October. While many of the activities and entertainments are similar, each fiesta highlights a different cooking contest: San Diego, the country-baked bread known as *pan de campo*; Benavides, a tortilla cook-off; and Concepción, a cabrito guisado (kid stew) cook-off. Musical performance has become another mainstay of the Duval County festivals, with headliners including the most celebrated names in Tejano music.[87]

The festivals have proven to be successful financial ventures for the communities, and the towns now charge admission and rent space to vendors. Estimates are that 10,000 to 15,000 participate in each festival, which typically runs for several days and attracts visitors especially from surrounding towns and counties but also from more distant locations. In San Diego, Mayor Alfredo Cardenas states that the Pan de Campo has become a combined festival and homecoming for former residents. In San Diego, the Pan de Campo is traditionally staged at the Plaza de Alcalá, but there is concern that the event may need to be relocated outside of town because the plaza space is too small to accommodate the burgeoning crowds, which typically exceed the population of the community.

If there is a single Texas Mexican festival that has become emblematic of the ethnic revival among Mexican Americans in the state, it is the Tejano Conjunto Festival inaugurated in San Antonio in 1982. Conjunto is a distinctive type of norteño music, a style common to northern Mexico that emerged in South Texas during the 1930s to become a symbol of the Texas Mexican working class.[88] The accordion is the basic instrument of the conjunto sound, although there is an ensemble of other instruments peculiar to the form. Manuel Peña, an ethnomusicologist and acknowledged expert on the history of the musical style, describes Texas Mexican conjunto as folk music rooted in an oral tradition, a style that became the signature of a collective ethnic identity.[89] Conjunto has remained a regionally distinctive music style in the Mexican American borderlands, one associated especially with Texas Mexicans, who have popularized it and carried it to other parts of the U.S. West where migrant farmworkers and urban working-class folk have relocated.[90]

While Tejano music in general has evolved to hybridize with other popular styles, the conjunto remains the most traditional popularized form.[91] And the overwhelming majority of conjunto musicians hail from South Texas, where 80 percent (75 of 94) of known Tejano conjunto

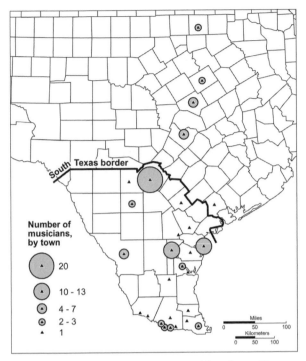

8.11. Birthplaces of Tejano conjunto musicians. Some 80 percent of performing conjunto musicians hail from South Texas.

performing artists were born (FIG. 8.11).[92] San Antonio is the clear capital for this music, but Corpus Christi and nearby Alice are cradles in coastal South Texas. In the Lower Rio Grande Valley, Hidalgo County is home to some eight Tejano conjunto musicians.

The Tejano Conjunto Festival is conjunto's major local, regional, national, and international forum. The festival serves to support and showcase Tejano conjunto music (FIG. 8.12). In 1997, the organizers boasted that some 140 different groups had performed at the festival since its inception. The six-day event is the largest gathering of its kind in the world and typically features more than forty hours of live performances by as many as thirty different conjuntos. The 1997 event was promoted as the "Sweet 16" of Tejano Conjunto Festivals. It included a symposium that brought together scholars, journalists, musicians, and promoters to discuss the relationships between conjunto and norteño music, a student accordion recital, and five days of musical extravaganza by the leading performers of this art form.

8.12. Conjunto master Valero Longoria performs at the Sixteenth Annual Tejano Conjunto Festival in San Antonio, 1997.

There are food and beverage booths, dancing, and games along with the music, so that the festival exudes a carnivalesque quality enjoyed by all age groups. The event is presented by the Guadalupe Cultural Arts Center of San Antonio and is organized by its director of Xicano Music, Juan Tejeda. It is staged at Rosedale Park on the West Side of the city and can draw as many as 50,000 revelers over the course of its celebration every May.

Conjunto has certainly been a folk component of South Texas for many generations, but the festival emerged only during the 1980s as part of a worldwide interest in "roots" music. Some conjunto practitioners have gained national and international notoriety, such as Flaco Jimenez, son of Santiago Jimenez Sr., an early pioneer of the style. Flaco, whose fiery accordion virtuosity is a favorite at the festival and usually the closing act, is a Grammy Award–winning musician who has performed and recorded with several nonconjunto musicians. Tejeda, the festival promoter, is optimistic that Tejano conjunto can reach beyond its chiefly Mexican American audience, but Peña, the scholar, is more reserved about its future. "I don't think it will make it into the mainstream. Conjunto is seen by mainstream people as working-class regional music. It will remain popular, yes, but only within its own base."[93] That base has historically been and continues to be Mexican American South Texas, a distinctive cultural region of the borderland.

Los Santos never wandered much once they settled in San Antonio. They never much needed or sought to know anything of the world that lay to the north of Elgin, east of Houston, west of Uvalde, in Texas, and south of Monclova, in Mexico. "This is where I'm from, right here," my father would say, surveying the live oak woods on the family's small ranch just outside of San Antonio, near Pleasanton, Texas. "This is the greatest place on the whole earth."

—JOHN PHILLIP SANTOS, *PLACES LEFT UNFINISHED AT THE TIME OF CREATION*, 1999

Tejano Cultural Province

There have been at least two-dozen serious plans to divide Texas into as many as five separate states. A proposal to make South Texas the forty-ninth state was publicly aired April 11, 1938, at Harlingen in Cameron County.[1] A brief set forth the fundamentals under which separate statehood was sought by people of Cameron, Willacy, Hidalgo, and Starr Counties. The organizers of this proclamation noted that there was no more similarity between the Lower Rio Grande Valley and the rest of Texas than there was between Texas and Minnesota. The region of the Lower Valley was declared to be isolated from San Antonio, Austin, and the rest of Texas, and a thriving agricultural economy was to be the foundation for the new state. Not a single Spanish-surnamed individual was given on the organizing committee and no mention was made about the Hispanic heritage of the region. This despite the fact that Starr County was more than 70 percent Mexican in 1930, or that Hidalgo and Willacy Counties each had a Mexican population that was greater than 50 percent in the same year.

In a proposal almost a half century later, South Texas was suggested as one of five states. South Texas was the area between the Gulf Coast on the east and the Rio Grande along the southwestern boundary. It would include some forty counties stretching from Val Verde in the west to Guadalupe in the northeast, and extending to Refugio on the Gulf of Mexico. San Antonio was imagined as the dominant urban center and potential capital of South Texas, a region now acknowledged as a stronghold of Mexican population.[2]

Today, it is popularly acknowledged that South Texas is a distinctive subregion of the Lone Star State, and the chapters above have made the case for this geographical claim. In this concluding chapter, I revisit the argument about South Texas as a cultural subregion of the Hispanic American borderland. That assertion is examined first from the perspective of political distinctiveness, how Mexican Americans of South Texas have allied themselves and how South Texas political geography distinguishes the subregion from other parts of Texas. Next, I investigate the issue of regional distinctiveness and its appropriateness to Mexican Americans in the borderland. Here I also examine how the expressions "Tejano" and "South Texas" have been used historically and the popular perception of them. Finally, I recount selected examples that signal how this subregion is culturally and geographically distinguishable from other Hispanic borderland areas, substantiating that Tejano South Texas is a separate cultural province.

POLITICAL DISTINCTIVENESS

In a political sense, South Texas is geographically different from subregions in the state.[3] Historically, the South Texas counties of Cameron, Hidalgo, Starr, Willacy, Kenedy, Kleberg, and Duval were the heart of the so-called *patrón* system, a semifeudal arrangement derived from Hispanic colonial roots. The *patrón* was a political overlord who controlled ranch *peones* (peons) through social and economic patronage. In the early twentieth century, this system survived almost exclusively in South Texas, where Anglo and Mexican American bosses like Jim Wells, Archie Parr, and

Manuel Guerra built county-based political machines on the foundations of the older Hispanic ranching system.[4]

South Texas has been a staging area for several Mexican and United States political movements. One was the short-lived Republic of the Rio Grande (1839-1840), whose sovereignty encompassed the Mexican states of Tamaulipas, Coahuila, and Nuevo León, as well as the disputed territory between the Rio Grande and the Nueces River. Its capital was Laredo.[5] A second was an irredentist movement sparked by the Plan of San Diego in 1915. Named after the town of San Diego in Duval County, this proclamation was likely drafted in Monterrey, Mexico. The manifesto called for a revolution against the United States to reclaim for Mexico land lost in 1836 and 1848—territory comprising Texas, New Mexico, Arizona, Colorado, and California. The rebellion was intended as a race war, with every Anglo American male over the age of sixteen to be put to death. The leaders of the movement in San Antonio scheduled Texas to be liberated first and distributed handbills urging Texas Mexicans to join them. For some ten months sporadic raids followed the proclamation, causing havoc and forcing perhaps half the population of the Lower Rio Grande Valley to leave the region. Although the leaders of the uprising aimed to establish an interim republic across the Southwest with eventual reannexation to Mexico, the rebellion faltered before year's end.[6]

The ethnic and racial overtones of early political struggles angered the rising middle-class Mexican Americans of Texas, who saw themselves as separate from the Mexican American laboring class and Mexican migrants. As a result, the middle class began to identify itself increasingly as "Latin American" or "Americans of Latin American descent." This referent gained political legitimacy in 1929, when they formed the League of United Latin American Citizens (LULAC) in Corpus Christi. LULAC based its creed on a duality: Mexican consciousness in culture and social activity, but U.S. consciousness in philosophy and politics. While LULAC favored the learning of English, it called for the maintenance of Spanish. Its agenda also advocated social and racial equality, the development of political power, and economic advancement. Although it was not a political party, it sponsored political, social, and cultural causes and events. LULAC currently has some 240 active councils and more than 200,000 members across the country, but it remains strongest in Texas.[7]

During the 1960s South Texas gave birth to the Chicano movement. Some Mexican Americans separated themselves from the cultural pluralist posture of LULAC and inaugurated a radical political agenda.

The catalyst for this awakening occurred when the control of local government in Zavala County shifted from Anglo American to Mexican American, an unprecedented event in the political history of the region.[8] Crystal City, the self-proclaimed Spinach Capital of the World, was then a small agricultural village in the Texas Winter Garden District. Some 85 percent of the town's population was Mexican American, yet the Anglo American minority dominated all aspects of community life, as it had since midwesterners founded the town in 1907. Politically powerless, the Mexican American majority consisted chiefly of farm laborers, cannery workers, and seasonal migrants. In 1963, Teamsters Union members joined with Chicano activists to defeat the Anglo ruling elite in a local election, which resulted in the establishment of Mexican American political control in the community. Victory was short-lived, however; the Anglo minority regained control of government just two years later. Yet in 1970 Mexican Americans organized La Raza Unida, a political party that proclaimed a platform of "Chicano nationalism" and gained control of the town council and school board. José Angel Gutiérrez, a native of Crystal City and a cofounder of MAYO, the San Antonio-based Mexican American Youth Organization, steered the Chicano campaign to political victory.[9] MAYO was formed in 1967 by several young Mexican Americans who advocated third party politics and local control of educational systems in Mexican American communities.

While the Raza Unida Party had some success in local and county elections in rural South Texas, it was unable to bring significant changes to this historically popular Democratic stronghold. In 1972 a Raza Unida Party candidate, Ramsey Muñiz of Corpus Christi, ran for governor, but garnered only 6 percent of the vote and won only Brooks County. Representing the Raza Unida Party, Muñiz ran again in the 1974 gubernatorial election, and this time he carried only Zavala County, although he finished second in fifteen other Texas counties, fourteen of which were in South Texas.[10]

In part, these election results reveal the social and economic variability that exists in the region despite the demographic dominance of Mexican Americans. For example, in border communities like Eagle Pass, Laredo, and Brownsville, places where Anglo and Mexican Americans have traditionally shared political leadership, Mexican Americans involved in local commerce have risen to middle- and even upper-class status. Because middle- and upper-class Mexican Americans lean to the two national political parties, especially the Democrats, the result has been that the Raza Unida Party fares poorly in these areas. As a consequence, Chicano political activity and the Raza Unida Party have had their greatest triumphs in inland towns like Crystal City, Carrizo Springs, and Cotulla, where Anglos have traditionally controlled local economies and government. Anglo minorities in these towns have long discriminated against Mexican Americans, and animosities served initially as the basis for ethnic politics, but ultimately third party popularity was unable to carry the region. In 1978 the party captured less than 2 percent of votes in the gubernatorial election. Philosophical splits within the party and the formation of Mexican American Democrats (MAD) in 1976 led to the demise of the Raza Unida Party at the state level. Although efforts had been made to have the party become national, its heart and greatest strength were in Texas, especially South Texas. In 1982 when the party expired in its Crystal City birthplace, its local influence came to an end.[11]

A legacy of the Chicano political movement in South Texas is the Southwest Voter Registration and Education Project (SVREP), which Willie Velásquez, a cofounder of MAYO, formed and directed after he left the Raza Unida Party in 1974. Headquartered in San Antonio, SVREP has probably done more to empower Mexican Americans than any other single political initiative. Intended as a grassroots organization to effect political change at the local level, SVREP brought together a coalition of civic, church, and neighborhood associations, labor groups, and volunteers to conduct door-to-door voter registration drives and education campaigns. In its first decade, SVREP helped increase the number of registered Hispanic voters in the Southwest by 1.6 million. In Texas alone the number increased from 488,000 to nearly 1 million.[12]

One measure of the success of the SVREP in Texas is the 240 percent increase in the number of Texas Mexicans elected to office between 1973 and 1990. Nearly half of all publicly elected Hispanic officials in the United States in 1990 were in Texas.[13] To a very great extent, the increase in the number of Mexican American officeholders was the result of SVREP lawsuits that forced cities, counties, and school boards to change from at-large systems of election to single-member districts. In 1990 most of the Hispanic elected officials in the state hailed from South Texas, including 745 school board members, 534 municipal officeholders, and 350 judges. All four United States congressional representatives and eighteen of twenty-seven Texas state legislators who were Hispanic in 1990 represented South Texas districts. Of Texas' 184 Hispanic county commissioners, clerks, treasurers, tax assessors, and other officials, 149, or

81 percent, held office in South Texas in 1990. Only one South Texas core county, Kenedy, did not then have a Hispanic county official.

The 1996 presidential election reinforced the half-century-long pattern of national Democratic allegiance in South Texas.[14] In that election only Kinney, Uvalde, Medina, Atascosa, McMullen, Live Oak, and Wilson Counties, among all South Texas counties, did not fall in line with Democrats.[15] This pattern of South Texas Democratic political expression in national elections is contrary to the recent Republican dominance that has colored presidential election voting in most other subregions of the state. South Texas remains a political subregion unlike the rest of Texas.

MEXICAN AMERICAN REGIONAL DISTINCTIVENESS

Scholarly examination of regional variation among Mexican Americans is beginning to emerge. Sociologists were among the earliest to question the need to differentiate the huge Mexican population in the United States. Leonard Broom and Eshref Shevky proposed the study of Mexican American source regions in the homeland and migration history as a first approximation of regional variability in 1952.[16] Fernando Peñalosa and Edward McDonagh in 1966 argued that upward mobility for Mexican Americans was more a matter of shedding class status than ethnic identity.[17] Their study of five population groups in Southern California concluded that ethnic subgroups were in a very real sense unique according to generation.

In 1982, historian Manuel Machado concluded that Mexican Americans were, in fact, a tricultural people with aboriginal, Spanish, and Anglo American complexities, and popular attempts to generalize a single group were compromised without that admission.[18] Recent sociological and economic analyses of Mexican Americans in Houston, Albuquerque, Laredo, and Tucson reveal consistent underclass characteristics, yet variability within the ethnic group persists.[19] Finally, Texas Mexican historian Arnoldo De León reflected that a recent turn in Tejano historiography is toward regional diversity, admitting that the experience of Texas Mexicans varies with place as well as time.[20]

Geographers too understand this reality. The distribution of the Mexican American population has been a function of historical inertia and migrations to areas of economic opportunity.[21] Mexican Americans evolved in different social and economic circumstances and at different times in the four hundred years of Hispanic occupation in North America. This differential process of social adaptation and economic development resulted in varied population groups within the Mexican American minority. Thus, Mexican Americans in South Texas are different from Mexican Americans in Chicago, and in turn both are different from the Mexican Americans of Arizona and California.

The patterns of social and economic diversity among Mexican American subgroups were differentiated and regionalized using 1970 data by geographers Thomas Boswell and Timothy Jones.[22] This study was based on a sample of Mexican Americans in U.S. counties and analysis of six major socioeconomic variables. These included median personal income, percentage of the population which was steadily employed, mean highest educational level, fertility ratio, percentage of the population over fourteen born in another state, and percentage of foreign-born population. Analysis revealed seven separate population regions, and these were mapped accordingly.

This regionalization showed the subgroups of Mexican American population that existed when measured by key social and economic variables. Two regional types accounted for almost 86 percent of the Mexican American population, most of it concentrated in the borderland states. For example, Mexican Americans in Southern California and Arizona generally ranked higher in all categories except fertility than their counterparts in Texas and southern New Mexico.

Although this regional analysis is several decades old, regional diversification of Mexican Americans is evident in other, more contemporary studies. Geographer Terrence Haverluk compared professional, managerial, and technical occupations for Mexican Americans in Webb, El Paso, Lubbock, and Deaf Smith Counties in Texas, Fresno County in California, and Yakima County in Washington.[23] These counties represent old and new Mexican American settlements, metropolitan areas and rural small towns, and concentrations of the minority ranging from 15 to 90 percent. In five of six counties, the percentage of occupations in professional, managerial, and technical fields increased significantly over some four decades; in Webb County the percentage grew from 1970-1980 but declined from 1980-1990. Nevertheless, by 1990 each county ranked differently in the percentage of Mexican Americans in these occupations: Webb 57 percent, El Paso 40 percent, Fresno 35 percent, Lubbock 34 percent, Yakima 25 percent, and Deaf Smith 23 percent. Similar measures of Mexican American income as a percentage of mean state income, as

TABLE 9.1   Selected Tejano Surnames in San Antonio and Los Angeles

NAME	SAN ANTONIO	LOS ANGELES
Arredondo	188	4
Benavides	204	35
Cadena	128	35
Cantú	525	19
Cavazos	178	6
Chapa	175	6
Elizondo	223	26
Garza	1,667	75
Guajardo	173	10
Hinojosa	153	30
Medina	453	2
Móntez	102	18
Sáenz	238	64
Treviño	842	25
Villareal	740	44

SOURCES: San Antonio Residence White Pages, *Greater San Antonio* (Southwestern Bell 1994); Pacific Bell White Pages, *Greater Los Angeles* (Pacific Bell 1991). *Greater Los Angeles* includes only area code 213, which encompasses the central city and parts of East Los Angeles.

well as median year of schooling completed in the same counties over four decades, showed comparable regional variation.

The cultural roots of Mexican American regional diversity are based in the regional homelands of Mexico, sometimes called *patrias chicas*, that have been the source areas for historic migrations north.[24] Time, isolation, adaptation to particular locales, and different interactions with neighboring populations created distinctive borderland Mexican Americans in varied subregions. That distinctiveness can be illustrated, for example, by differences in surnames. A comparison of Spanish surnames found in San Antonio with those in Los Angeles provides evidence of this differentiation (TABLE 9.1). Surname differences have resulted from different homeland roots; Los Angeles surnames came from the western Mexico states of Jalisco, Guanajuato, and Zacatecas, while those in San Antonio came from the northeastern Mexico states of Nuevo León, Coahuila, and Tamaulipas. South Texas, including San Antonio, is therefore a subregion of the Mexican American borderland, and "Tejano" has emerged as the distinctive self-referent for this particular Mexican American subgroup.

"Tejano" is the Spanish-language term that denotes a Texan of Mexican descent, that is, a Texas Mexican.[25] Perhaps the earliest uses of the term appear in the 1820s and 1830s. Historians especially have applied the term to Texas Mexicans in Spanish colonial Texas to distinguish them from Mexicans of other regions, and in Texas to differentiate Texas Mexicans from Texians, that is, Anglo American residents. The term has become popularized especially since the 1960s, and is now considered a naturalized part of the Texas lexicon.

South Texas by comparison has not developed an equivalent utility in historical context (see Chap. 2). Nevertheless, the expression is popular as a regional identifier, especially in commercial advertising. A survey of metropolitan telephone directories in the region suggests that "South Texas" as a business name is most popular in the Rio Grande Valley and least so in the extreme northwest of the region (TABLE 9.2). In the largest metro areas, San Antonio and Laredo, the local place name far surpasses the popularity of the regional label among business names. This is a telling clue to the geographical mosaic that exists even within the boundaries of the South Texas region. As early as 1973, the Greater South Texas Cultural Basin Commission recommended dividing South Texas into five subareas: Alamo, centered on San Antonio; South Texas, focused on Laredo; Coastal Bend, highlighting Corpus Christi, Lower Rio Grande, encompassing McAllen and Brownsville; and Middle Rio Grande pivoting on Eagle Pass, Del Rio, and surrounding counties of the Winter Garden.[26] That the perceptual

TABLE 9.2 "South Texas" as a Business Name in Metropolitan Telephone Directories

DIRECTORY	"SOUTH TEXAS"	OTHER BUSINESS NAMES
Rio Grande Valley	190	—
Greater San Antonio	161	421 ("San Antonio")
Corpus Christi Bay Area	98	69 ("Coastal Bend")
Laredo, Encinal Region	33	211 ("Laredo")
Eagle Pass	3	21 ("Eagle Pass")
		5 ("Southwest Texas")
Del Rio	0	65 ("Del Rio")
		11 ("Southwest Texas")

SOURCES: *Rio Grande Valley* (Southwestern Bell, 1993); *Greater San Antonio, October 1997* (Southwestern Bell, 1996); *Corpus Christi Bay Area, April 1992–93* (Southwestern Bell, 1992); *Laredo, Encinal Region, March '97* (Southwestern Bell, 1996); *Eagle Pass* (Southwestern Bell, 1996); *Del Rio, November 1996* (GTE Southwest, 1996).

boundaries of the South Texas subregion remain fluid is evident by the new subregional term "Laredo Borderplex," which was used for an areawide telephone book published for the year 1996-97 that contains listings for Webb County and surrounding Zapata, La Salle, and Dimmit Counties.

CIS–RIO GRANDE CULTURAL PROVINCE

Tejano South Texas is a cultural province of the Hispanic American borderland. In the original Latin use of the term, a province is a territory outside the boundaries of a political domain yet governed by a capital in that domain. Tejano South Texas is outside of Mexico, yet its cultural ancestry is rooted in that homeland. Nevertheless, the province is part of Texas and has political allegiance to the United States. Tejano South Texas is a cis–Rio Grande cultural province because it is geographically defined by its position on the U.S. side of the Rio Grande, although its cultural heritage is linked to Mexico.

Two cultural conditions and their geographical circumstances reinforce the link between Tejano South Texas and its motherland: Spanish-language tolerance and encouragement, and willingness to recognize and celebrate the Mexican heritage of place. These conditions are different from the ways in which Hispanic American subcultures are accommodated in other borderland states.

Nowhere in the Hispanic American borderland is the Spanish language as geographically resilient as it is along the South Texas borderland.[27] Only northern New Mexico comes close, but it falls short in comparison with the geography of Spanish language use in South Texas, where some eighteen counties are predominantly Spanish-speaking (FIG. 9.1). In California and Arizona, just two counties combined meet the same criteria. Sociolinguists agree that varieties of Spanish language occur in the southwestern United States, and that subregions exist for Texas, Arizona, California, and New Mexico and southern Colorado.[28] Some 7,000 words and phrases used in the Spanish of Texas suggest that regional variation may be pronounced.[29]

South Texas communities are setting a precedent in the legal and popular uses of Spanish language at a time when English-only advocates are crowding the news in other borderland states. In 1999 El Cenizo, a colonia of 7,500 residents south of Laredo, made Spanish the official language. The mayor and city commissioners agreed to the ordinance because 80 percent of the town population speaks only Spanish.[30] In San

Antonio, the Hispanic Chamber of Commerce initiated a campaign to make the city an English/Spanish-speaking town officially. Lorena González, the director of the chamber, is calling for schools in San Antonio to integrate Spanish into their curricula over the next five years, and so far the school districts and the business community are supportive. The idea is to have both English-speakers and Spanish-speakers fluent and literate in two languages and two cultures. Texas companies presently export $21.9 billion of goods to Mexico, approximately three times what California exports to Mexico.[31] González says, "Employers are now paying more here in San Antonio if you have a second language, preferably Spanish, because of our proximity to Mexico."

The recognition of language as a rooted element of Tejano subculture is coupled in South Texas with a pride of place that is unusual in the Hispanic American borderland. The town plaza, a symbolic place in South Texas communities, has been established as a nearly unique institution in the region (see Chap. 5). Along the Rio Grande, Los Caminos del Rio Heritage Project, a decade-long undertaking, is emblematic of the South Texas commitment to cultural resource preservation and regional under-

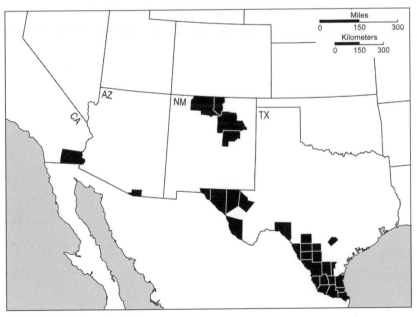

9.1. Counties in the borderland where Spanish is the primary language spoken at home.

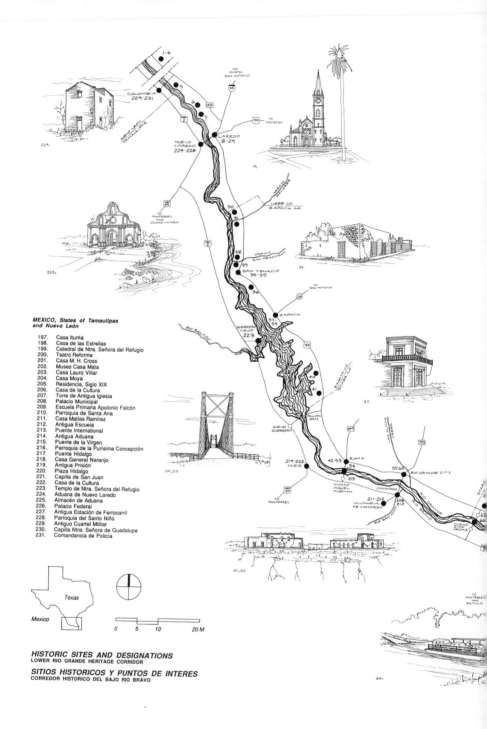

MEXICO, States of Tamaulipas and Nuevo León

197. Casa Iturria
198. Casa de las Estrellas
199. Catedral de Ntra. Señora del Refugio
200. Teatro Reforma
201. Casa M. H. Cross
202. Museo Casa Mata
203. Casa Lauro Villar
204. Casa Moya
205. Residencia, Siglo XIX
206. Casa de la Cultura
207. Torre de Antigua Iglesia
208. Palacio Municipal
209. Escuela Primaria Apolonio Falcón
210. Parroquia de Santa Ana
211. Casa Matías Ramírez
212. Antigua Escuela
213. Puente International
214. Antigua Aduana
215. Puente de la Virgen
216. Parroquia de la Purísima Concepción
217. Puente Hidalgo
218. Casa General Naranjo
219. Antigua Prisión
220. Plaza Hidalgo
221. Capilla de San Juan
222. Casa de la Cultura
223. Templo de Ntra. Señora del Refugio
224. Aduana de Nuevo Laredo
225. Almacén de Aduana
226. Palacio Federal
227. Antigua Estación de Ferrocarril
228. Parroquia del Santo Niño
229. Antiguo Cuartel Militar
230. Capilla Ntra. Señora de Guadalupe
231. Comandancia de Policía

Texas

Mexico

0   5   10   20 M

HISTORIC SITES AND DESIGNATIONS
LOWER RIO GRANDE HERITAGE CORRIDOR

SITIOS HISTORICOS Y PUNTOS DE INTERES
CORREDOR HISTORICO DEL BAJO RIO BRAVO

9.2. Historic sites and designations of the Lower Rio Grande heritage corridor.

UNITED STATES, State of Texas

1. Chupadera Ranch
2. Untitled Property
3. Pilotes Ranch
4. San Jose de Palafox
5. Dolores Ranch
6. Leyendecker
7. Untitled Property
8. Marker for Bishop Peter Verdaguer
9. Old Fort McIntosh Historic District
10. Fort McIntosh Barracks
11. Fort McIntosh Marker
12. Richter Mansion
13. Casa Vidaurri
14. Marker for Benavides Brothers
15. Capitol, Republic of the Rio Grande
16. Casa Ortiz
17. Election Riot Marker
18. Republic of the Rio Grande
19. St. Agustín Church
20. San Agustín Historic District
21. Webb County Courthouse
22. Leyendecker/Salinas House
23. Bertini House
24. De Leal House
25. De la Garza House
26. Montemayor House
27. El Azteca/Ranchero Neighborhood
28. Casa Zaragoza
29. Villa de Laredo Marker
30. Dolores Nuevo
31. Dolores Viejo
32. Corralitos Ranch
33. San Francisco Ranch

34. Treviño House
35. San Ygnacio Historic District
36. Old Ramireño
37. Mission Revilla
38. Old Zapata
39. Colonization of Lower Rio Grande
40. Old Lopeño
41. Old Falcón
42. Noah Cox House
43. Commercial Building
44. First Chapel of Roma
45. Old Garcia House
46. Our Lady of Refuge Church
47. Manuel Guerra Store
48. Knights of Columbus Hall
49. Ramirez Hall
50. Ramirez Hospital
51. Roma City Hall
52. Old Roma Convent
53. Roma Historic District
54. Roma-San Pedro International Bridge
55. Bass House
56. Cortina Battle Site
57. Marker for Jose de Escandon
58. Fort Ringgold
59. Fort Ringgold Hospital
60. J. Gonzales House
61. J.P. Kelsey House
62. Robert E. Lee House
63. Rio Grande City, C.S.A.
64. La Borde Hotel
65. De la Peña Drugstore/Post Office
66. Los Ebanos Ferry
67. First County Oil Well
68. Town of Havana
69. Town of Peñitas
70. Bentsen-Rio Grande Valley State Park
71. Chimney Park
72. Spiderwebb Railroad
73. La Lomita Historic District
74. Hidalgo Pumphouse

75. El Granjeno Cemetery
76. Rio Theatre
77. Gregg Wood Home
78. Oblate Park
79. Texas Citrus Fiesta
80. Wm. Jennings Bryan House
81. John H. Shary House
82. Vela Building
83. Hidalgo-Reynosa Bridge
84. Old Hidalgo Courthouse
85. Old Hidalgo School Teacherage
86. Old Hidalgo School
87. McAllen Park
88. Quinta Mazatlán
89. McAllen Post Office
90. Sacred Heart Church
91. Southern Pacific Depot
92. Bessie Steamboat Bell
93. "Fighting 69th" Camp Site
94. Archer Park
95. Casa De Palmas
96. McAllen 1st Methodist Church
97. Marker for W.L. Lipscomb
98. Marker for Father Hidalgo
99. El Sal del Rey
100. Edinburg Jr. College Auditorium
101. Everitt Building
102. Pharr Kiwanis Club
103. Old Pharr City Hall
104. First Pharr-San Juan-Alamo School
105. First Pharr School
106. San Juan Townsite
107. San Juan Hotel
108. Camp Ebenezer
109. St. Joseph's Catholic Church
110. Jackson Ranch Church
111. San Juan Plantation
112. Donna Townsite
113. Donna American Legion
114. Donna Public Schools
115. Weslaco City Hall
116. Weslaco Water Tower
117. Citrus Fruit Marker
118. Camp Llano Grande
119. Marker for Father Keralum
120. Town of Weslaco
121. National Guard Marker, Weslaco
122. Immanuel Lutheran Cemetery
123. American Co. Land & Irrigation

124. National Guard Marker
125. Hidalgo County Bank & Trust
126. Spiderwebb Railroad Station Site
127. Rancho Toluca
128. Relampago Ranch
129. Thornton Skirmish
130. Our Lady of Visitation Church
131. Rancho Santa María
132. Dunlap House
133. First Bank in La Feria
134. Town of La Feria
135. Rosalio Longoria House
136. Las Rucias
137. Routes of Alonso de Leon
138. City of Harlingen
139. Harlingen Hospital
140. Lon C. Hill House
141. Sam Houston School
142. Planters State Bank
143. Santos Lozano Building
144. A.C. Purvis House
145. Col. Sam Roberton House
146. St. Benedict's Church
147. City of San Benito
148. San Benito Bank & Trust Co.
149. Landrum House
150. Rancho Viejo
151. Marker for Cameron County
152. Santa Rita Settlement
153. Palo Alto Battlefield
154. Resaca de la Palma Battlefield
155. Marker for Jefferson Davis
156. Manatou House
157. Tijerina House
158. Browne-Wagner House
159. Celaya-Creager House
160. Southern Pacific Railroad Depot
161. Our Lade of Lourdes Grotto
162. Cavazos House
163. Kowalski-Dennett House
164. Augustine-Celaya House
165. Samuel Brooks House
166. Incarnate Word Convent, Former Site
167. La Madrileña Store
168. Cameron County Courthouse, 1912
169. Cameron County Courthouse, 1883
170. La Nueva Libertad Store
171. Immaculate Conception Church
172. San Roman Building
173. Charles Stillman House
174. Brownsville, C.S.A.
175. Yturria Bank
176. Bagdad-Matamoros, C.S.A.
177. Brownsville Public Market
178. Fort Brown
179. Commissary, Fort Brown
180. First U.S. Army Warplane Site
181. Medical Lab, Fort Brown
182. Morgue Building, Fort Brown
183. Post Hospital, Fort Brown
184. Neale House
185. Blind Flying School
186. Brulay Plantation
187. Port of Brownsville
188. Palmito Hill Battlefield
189. Palmito Pilings
190. Point Isabel Lighthouse
191. Point Isabel, C.S.A.
192. Point Isabel Coast Guard Building
193. Port Isabel Site
194. Brazos Santiago
195. Brazos Santiago Depot
196. Historic Shipwrecks

Map & Drawings by Mario L. Sánchez
Historical Research by Martha Doty Freeman (U.S.A.)
and Javier Sánchez Garcia (Mexico)

Produced by the Lower Rio Grande Heritage Project and
the Texas Historical Commission, funded by the Meadows Foundation
Copyright, 1990

standing. The enterprise, a model binational collaboration, has no equivalent anywhere along the borderland. That Mexico and Texas cooperate at this level is further proof of how Tejano South Texas is a distinctive cultural province, unlike borderland subregions in California, Arizona, and New Mexico.

Los Caminos del Rio is dedicated to the preservation and enhancement of cultural and natural resources of the Lower Rio Grande/Río Bravo region of Texas and Mexico.[32] Launched in 1990, the project defines the region as a heritage corridor that transcends political boundaries.

Conceived as a partnership of public agencies and private philanthropy, the enterprise was given an early incentive by Texas Governor Ann W. Richards, who by executive order in 1991 created the Texas Task Force for Los Caminos del Rio Heritage Project. The Task Force was steered by representatives from four Texas departments, including Historical Commission, Parks and Wildlife, Commerce, and Transportation. The Task Force expanded to include support from the Rivers, Trails, and Conservation Assistance Program of the National Park Service, the U.S. Fish and Wildlife Service, Institute of Texan Cultures, and The Conservation Fund. Mexico's participation includes the Comisión Intersecretarial Federal, a governing body that represents agencies of Tourism, Anthropology and History, Finance, Urban Development and Environment, Communication and Transportation, Interior Affairs, and Foreign Relations. The State of Tamaulipas is represented through the Subsecretaría de Desarrollo Turístico. Private sector support was organized by the Meadows Foundation of Dallas as the binational, nonprofit body Los Caminos del Rio of Texas, Inc. and Mexico, A.C., whose mission is to stimulate broad public awareness of the project and assist in the enhancement and promotion of its resources.[33]

The river and the historic communities of the region create a corridor of shared heritage that is the focus of the project. Initial surveys and inventories conducted by the Texas Historical Commission declared some 231 sites in the corridor, a zone that stretches from Colombia, Nuevo León—upriver from Laredo and Nuevo Laredo—to the mouth of the Rio Grande/Río Bravo below Matamoros and Brownsville (FIG. 9.2). Almost 90 percent of these sites are in Texas and generally follow the routes of U.S. Highways 83 and 281. The sites are defined according to heritage themes that link Texas and Tamaulipas such as colonial river settlements, ranching, river trade, agriculture, and military history.[34] Especially significant to the cultural geography of Tejano South Texas are the historic districts in Laredo, San Ygnacio, and Roma, all in the National Register of Historic Places and included within the corridor.[35] These sites contain important numbers of historic structures and spaces that are part of the cultural legacy of Hispanic occupancy in the region.

Los Caminos del Rio Heritage Project is more than historic architectural preservation; it is concerned with the region's cultural patrimony as embraced by its people. Integral to the project are community development and heritage tourism, folklife expressions and resources, and heritage education. As observed by Mexico's tourism secretary, Margarita Robleda, in 1994, Los Caminos del Rio is a long-term endeavor that will succeed once it ceases to be called "The Project" and becomes "Their Project."[36]

EPILOGUE

Regional differences and fluctuating regionalisms are said to be persistent features of U.S. life.[37] Tejano South Texas has been and continues to be part of that ever-changing cultural mosaic. It is a distinctive part of Texas and a unique subregion of the broad Hispanic American borderland. This is not to suggest that Tejano South Texas is somehow at risk in the riptide of changing geography in the United States of the twenty-first century, because ultimately all places and landscapes change. Neither do I pretend to believe that South Texas is not influenced by other than Hispanic culture.

In these few pages I have argued for the recognition of Tejano South Texas as a cultural province, one unlike the Mexican American subregions of neighboring borderland states like California, Arizona, and New Mexico. In the end, that regional distinctiveness must be appreciated, preserved, and celebrated by Tejanos, for it is their past and their future, their *tierra tejana*. A wise voice once advised that a place can establish bonds between people, and the characteristics of those bonds give a landscape its uniqueness, its style.[38] These qualities make us recall it with emotion, and it is when we begin to participate emotionally in a place that its uniqueness and beauty are revealed to us.

Notes

CHAPTER 1

1. *Bryan–College Station Eagle*, "Lawyer Wants Mexican Flag Out of City Hall," A3. This chapter also draws from Daniel D. Arreola, "The Texas-Mexican Homeland," 61–62.

2. *San Antonio Light*, "Weather," E8; *Wall Street Journal*, "Border Midwives Bring Baby Boom to South Texas," A1, A12; *Austin American-Statesman*, "Boom on Border: Flood of Students Washes across Rio Grande Valley," A1, A5.

3. Richard L. Nostrand, "The Hispanic-American Borderland: Delimitation of an American Culture Region," 638–661; Daniel D. Arreola, "Mexican Americans," Table 4.1; John R. Chávez, *The Lost Land: The Chicano Image of the Southwest*, 1–5; Z. Anthony Kruszewski, "Territorial Minorities: Some Sociopolitical and International Aspects and Their Possible Implications," 268.

4. John G. Bourke, "The American Congo," 590, 592.

5. Joel Garreau, *The Nine Nations of North America*, 207–244; Jerry Adler and Tim Padgett, "Mexamerica: Selena Country," 76–79.

6. Arreola, "Texas-Mexican Homeland," 61–74; Daniel D. Arreola, "Mexican Texas: A Distinctive Borderland," 3–9; Daniel D. Arreola, "*La Tierra Tejana*: A South Texas Homeland."

7. Major texts include Philip L. Wagner and Marvin W. Mikesell, eds., *Readings in Cultural Geography*; Peter Jackson, *Maps of Meaning: An Introduction to Cultural Geography*; Kenneth E. Foote, Peter J. Hugill, Kent Mathewson, and Jonathan M. Smith, eds., *Re-reading Cultural Geography*; Mike Crang, *Cultural Geography*; and William Norton, *Cultural Geography: Themes, Concepts, Analyses*.

8. Don Mitchell, *Cultural Geography: A Critical Introduction*, 3–65.

9. Clifford Geertz, "Thick Description: Toward an Interpretive Theory of Culture," 5.

10. Crang, *Cultural Geography*, 7.

11. Carl O. Sauer, "The Personality of Mexico," 353.

12. Philip L. Wagner, "Cultural Landscapes and Regions: Aspects of Communication"; D. W. Meinig, "The Shaping of America, 1850–1915."

13. Wilbur Zelinsky, "The Changing Character of North American Culture Areas"; Garreau, *Nine Nations of North America*.

14. See, for example, George J. Sánchez, *Becoming Mexican American: Ethnicity, Culture, and Identity in Chicano Los Angeles, 1900–1945*; Thomas E. Sheridan, *Los Tucsonenses: The Mexican Community in Tucson, 1854–1941*; Mario T. García, *Desert Immigrants: The Mexicans of El Paso, 1880–1920*; Arnoldo De León, *The Tejano Community, 1836–1900*; David Montejano, *Anglos and Mexicans in the Making of Texas, 1836–1986*; and Richard Griswold del Castillo, "Tejanos and California Chicanos: Regional Variations in Mexican American History."

15. D. W. Meinig, "Environmental Appreciation: Localities as a Humane Art"; David Sopher, "Place and Location: Notes on the Spatial Patterning of Culture"; J. Nicholas Entrikin, *The Betweeness of Place: Towards a Geography of Modernity*; James Duncan and David Ley, eds., *Place/Culture/Representation*.

16. D. W. Meinig, ed., *The Interpretation of Ordinary Landscapes: Geographical Essays*; William Norton, *Explorations in the Understanding of Landscape: A Cultural Geography*; Paul Groth and Todd W. Bressi, eds., *Understanding Ordinary Landscapes*.

17. Denis Cosgrove, "Prospect, Perspective, and the Evolution of the Landscape Idea"; Lester B. Rowntree, "The Cultural Landscape Concept in American Human Geography."

18. D. W. Meinig, "The Beholding Eye: Ten Versions of the Same Scene," 33–48; Peirce F. Lewis, "Axioms for Reading the Landscape: Some Guides to the American Scene," 11–32.

19. James S. Duncan, Jr., "Landscape Taste as a Symbol of Group Identity: A Westchester County Village"; James S. Duncan, Jr., "Landscape and the Communication of Social Identity."

20. James S. Duncan, *The City as Text: The Politics of Landscape Interpretation in the Kandyan Kingdom*, 17.

21. Eric Issac, "The Act and the Covenant," 12–17; Henry H. Glassie, *Passing Time in Ballymenone: Culture and History of an Ulster Community*.

22. John A. Agnew, John Mercer, and David E. Sopher, eds. *The City in Cultural Context*. Also, the contributions of Deryck Holdsworth, Don Mitchell, David Ley, and Caroline Mills in Duncan and Ley, eds. *Place/Culture/Representation*, 95–170.

23. Duncan and Ley, eds., *Place/Culture/Representation*, 332.

24. Wilbur Zelinsky, *The Cultural Geography of the United States*, 30–31, 118–119, 120–140.

25. Nostrand, "The Hispanic-American Borderland," 638–661. See also Richard L. Nostrand, "Mexican Americans Circa 1850," 378–390, and Richard L. Nostrand, "A Changing Culture Region," 6–15.

26. Richard L. Nostrand, "The Hispano Homeland in 1900," 382–396; Richard L. Nostrand, *The Hispano Homeland*.

27. See, for example, Alvar W. Carlson, *The Spanish-American Homeland: Four Centuries in New Mexico's Río Arriba*; Jeffrey S. Smith, "Spanish-American Village Anatomy"; and Terrence W. Haverluk, "Hispanic Community Types and Assimilation in Mex-America."

28. Terry G. Jordan, "The Concept and the Method," 11.

29. Trevor Barnes and Derek Gregory, "Place and Landscape," 292–298.

CHAPTER 2

1. John H. Jenkins, *Basic Texas Books*.

2. Matt S. Meier and Feliciano Rivera, *Dictionary of Mexican American History*.

3. Ron Tyler, ed., *The New Handbook of Texas*, vol. 5, 1163–1164.

4. Mike Kingston, ed. *1990–91 Texas Almanac*, 602.

5. Federal Writers' Project, Texas, *The WPA Guide to Texas*.

6. Ray Miller, *The Eyes of Texas Travel Guide, San Antonio/Border Edition*.

7. Robert R. Rafferty, *Texas*, xii.

8. Terry G. Jordan, "Perceptual Regions in Texas," 305; De Léon, *The Tejano Community, 1836–1900*, 78–79.

9. This chapter is adapted from Daniel D. Arreola, "Beyond the Nueces: The Early Geographical Identity of South Texas," 46–60.

10. For early use of the word "geosophy," see John Kirtland Wright, "*Terrae Incognitae*: The Place of Imagination in Geography," 14–15.

11. For an introduction to the native worlds as they relate to South Texas, see Thomas R. Hester, *Digging into South Texas Prehistory*; William W. Newcomb, Jr., *The Indians of Texas: From Prehistoric to Modern Times*; and Martín Salinas, *Indians of the Rio Grande Delta: Their Role in the History of Southern Texas and*

Northeastern Mexico. Early Spanish contacts with South Texas are summarized in Robert S. Weddle, *Spanish Sea: The Gulf of Mexico in North American Discovery, 1500–1685,* 185–207, 333–349.

12. Weddle, *Spanish Sea,* 95–108.

13. Robert S. Weddle, *San Juan Bautista: Gateway to Spanish Texas,* 3–18.

14. Ibid., 3–18.

15. The single best summary of travelers' accounts of South Texas is Jack M. Inglis, *A History of Vegetation on the Rio Grande Plain.*

16. Frederick Law Olmsted, *A Journey through Texas,* 441–442.

17. Jean Louis Berlandier, *Journey to Mexico during the Years 1826 to 1834,* vol. 2, 569.

18. Benjamin Lundy, *Life, Travels, and Opinions of Benjamin Lundy, Including His Journeys to Texas and Mexico,* 97.

19. While South Texas is generally classified as subtropical and receives between 15 and 30 inches of annual rainfall, climatologists have further distinguished subhumid and semiarid parts of the region. See Richard Joel Russell, "Climates of Texas," 37–52, and Jim Norwine and Ralph Bingham, "Frequency and Severity of Droughts in South Texas: 1900–1983," 1–17.

20. Del Weniger, *The Explorers' Texas: The Lands and Waters,* 60–61.

21. V. Havard, "Report on the Flora of Western and Southern Texas," 450.

22. Berlandier, *Journey to Mexico during the Years 1826 to 1834,* vol. 2, 541–543.

23. L. F. Brown Jr. et al., *Environmental Geologic Atlas of the Texas Coastal Zone—Brownsville-Harlingen Area,* 20, 23–24.

24. Frederick R. Gehlbach, *Mountain Islands and Desert Seas: A Natural History of the U.S.-Mexican Borderlands,* 21–42.

25. William H. Emory, *Report on the United States and Mexican Boundary Survey,* vol. 1, 59.

26. Ibid., 65–68; Pat Kelley, *River of Lost Dreams: Navigation on the Rio Grande.*

27. Terry G. Jordan, with John L. Bean, Jr., and William M. Holmes, *Texas: A Geography,* 40.

28. Olmsted, *Journey through Texas,* 245, 247, 259.

29. Berlandier, *Journey to Mexico during the Years 1826 to 1834,* vol. 2, 555, 373.

30. Marshall C. Johnston, "Past and Present Grasslands of Southern Texas and Northeastern Mexico," 456–466.

31. Berlandier, *Journey to Mexico during the Years 1826 to 1834,* vol. 2, 549.

32. Ibid., vol. 1, 286.

33. *A Twentieth Century History of Southwest Texas, Illustrated,* vol. 1, i–ii.

34. Frederic William Simonds, *The Geography of Texas, Physical and Political,* 19–20. Simonds was a professor of geology at the University of Texas. The physical geography sections of this book are drawn especially from Robert T. Hill's contribution on Texas' physical geography in *Topographic Atlas of the United States,* published by the United States Geological Survey in 1900.

35. Elmer H. Johnson, *The Natural Regions of Texas*, 133–141. Johnson was an industrial geographer, and this volume was the first in a series of publications by the Bureau of Business Research at the University of Texas. The stated purpose of the work was "to delineate Texas regions as units which are necessary not only in making an analysis of the commercial aspects of the natural resources of the State, but also in establishing bases for the analysis of the economic development of the various sections of Texas ...The method employed ... [is] *geographic correlation*, that is, the interpretation of the areal extent and characteristics of regions in terms of relationships between the elements of the regional environment." E. H. Johnson, *Natural Regions*, 5.

36. William T. Chambers, "Geographic Regions of Texas," 9–11.

37. W. Frank Blair, "The Biotic Provinces of Texas," 98, 102–105.

38. Carey McWilliams, *North from Mexico: The Spanish-Speaking People of the United States*, 84–88; Robert H. Talbert, *Spanish-Name People in the Southwest and West*, 26.

39. D. W. Meinig, *Imperial Texas: An Interpretive Essay in Cultural Geography*, 93, 98–101.

40. Terry G. Jordan-Bychkov and Mona Domash, *The Human Mosaic: A Thematic Introduction to Cultural Geography*, 8–10.

41. Jordan, with Bean and Holmes, *Texas: A Geography*, 91.

42. Lauro Cruz, *Developing South Texas: A Report to the Governor and Legislature—Executive Summary*, 1–3, 6.

43. Hester, *Digging into South Texas Prehistory*, 4–5.

44. Armando C. Alonzo, *Tejano Legacy: Rancheros and Settlers in South Texas, 1734–1900*, 5–13.

CHAPTER 3

1. Peter Gerhard, *The North Frontier of New Spain*, 325–368, discusses Coahuila, Texas, Nuevo León, and Nuevo Santander.

2. See, for example, Eugenio del Hoyo, *Historia del nuevo reino de León (1577–1723)*, vol. 1; David J. Weber, *The Spanish Frontier in North America*, 147–171; Robert S. Weddle, *The French Thorn*, 258–285; and David M. Pletcher, *The Diplomacy of Annexation*, 113–392.

3. Elizabeth A. H. John, *Storms Brewed in Other Men's Worlds*, discusses the conflicts between Indians and Spanish on the Rio Grande frontier.

4. Gerhard, *North Frontier of New Spain*, Table B, 24 gives the following estimates: Coahuila 50,000 in 1519, 22,500 in 1821; Nuevo León 100,000 in 1519, 74,000 in 1821; Texas 20,000 in 1519, 8,800 in 1821; and Nuevo Santander 190,000 in 1519, 62,000 in 1821.

5. Donald E. Chipman, *Nuño de Guzmán and the Province of Pánuco in New Spain, 1518–1533*, 26.

6. Robert C. West and John P. Augelli, *Middle America: Its Lands and Peoples*, 209–211.

7. See Map 5b in Gerhard, *North Frontier of New Spain*, 13.

8. Enriqueta García de Miranda, *Nuevo atlas Porrúa de la República Mexicana*, 65; Robert C. West, "Surface Configuration and Associated Geology of Middle America," 37.

9. T. N. Campbell, *The Indians of Southern Texas and Northeastern Mexico*, 39–59; Gerhard, *North Frontier of New Spain*, 345–346.

10. Gerhard, *North Frontier of New Spain*, 325–326.

11. García de Miranda, *Nuevo atlas Porrúa*, 35; West, "Surface Configuration," 37.

12. Campbell, *Indians of Southern Texas and Northeastern Mexico*, 39–59; Gerhard, *North Frontier of New Spain*, 325–328, 331–333.

13. Vito Alessio Robles, *Coahuila y Texas en la Epoca Colonial*, 1–6; Gerhard, *North Frontier of New Spain*, 358.

14. Daniel D. Arreola, "Texas," 1069–1070.

15. Herbert Eugene Bolton, *Texas in the Middle Eighteenth Century: Studies in Spanish Colonial History and Administration*, 1–13.

16. Newcomb, *Indians of Texas*, 29–57.

17. Gerhard, *North Frontier of New Spain*, 358–360.

18. Campbell, *Indians of Southern Texas and Northeastern Mexico*, 39–59; Salinas, *Indians of the Rio Grande Delta*, 164.

19. I. J. Cox, "The Southwest Boundary of Texas," 85–86.

20. Guevara's map, the original of which is in the Archivo General de Indias in Seville, is reproduced as Fig. 15 in Weddle, *French Thorn*, 262–263.

21. Escandón's *Mapa* is reproduced from the original in the Archivo General de Indias as Fig. 16 in Weddle, *French Thorn*, 266–267.

22. For the principal map of the Tienda de Cuervo inspection (titled *Mapa General Ychnographico de la nueba Colonia Santander*), see Dennis Reinhartz, "Two Manuscript Maps of *Nuevo Santander* in Northern New Spain from the Eighteenth Century," 57. The Haro map is reproduced in Robert S. Weddle, *Changing Tides: Twilight and Dawn in the Spanish Sea, 1763–1803*, 40. Finally, *Mapa de la Sierra Gorda y costa de el Seno Mexicano* and attributed to Escandón is reproduced in color as a foldout in *Estado general de las fundaciones hechas por D. José de Escandón en la colonia del Nuevo Santander, costa del Seno Mexicano*, vol. 1, opposite 536.

23. The map is titled *Mapa de la frontera del vireinato [sic] de la Nueva España* and is reproduced as a foldout at the back of Nicolás de La Fora, *Relación del viaje que hizo a los presidios internos situados en la frontera de la América Septentrional perteneciente al rey de España*. Alessio Robles, *Coahuila y Texas en la Epoca Colonial*, gives details on the publication history of the map in notes on 12–13; the signed original is said to be in the Ministry of War in Madrid. Curiously, in text 236, La Fora gives the Río Grande del Norte as the boundary of Colonia del Nuevo Santander.

24. Lawrence Kinnaird, *The Frontiers of New Spain: Nicolas de Lafora's Description, 1766–1768*, 186.

25. Alejandro de Humboldt, *Ensayo político sobre el reino de la Nueva España*, vol. 5, map 2 and pp. 16–17.

26. The map is titled *Mapa de las provincias internas de Oriente* and appears in Alessio Robles, *Coahuila y Texas en la Epoca Colonial*, facing p. 268.

27. A copy of the J. H. Young map is housed in the Center for American History, the University of Texas at Austin. Earlier published copies of this map exist. See Meinig, *Imperial Texas*, map 4 facing p. 40, which reproduces a detail of an 1835 edition.

28. See William Campbell Binkley, *The Expansionist Movement in Texas, 1836–1850*, map 1 facing p. 8.

29. The original Antonio García Cubas map is colored and appears in *Atlas geográfico* as "Carta [map] VI, Tamaulipas."

30. Bolton, *Texas in the Middle Eighteenth Century*. The map is a foldout following p. 501 and is titled "Map of Texas and Adjacent Regions in the Eighteenth Century." In the legend Bolton states, "Boundary lines as on La Fora map, 1771." In Herbert E. Bolton, *Guide to Materials for the History of the United States in the Principal Archives of Mexico*, 365, the author gives a full description of the map. The original, according to Bolton, is in the Secretaría de Fomento, Mexico, Sección de Cartografía, map no. 1138, and measures 64 × 128 inches. Bolton notes that there is a second copy of the map in the Archivo de Indias, see *Texas in the Middle Eighteenth Century*, 378.

31. Wolfgang Trautman, "Geographical Aspects of Hispanic Colonization on the Northern Frontier of New Spain," 243.

32. See Herbert E. Bolton, "The Spanish Occupation of Texas, 1519–1690"; Odie B. Faulk, *The Last Years of Spanish Texas, 1778–1821*; and Kathleen Gilmore, "Spanish Colonial Settlements in Texas."

33. Weddle, *San Juan Bautista*, 21–28.

34. Gerald E. Poyo and Gilberto M. Hinojosa, eds., *Tejano Origins in Eighteenth-Century San Antonio*; Kathryn Stoner O'Conner, *The Presidio La Bahía del Espíritu Santo de Zuñiga, 1721 to 1846*.

35. Alicia Vidaurreta, "Evolución urbana de Texas durante el Siglo XVIII," 605–636.

36. Inglis, *Vegetation on the Rio Grande Plain*, Figs. 3, 4; J. W. Williams, *Old Texas Trails*, map titled "San Antonio Roads," facing p. 128.

37. Lawrence Francis Hill, *José de Escandón and the Founding of Nuevo Santander: A Study in Spanish Colonization*; Florence Johnson Scott, "The Colonial Period: Spanish Colonization of the Lower Rio Grande."

38. *Estado general de las fundaciones hechas por D. José de Escandón*, vol. 1, 13–38; Carlos E. Castañeda, *Our Catholic Heritage in Texas, 1519–1936*, vol. 3, 130–188; Florence Johnson Scott, *Historical Heritage of the Lower Rio Grande*, 25–46.

39. See maps of *porciones* in Jack Jackson, *Los Mesteños: Spanish Ranching in Texas, 1721–1821*, 445, and Scott, *Historical Heritage of the Lower Rio Grande*, facing p. 78.

40. Scott, *Historical Heritage of the Lower Rio Grande*, 47–71.

41. Florence Johnson Scott, *Royal Land Grants North of the Río Grande, 1777–1821*, 22.

42. For details on the conditions of ranching in Spanish colonial Nuevo Santander and Texas, see Terry G. Jordan, *North American Cattle-Ranching Frontiers: Origins, Diffusion, and Differentiation*, especially 134; Sandra L. Myres, *The Ranch in Spanish Texas, 1691–1800*; and Jack Jackson, *Los Mesteños*.

43. David J. Weber, *The Mexican Frontier 1821–1846: The American Southwest under Mexico*, 163.

44. A. B. J. Hammett, *The Empresario Don Martin De León*, 2, 16, 28; Juan N. Almonte, "Statistical Report on Texas [1835]," 186.

45. William H. Oberste, *Texas Irish Empresarios and Their Colonies*, 15–16, 60–61.

46. Almonte, "Statistical Report on Texas [1835]," 186.

47. Hobart Huson, *Refugio: A Comprehensive History of Refugio County*, vol. 1, 178.

48. Leroy P. Graf, "Colonizing Projects in Texas South of the Nueces, 1820–1845."

49. Almonte, "Statistical Report on Texas [1835]," does not reference this settlement in his 1834 report.

50. Jean Y. Fish, *Zapata County Roots Revisited*, 108.

51. José Raúl Canseco Botello, *Historia de Matamoros*; W. H. Chatfield, *The Twin Cities of the Border and the Country of the Rio Grande*; Frank G. Pierce, *A Brief History of the Lower Rio Grande Valley*, 137–138.

52. David M. Vigness, "Indian Raids on the Lower Rio Grande, 1836–1837."

53. Almonte, "Statistical Report on Texas [1835]," 191.

54. H. S. Thrall, *A Pictorial History of Texas*, cited in V. W. Lehmann, *Forgotten Legions: Sheep on the Rio Grande Plain of Texas*, 22.

55. México, Comisión Pesquisidora de la Frontera del Norte, *Reports of the Committee of Investigation, Sent in 1873 by the Mexican Government to the Frontier of Texas*, foldout map facing p. 400. See also De León, *The Tejano Community, 1836–1900*, 223 which lists from the 1880 U.S. Census Schedules 49 ranchos for Hidalgo County and 44 ranchos for Zapata County. Rancho geography is discussed and mapped in Chapter 5.

56. See Terry G. Jordan, "A Century and a Half of Ethnic Change in Texas, 1836–1986," Fig. 4, "Largest Cultural or Ethnic Group, by County, 1887," 396.

57. Robert C. Spillman, *A Historical Geography of Mexican American Population Patterns in the South Texas Hispanic Borderland*, 36, 38.

58. Richard Griswold del Castillo, *La Familia: Chicano Families in the Urban Southwest, 1848 to Present*, 19.

59. Milo Kearney and Anthony Knopp, *Border Cuates: A History of the U.S.-Mexican Twin Cities*, 74–80; J. Lee Stambaugh and Lillian J. Stambaugh, *The Lower Rio Grande Valley of Texas: Its Colonization and Industrialization, 1518–1953*, 96.

60. Bourke, "The American Congo," 592.

61. Arnoldo De León, *Benavides: The Town and Its Founder, 1880*, 3–7; Arnoldo De León, "A Social History of Mexican Americans in Nineteenth-Century Duval County," 1. See also the discussion of San Diego in Chapter 6.

CHAPTER 4

1. Arreola, "Texas-Mexican Homeland," 64; Arreola, "Mexican Texas: A Distinctive Borderland," 3–4.

2. Leo Grebler, Joan W. Moore, Ralph C. Guzman, *The Mexican-American People: The Nation's Second Largest Minority*, 63; Elizabeth Broadbent, *The Distribution of Mexican Population in the United States*, 15. Broadbent cites Mexican immigrant totals from the annual reports of the Commissioner General of Immigration, which show that Texas received over 80 percent of all Mexican immigrants to the United States in 1909 and 1910, see Table 5.

3. Samuel N. Dicken, "Cotton Regions of Mexico," 363–371; Peter J. Hugill, "The Macro-Landscape of the Wallerstein World-Economy: 'King Cotton' and the American South," 77–84.

4. Emilio Zamora, *The World of the Mexican Worker in Texas*, 16.

5. I borrow the terms "stronghold" and "domain" as used by Richard L. Nostrand in his assessment of Hispano population geography in New Mexico and D. W. Meinig in his analysis of the Mormon culture region, respectively. See Nostrand, *The Hispano Homeland*, 46–47, 127–129, and D. W. Meinig, "The Mormon Culture Region: Strategies and Patterns in the Geography of the American West, 1847–1964," 214–215.

6. See Fig. 15 in Robert C. Spillman, *A Historical Geography of Mexican American Population Patterns in the South Texas Hispanic Borderland*, 51.

7. R. B. Cunninghame [Graham], *The North American Sketches of R. B. Cunninghame Graham*, 37.

8. Douglas E. Foley et al., *From Peones to Políticos: Ethnic Relations in a South Texas Town, 1900–1977*, 6–13.

9. De León, *The Tejano Community, 1836–1900*, 84–85. Paul H. Carlson, *Texas Woollybacks: The Range Sheep and Goat Industry*, 102; on p. 115 is a map that shows Val Verde County as one of the principal sheep ranching counties in 1900.

10. Paul S. Taylor, *An American-Mexican Frontier: Nueces County, Texas*, 92–93.

11. See Table 4.1 in Grebler, Moore, and Guzman, *The Mexican-American People*,

64; see Table 1 in Thomas D. Boswell, "The Growth and Proportional Redistribution of the Mexican Stock Population in the United States, 1900–1970," 60; Robert R. McKay, "Mexican Americans and Repatriation," 676–679.

12. Max Sylvius Handman, "The Mexican Immigrant in Texas," 34.

13. Michael M. Smith, "Beyond the Borderlands: Mexican Labor in the Central Plains, 1900–1930"; Neil Foley, "Mexican Migrant and Tenant Labor in Central Texas Cotton Counties, 1880–1930."

14. See Table 6.4 in Grebler, Moore, and Guzman, *The Mexican-American People*, 111; Talbert, *Spanish-Name People in the Southwest and West*, 34.

15. See Table 8 in Manuel Gamio, *Mexican Immigration to the United States: A Study of Human Migration and Adjustment*, 13.

16. Data based on Mexican born birth parents. Arreola, "Mexico Origins of South Texas Mexican Americans, 1930," 55.

17. Mark Reisler, *By the Sweat of Their Brow: Mexican Immigrant Labor in the United States, 1900–1940*, 77–78.

18. Edwin J. Foscue, "Land Utilization in the Lower Rio Grande Valley of Texas," 1–11.

19. Stambaugh and Stambaugh, *Lower Rio Grande Valley*, 195.

20. Stanley A. Arbingast et al., *Atlas of Texas*, 127; McWilliams, *North from Mexico*, 169–173; Neil Foley, *White Scourge: Mexicans, Blacks and Poor Whites in Texas Cotton Culture*, 40–63.

21. See Fig. 1 in Arreola, "Mexico Origins of South Texas Mexican Americans, 1930," 51.

22. See Table 2 in Taylor, *An American-Mexican Frontier*, 84, 92.

23. See inside cover map of the King Ranch in its centennial year, 1953, in Tom Lea, *The King Ranch*, vol. 2.

24. See Table 17 in U.S. Bureau of the Census, *Fifteenth Census of the United States, 1930*, 1014–1015.

25. James L. Allhands, *Gringo Builders*, 89–97; Pierce, *Lower Rio Grande Valley*, 128–135.

26. Paul S. Taylor, *Mexican Labor in the United States: Dimmit County, Winter Garden District South Texas*, 295, 303–304.

27. Arbingast et al., *Atlas of Texas*, 127.

28. Talbert, *Spanish-Name People in the Southwest and West*, 34–35.

29. Daniel D. Arreola and James R. Curtis, *The Mexican Border Cities*, 26–27.

30. Sheldon C. Menefee, *Mexican Migratory Workers of South Texas*; Pauline R. Kibbe, *Latin Americans in Texas*, 168–169; U.S. Bureau of the Census, *Special Report, Population Mobility, States and Economic Areas*, Table 19.

31. Carey McWilliams, *Ill Fares the Land: Migrants and Migratory Labor in the United States*, 231.

32. See Table 10 in Lyle Saunders and Olen E. Leonard, *The Wetback in the Lower Rio Grande Valley of Texas*, 31.

33. Ibid., see Tables 17 and 18 on pp. 37, 38.

34. Ibid., 44.

35. Kibbe, *Latin Americans in Texas*, 174.

36. Menefee, *Mexican Migratory Workers of South Texas*, 12–13.

37. Ibid., 21.

38. Kibbe, *Latin Americans in Texas*, 201–206.

39. Terry G. Jordan, "The Anglo-Texan Homeland," 84.

40. Sidney Weintraub and Gilberto Cardenas, *The Use of Public Services by Undocumented Aliens in Texas*, xxviii.

41. Richard C. Jones, "Changing Patterns of Undocumented Mexican Migration to South Texas," 468–469.

42. Terrence William Haverluk, "A Descriptive Model for Understanding the Wider Distribution and Increasing Influence of Hispanics in the American West," 55.

43. Joe S. Graham, "Folk Medicine and Intercultural Diversity among West Texas Mexican Americans," 168–193.

CHAPTER 5

1. Jan O. M. Broek and John W. Webb, *A Geography of Mankind*, 306.

2. Christopher L. Salter, *The Cultural Landscape*, iv.

3. Cited in Willard B. Robinson, "Colonial Ranch Architecture in the Spanish-Mexican Tradition," 125.

4. Joe S. Graham, *El Rancho in South Texas: Continuity and Change from 1750*, 22, 30; see also Alonzo, *Tejano Legacy: Rancheros and Settlers in South Texas, 1734–1900*, and Andrés Tijerina, *Tejano Empire: Life on South Texas Ranchos*.

5. Joe B. Frantz and Mike Cox, *Lure of the Land: Texas County Maps and the History of Settlement*, 20–47.

6. Graham, *El Rancho in South Texas*, 23.

7. Robinson, "Colonial Ranch Architecture," 126–127.

8. Scott, *Historical Heritage of the Lower Rio Grande*, 88, 99.

9. Armando Alonzo, "Change and Continuity in Tejano Ranches in the Trans-Nueces, 1848–1900," 53–68.

10. *Monitor* (McAllen), "Old San Isidro," A1, A16.

11. *Monitor* (McAllen), "El Sauz Folks Relish Small-Town Life," A17, A18.

12. Francois Chevalier, *Land and Society in Colonial Mexico: The Great Hacienda*.

13. Charles H. Harris III, *A Mexican Family Empire: The Latifundio of the Sánchez Navarro Family, 1765–1867*.

14. Jean Y. Fish, *José Vásquez Borrego and La Hacienda de Nuestra Señora de Dolores*.

15. Jovita González, *Social Life in Cameron, Starr, and Zapata Counties*.

16. Lea, *The King Ranch*.

17. Robinson, "Colonial Ranch Architecture," 130; Joe S. Graham, "The *Jacal* in South Texas: The Origins and Forms of a Folk House," 294; Joe S. Graham, "The Built Environment in South Texas: The Hispanic Legacy," 61–68.

18. Mary Anna Casstevens, "Randado: The Built Environment of a Texas-Mexican Ranch," 318.

19. Robinson, "Colonial Ranch Architecture," 142–143.

20. Casstevens, "Randado," 318; Graham, "Built Environment in South Texas," 70, 74.

21. Elena Zamora O'Shea, *El Mesquite*, 12.

22. Graham, *El Rancho in South Texas*, 52, 97.

23. Ibid., 67, 70.

24. This section draws heavily from Daniel D. Arreola, "Plaza Towns of South Texas," 56–73.

25. John W. Reps, *Cities of the American West: A History of Frontier Urban Planning*, 117–122.

26. Dora P. Crouch, Daniel J. Garr, and Axel I. Mundigo, *Spanish City Planning in North America*, 13–14.

27. Gilbert R. Cruz, *Let There Be Towns: Spanish Municipal Origins in the American Southwest, 1610–1810*, 97.

28. Reps, *Cities of the American West*, 117.

29. Mario L. Sánchez, ed., *A Shared Experience: the History, Architecture, and Historic Designations of the Lower Rio Grande Heritage Corridor*, 84.

30. Kathleen Da Cámara, *Laredo on the Rio Grande*, 24.

31. Jorge González, personal communication; Luciano Guajardo, personal communication.

32. Jorge E. Hardoy, "La forma de las ciudades coloniales en la América Española," 315–344.

33. Sanborn Map Company, *Del Rio, Val Verde County, Texas* (1924).

34. A. P. Johnson, *Map of Carrizo Springs, Dimmit County, 1914*.

35. Florence J. Scott, "Early History of Starr County," 34.

36. Sanborn-Perris Map Company, *Roma, Starr County, Texas* (1894); David Hoffman, *Roma*, 10, 17.

37. Sanborn-Perris Map Company, *Rio Grande City, Starr County, Texas* (1894); *Rio Grande City* (map, 1910); see photograph "Britton Avenue, Rio Grande City" in the Hidalgo County Historical Museum Archive; Scott, "Early History of Starr County," 32.

38. Daniel D. Arreola, "Nineteenth-Century Townscapes of Eastern Mexico," 1–19.

39. J. A. Dabbs, *The French Army in Mexico, 1861–1867: A Study in Military Government*, 252–255.

40. Douglas Lee Robertson, *A Behavioral Portrait of the Mexican Plaza*.

41. "Quiosco," *Enciclopedia universal ilustrada europeo-americana*, 1416.

42. Patsy J. Byfield, *Falcon Dam and the Lost Towns of Zapata.*

43. Jerry Thompson, *Laredo: A Pictorial History*, 17, 258.

44. Sanborn-Perris Map Company, *Laredo, Webb County, Texas* (1905).

45. P. D. Spreiregen, *Urban Design: The Architecture of Towns and Cities*, 19.

46. Robertson, *Mexican Plaza.*

47. Charles Malcolm Flandrau, *¡Viva México!*, 277–278.

48. Da Cámara, *Laredo on the Rio Grande*, 76–77.

49. Q. Mitchell, *50th Anniversary, Jim Hogg County 1913–1963.*

50. John M. Jones, ed., *La Hacienda; Spirit of Val Verde*, 20.

51. De León, *The Tejano Community, 1836–1900*, 176.

52. Ibid., 177.

53. Jones, *La Hacienda*; a photograph of Orquesta Aguilar performing in the plaza at Old Zapata is on exhibit at the La Paz Museum in San Ygnacio, Texas.

54. Daniel D. Arreola, "Plazas of San Diego, Texas: Signatures of Mexican-American Place Identity," 82–84.

55. Joe S. Graham, *Hispanic-American Material Culture: An Annotated Directory of Collections, Sites, Archives, and Festivals in the United States*, 228–234.

56. Webb County Heritage Foundation, "A Walking Tour."

57. Sánchez, *A Shared Experience*, 144–155.

58. Lawrence A. Herzog, "Mexican-Americans and the Evolution of the San Diego, California, Built Environment," 117; Brian J. Godfrey, *Neighborhoods in Transition*, 136.

59. Arthur J. Rubel, *Across the Tracks: Mexican-Americans in a Texas City*, 3–24; William Madsen, *The Mexican-Americans of South Texas*, 12–13; Ozzie G. Simmons, *Anglo Americans and Mexican Americans in South Texas*, 124–153.

60. Madsen, *Mexican-Americans of South Texas*, 12.

61. Rubel, *Across the Tracks*, 12.

62. Ibid., 8–9.

63. James R. Curtis, "Central Business Districts of the Two Laredos," 59–60.

64. City of Laredo, *Historic Preservation Plan*, 15.

65. John W. Clark Jr. and Ana Maria Juárez, *Urban Archaeology: A Culture History of a Mexican-American Barrio in Laredo, Webb County, Texas*, 139–159.

66. Peter Ward, *Colonias and Public Policy in Texas and Mexico: Urbanization by Stealth*, 13–64.

67. Christopher S. Davies and Robert K. Holtz, "Settlement Evolution of 'Colonias' along the U.S.-Mexico Border: The Case of the Lower Rio Grande Valley of Texas"; Texas Water Development Board, *Water and Wastewater Needs of Texas Colonias.*

68. Kingsley E. Haynes, *Colonias in the Lower Rio Grande Valley of South Texas: A Summary Report*, 9.

69. See Fig. 2, "Distribution of Colonias, 1990," in Davies and Holtz, "Settlement Evolution of 'Colonias.'"

70. J. R. Beard, *Map 17, City of McAllen, Hidalgo County, Texas, 1946*; J. R. Beard, *Map 17, City of McAllen, Hidalgo County, Texas, 1960*.

71. Davies and Holtz, "Settlement Evolution of 'Colonias'," suggest that typical colonia plots sold for $1000–2500 in the mid-1970s. In 1994, colonia lot prices in Hidalgo County averaged $10,000. See *Monitor* (McAllen), "New Types of Development: Much Like Old," A1.

72. *Christian Science Monitor*, "*Colonia* Families Put up with Much to Own Land," 32.

73. Haynes, *Colonias in the Lower Rio Grande Valley*, 9; Davies and Holtz, "Settlement Evolution of 'Colonias'"; *Monitor* (McAllen), "Town inside a Town Has a Long Way to Go," A8.

74. *Monitor* (McAllen), "Lack of Standards: Helter-Skelter Housing," A1, A6.

75. Arreola and Curtis, *Mexican Border Cities*, 68–69, 180–181.

76. Davies and Holtz, "Settlement Evolution of 'Colonias.'"

77. Ward, *Colonias and Public Policy in Texas and Mexico*, 260.

CHAPTER 6

1. George Foster, *Culture and Conquest: America's Spanish Heritage*, 34–35.

2. Dan Stanislawski, *The Anatomy of Eleven Towns in Michoacán*, 71–75.

3. Samuel N. Dicken, "Galeana: A Mexican Highland Community," 140–147; Leslie Hewes, "Huepac: An Agricultural Village of Sonora, Mexico," 284–292.

4. Fish, *Zapata County Roots Revisited*, 108.

5. Byfield, *Falcon Dam and the Lost Towns of Zapata*, 3; Lori Brown McVey, *Guerrero Viejo: A Photographic Essay*, 7–8.

6. Kelley, *Navigation on the Rio Grande*, 75; Fish, *Zapata County Roots Revisited*, 109.

7. Adrián Martínez, *Adrián: An Autobiography*, 45, 47.

8. *Laredo News*, "Old San Ygnacio Customhouse 'Made it Legal Two Days a Week'"; *Laredo Times*, "Holiday Excursionists See Typical Border Community," 5.

9. Martínez, *Adrián: An Autobiography*, 76.

10. Dick D. Heller Jr., "San Ygnacio, Texas," 894; Pierce, *Lower Rio Grande Valley*, 134.

11. Heller, "San Ygnacio, Texas," 894.

12. Virgil N. Lott and Mercurio Martínez, *The Kingdom of Zapata*, 70.

13. U.S. Bureau of the Census, *1990 Census of Population and Housing, Texas*, Zapata County, San Ygnacio Subdivision, STF 3A.

14. Ibid.

15. *Brownsville Herald*, "San Ygnacio Has Ghost-Like Quality," C1.

16. *Laredo Times*, "Tourists Favor San Ygnacio," D2.

17. San Ygnacio, Texas, *Mapa: terreno especial y pueblo de San Ygnacio, Tex.*, 1917.

18. I. T. Frary, "Picturesque Towns of the Borderland," 382–384.

19. San Ygnacio, Texas, *Historic American Building Survey, Zapata County, 1936*.

20. Sánchez, *A Shared Experience*, 84; South Texas Development Council, *Regional Historic Sites Survey and Development Plan*, 22.

21. William Clayton Barbee, *A Historical and Architectural Investigation of San Ygnacio, Texas*, 76–94; *Laredo Times*, "San Ygnacio: Sleepy South Texas Town Is Rich in History, Tradition."

22. Martínez, *Adrián: An Autobiography*, 21.

23. Ibid.

24. Fish, *Zapata County Roots Revisited*, 107–110.

25. *Laredo News*, "Uribe Event Sets Record," 1, A6; Joel Uribe, personal communication.

26. *Laredo Times*, "There Was a Homecoming in San Ygnacio."

27. The church or *capilla* is marked on the town plat. See San Ygnacio, Texas, *Plano de Rancho San Ignacio, Zapata Co., Texas, 1874*.

28. Sheri Fowler, "Tested by Fire: A South Texas Town Rebuilds Its Church with Faith, Hope, and Lots of Charity," 72–73.

29. *Laredo Times*, "Hundreds Gather to Honor Virgen de San Juan," C10.

30. The precise number of years this procession has been celebrated is a matter of several opinions. When I witnessed and participated in the event on March 28, 1997, residents informed me that the *procesión* had been part of San Ygnacio from its earliest days. See *South Texas People*, "70–Year Traditional Religious Procession Practiced," 1.

31. *Guide to Spanish and Mexican Land Grants in South Texas*, entry 78.

32. Martin Donell Kohout, "San Diego, Texas," 832–833; Agnes G. Grimm, *Llanos Mesteños: Mustang Plains*, 83; Alfredo E. Cardenas, "A Brief History of Duval County." Cardenas gives the following as the first resident families of Perezville: García Pérez, Juan Bautista, Martín Pérez, Jesús Solis.

33. A. E. Cardenas, "Brief History of Duval County."

34. Kohout, "San Diego, Texas," 833; Sister Mary Xavier [Holworthy], *Father Jaillet, Saddlebag Priest of the Nueces*, 18–21.

35. *Corpus Christi Caller-Times*, "San Diego Gets Lots of Notice for Town of Only 5,000 People," D16; *San Antonio Express*, "San Diego Has Romantic Past, Bright Future," C1.

36. A. E. Cardenas, "Brief History of Duval County."

37. Elena Bilbao and María Antonieta Gallart, *Los Chicanos*, 101; Kohout, "San Diego, Texas," 833.

38. Sanborn Map Company, *San Diego, Duval County, Texas* (1910); Sanborn Map Company, *San Diego, Duval and Jim Wells Counties, Texas* (1932).

39. Richard Tangum and Dixie Watkins, *San Diego: Economic and Environmental Design Analysis*, 7.

40. U.S. Bureau of the Census, *1990 Census*, Table 71.

41. Harold Owen Brown, *The Building of the Texas-Mexican Railroad*.

42. Sanborn Map Company, *San Diego, Duval County, Texas* (1922).

43. Evan Anders, *Boss Rule in South Texas: The Progressive Era*, 171–193.

44. Alfredo E. Cardenas, personal communication.

45. Ibid.

46. This section is chiefly based on Arreola, "Plazas of San Diego, Texas," 80–87.

47. Sanborn Map Company, *San Diego, Duval County, Texas*, (1885); Sanborn Map Company, *San Diego, Duval County, Texas* (1922); Sanborn Map Company, *San Diego, Duval and Jim Wells Counties, Texas* (1932).

48. *Houston Chronicle*, "Perpetual City."

49. *La Onda de Corpus Christi*, "San Diego Celebrates Annual Pan de Campo Fiesta."

50. Tangum and Watkins, *San Diego*, 3.

51. Everett G. Smith, "Decent Places off the Beaten Path," 16–28.

52. Annette Martin Ludeman, *La Salle: A History of La Salle County 1856–1975*, 8–9.

53. Stanley H. Holm, *La Salle County Scrapbook*.

54. The concept of housescape is fully elaborated in Daniel D. Arreola, "Mexican American Housescapes," 299–315.

55. The dual town idea in the Southwest is advanced in D. W. Meinig, *Southwest: Three Peoples in Geographical Change, 1600–1970*, 48.

56. Higinio Martínez Jr., personal communication.

57. Sánchez, *A Shared Experience*.

58. Texas Department of Parks and Wildlife, *San Ygnacio: A Proposal to Preserve an Hispanic Borderlands Settlement*, 1–44.

CHAPTER 7

1. James P. Allen and Eugene Turner, "The Most Ethnically Diverse Places in the United States," 523–539.

2. Martha A. Reddy, ed., *Statistical Record of Hispanic Americans*, 165; *2000 Census of Population and Housing*.

3. James P. Allen and Eugene Turner, *The Ethnic Quilt: Population Diversity in Southern California*, 100–106.

4. U.S. Bureau of the Census, *Fifteenth Census*, Tables 17 and 23.

5. Harriet Prescott Spofford, "San Antonio de Bexar," 838–839; Max Sylvius Handman, "San Antonio: The Old Capital City of Mexican Life and Influence," 163; Carey McWilliams, "Mexicans to Michigan," 5.

6. Bolton, *Texas in the Middle Eighteenth Century*, 5.

7. Vidaurreta, "Evolución urbana de Texas durante el siglo XVIII," 605–636.

8. Alicia V. Tjarks, "Comparative Demographic Analysis of Texas, 1777–1793," 241–338.

9. G. R. Cruz, *Let There Be Towns*, 52–80.

10. Reps, *Cities of the American West*, plate 4.

11. Ygnacio de Labastida, *Plano de la Ciudad de Béjar y fortificación del Alamo*.

12. Jesus F. de la Teja and John Wheat, "Béxar: Profile of a Tejano Community, 1820–1832," 7–9; Carland Elaine Crook, *San Antonio, Texas, 1846–1861*, 1–7.

13. Donald E. Everett, *San Antonio: The Flavor of Its Past, 1845–1898*, 5.

14. Jerry Lochbaum, ed., *Old San Antonio, History in Pictures*, 36–38; Cecelia Steinfeldt, *San Antonio Was: Seen through a Magic Lantern*, 32–56.

15. Reps, *Cities of the American West*, plate 4.

16. M. Pattan, *Town of San Antonio de Bejar* (map); G. Freisleben, *San Antonio and Its Ancient Wards* (map); W. C. A. Thielepape, *Map of Land Lying within the Corporation Limits of the City of San Antonio, Surveyed and Divided in 1852*.

17. William Corner, *San Antonio de Bexar: A Guide and History*.

18. Cited in Steinfeldt, *San Antonio Was*, 50.

19. G. R. Cruz, *Let There Be Towns*, 52–80.

20. Samuel A. Maverick, *Plat of Grand Plaza*; H. M. Mason, *A Century on Main Plaza*.

21. Sanborn-Perris Map Co., *San Antonio, Bexar County, Texas* (1892).

22. De León, *The Tejano Community, 1836–1900*, 29.

23. Daniel D. Arreola, "The Mexican American Cultural Capital," 17–34.

24. Pearson Newcomb, *The Alamo City*, 145.

25. Federal Writers' Project, Texas, *San Antonio: An Authoritative Guide to the City and Its Environs*, 62.

26. Green Peyton, *San Antonio, City in the Sun*, 146–147.

27. Mary Ann Noonan Guerra, *The History of San Antonio's Market Square*, 67.

28. Federal Writers' Project, *San Antonio*, 64.

29. Richard A. García, *Rise of the Mexican American Middle Class: San Antonio, 1929–1941*, 38–46.

30. J. C. Sologaistoa, *Guía general y directorio mexicano de San Antonio, Texas*.

31. Frances Jerome Woods, *Mexican Ethnic Leadership in San Antonio, Texas*, 20–21.

32. Arreola, "Mexican American Cultural Capital," 26.

33. *San Antonio Light*, "Famed S.A. Surgeon Is Dead. Urrutia, 103, a 'Legend'," 1, 20.

34. Nicolás Kanellos, *A History of Hispanic Theatre in the United States: Origins to 1940*, 80–86.

35. Freiselben, *San Antonio and Its Ancient Wards* (map); de la Teja and Wheat, "Béxar: Profile of a Tejano Community," 8–9.

36. Gerald E. Poyo, "Immigrants and Integration in Late Eighteenth-Century Béxar," 89–90.

37. Robert H. Thonhoff, *San Antonio Stage Lines, 1847–1881*.

38. W. Eugene Hollon and Ruth Lapham Butler, *William Bollaert's Texas*,

208–241; Ferdinand Roemer, *Roemer's Texas*, 117–134; Olmstead, *Journey through Texas*, 156–162.

39. Dorothy Steinbomer Kendall and Carmen Perry, *Gentilz: Artist of the Old Southwest*, 35.

40. Spofford, "San Antonio de Bexar," 837.

41. Berlandier, *Journey to Mexico during the Years 1826–1834*, vol. 2, 290–291.

42. Spofford, "San Antonio de Bexar," 838.

43. Manuel Gamio, *The Life Story of the Mexican Immigrant*, 68–69.

44. Audrey Granneberg, "Maury Maverick's San Antonio," 423.

45. R. A. García, *Rise of the Mexican American Middle Class: San Antonio, 1929–1941*, 24–25, 39; W. P. Clarke, *Map of San Antonio, 1924*.

46. William T. Chambers, "San Antonio, Texas," 297–298.

47. Harold Arthur Shapiro, "The Pecan Shellers of San Antonio, Texas," 229–244; Donald L. Zelman, "Alazan-Apache Courts: A New Deal Response to Mexican American Housing Conditions in San Antonio," 132.

48. Thomas Guy Rogers, *The Housing Situation of Mexicans in San Antonio, Texas*, 41–52, cited in Zelman, "Alazan-Apache Courts," 126–127.

49. Zelman, "Alazan-Apache Courts," 141.

50. R. A. García, *Rise of the Mexican American Middle Class: San Antonio, 1929–1941*, 72.

51. Joe Bernal, personal communication.

52. Robert Garland Landolt, *The Mexican-American Workers of San Antonio, Texas*, map 2, p. 378; Robert Sargent Bacon, *The Factorial Ecology of the Mexican-American Barrio*, Fig. 7, p. 79.

53. Robert Brischetto, Charles L. Cotrell, and R. Michael Stevens, "Conflict and Change in the Political Culture of San Antonio in the 1970s," 76.

54. Wilbur E. Garrett, ed., "A Grand Fiesta Called Hispanics," 72.

55. Daniel D. Arreola, "Urban Ethnic Landscape Identity," 524–528.

56. See, for example, Kenneth Woodward, "In Old San Antonio, *Mestizaje* Nurtures New American Way," 115–127; Richard West, "San Antonio: The *Barrio*," 53–88; and *Los Angeles Times*, "A Cultural Diamond in the Rough. San Antonio Has Emerged as an Artistic and Political Mecca for Latinos," A1.

57. Chris Carson and William McDonald, eds., *A Guide to San Antonio Architecture*, 9.

58. Ibid., 82.

59. Kell-Muñoz-Wigodsky, Architects, "*Mestizo* Regionalism: Cultural Activism in the Built Environment along the Texas-Mexico Border," 10.

60. *San Antonio Express-News*, "'Mestizo' Style's Roots Too Short"; *San Antonio Express-News*, "Chicano Architecture Shows Off New Takes on Hispanic Tradition."

61. Sandra Cisneros, "Purple Casa (Casa violeta)," 34.

62. *San Antonio Express-News,* "Purple Politics," J1, J5; *Los Angeles Times,* "Purple Passions Swirl about Texas Abode," A1, A13; *New York Times,* "Novelist's Purple Palette Is Not to Everyone's Taste," A14.

63. Cisneros, "Purple Casa," 37.

64. Texas Center for Border Economic and Enterprise Development, "Texas Truck Crossing Information, Monthly/Yearly"; Juan Carlos Espinosa Rescala, Rob Harrison, and B. F. McCullough, *Effect of the North American Free Trade Agreement on the Transportation Infrastructure in the Laredo–Nuevo Laredo Area,* 60.

65. G. R. Cruz, *Let There Be Towns,* 94.

66. Gilberto Miguel Hinojosa, *A Borderlands Town in Transition: Laredo, 1755–1870,* 10, 59.

67. G. R. Cruz, *Let There Be Towns,* 97; Hinojosa, *A Borderlands Town in Transition,* 17, 23, 29.

68. Hinojosa, *A Borderlands Town in Transition,* 39, 41, 43.

69. Ibid., 71, 74.

70. Isidro Vizcaya Canales, *Los orígenes de la industrialización de Monterrey,* 4–5.

71. J. B. Wilkinson, *Laredo and the Rio Grande Frontier,* 272, 326.

72. James W. Daddysman, *The Matamoros Trade,* 31–35; Pat Kelly, *Navigation on the Rio Grande,* 73–74.

73. Wilkinson, *Laredo and the Rio Grande Frontier,* 363.

74. Brown, *Building of the Texas-Mexican Railway,* 31; Wilkinson, *Laredo and the Rio Grande Frontier,* 366; Thompson, *Laredo: A Pictorial History,* 56–58.

75. Chester C. Wine, *Description of Laredo, Texas: The Great International Gateway of the Two Republics.*

76. E. R. Tarver, *Laredo the Gate Way between the United States and Mexico: An Illustrated Description of the Future City of the Great Southwest* (1889); J. W. Falvella, *A Souvenir Album of Laredo the Gateway to Mexico* (1917); Laredo, Chamber of Commerce, *The Gateway to Mexico, Laredo South Texas* (1926); Jack Dunson, ed. *The Gateway* (1931).

77. Montejano, *Making of Texas, 1836–1986,* 106–110, 197–201.

78. Burt C. Blanton, *Industrial and Economic Survey of the City of Laredo and Webb County, Texas,* 95–98.

79. *México en cifras (Atlas estadístico), 1934,* 76.

80. Frances Toor, *Frances Toor's Motor Guide to Mexico,* 42; *South Texan,* "Laredo Offers Hospitality to Centennial Tourists; Gateway to Mexico Affords Varied Services and Modern Accommodations," 1.

81. Thompson, *Laredo: A Pictorial History,* 264.

82. Anita Brenner, *Your Mexican Holiday: A Modern Guide,* map facing p. 66; Toor, *Frances Toor's Motor Guide to Mexico,* maps 1–3.

83. Daniel D. Arreola, "Across the Street Is Mexico: The Invention and Persistence of the Border Town Curio Landscape," 15.

84. Federal Writers' Project, *WPA Guide to Texas*, 306–307.

85. Avelardo Valdez, "Persistent Poverty, Crime, and Drugs: U.S.-Mexican Border Region," 177.

86. Haverluk, "Hispanic Community Types and Assimilation in Mex-America," 470.

87. Ibid., table 1, 468.

88. Montejano, *Making of Texas, 1836–1986*, 36, 80.

89. Hinojosa, *A Borderlands Town in Transition*, 120.

90. Arnoldo De León and Kenneth L. Stewart, *Tejanos and the Numbers Game: A Socio-Historical Interpretation from the Federal Censuses, 1850–1900*, Table 5.8, 87.

91. Grebler, Moore, and Guzman, *The Mexican-American People: The Nation's Second Largest Minority*, Table 12–1, 275.

92. See "Urbanization of Laredo from 1767 to 1955," (map) in City of Laredo, *Historic Preservation Plan*.

93. U.S. Bureau of the Census, *Census of Population and Housing: 1970, Census Tracts, Laredo, Tex. SMSA*, Table P-7, 11–12.

94. Eduardo Alarcón Cantú, *Interpretación de la estructura urbana de Laredo y Nuevo Laredo*, map 10, "Etapas de crecimiento," 90, and map 4, "Distribución por nivel socioeconómico," 84.

95. Hinojosa, *A Borderlands Town in Transition*, 95–96.

96. Wilkinson, *Laredo and the Rio Grande Frontier*, 165–174.

97. Alan M. Klein, *Baseball on the Border: A Tale of Two Laredos*, 26.

98. Alan Weisman, *La Frontera: The United States Border with Mexico*, 37.

99. Curtis, "Central Business Districts of the Two Laredos," 54–65; John W. Sloan and Jonathan P. West, "Community Integration and Policies among Elites in Two Border Cities: Los Dos Laredos," 451–474.

100. A. J. Weissmann et al., *Overview of the Texas-Mexico Border: Assessment of Traffic Flow Patterns*, 154.

101. Klein, *Baseball on the Border*, 261–263.

102. Norma Elia Cantú, *Canícula: Snapshots of a Girlhood en La Frontera*, 5–9.

CHAPTER 8

1. Frank D. Bean and Marta Tienda, *The Hispanic Population of the United States*, 38, Table 3.7, 93; Grebler, Moore, and Guzman, *The Mexican-American People: The Nation's Second Largest Minority*, 423–428, 473–477; Jane MacNab Christian and Chester C. Christian, Jr., "Spanish Language and Culture in the Southwest," 280–317.

2. Roberto A. Galván and Richard V. Teschner, *El diccionario del español de Tejas / The Dictionary of the Spanish of Texas*; Craig M. Carver, *American Regional Dialects: A Word Geography*; Américo Paredes, *Folklore and Culture on the Texas-Mexican Border*, 235–246.

3. Floyd M. Henderson, "Foodways," 225–233.

4. Wilbur Zelinsky, "The Roving Palate: North America's Ethnic Restaurant Cuisines," 51–72.

5. Linda Keller Brown and Kay Mussell, eds. *Ethnic and Regional Foodways in the United States: The Performance of Group Identity*, 3–15; Anne R. Kaplan, Marjorie A. Hoover, and Willard B. Moore, "Introduction: On Ethnic Foodways," 121–133.

6. Jeffrey M. Pilcher, *¡Que Vivan los Tamales! Food and the Making of Mexican Identity*, 1–6.

7. Barbara G. Shortridge and James R. Shortridge, eds., *The Taste of American Place: A Reader on Regional and Ethnic Foods*, 7.

8. William H. Beezley, Cheryl English Martin, and William E. French, eds., *Rituals of Rule, Rituals of Resistance: Public Celebrations and Popular Culture in Mexico*, xiv.

9. John O. West, *Mexican-American Folklore*, 159.

10. Margarita B. Melville, "The Mexican-American and the Celebration of the *Fiestas Patrias*: An Ethnohistorical Analysis," 107–116.

11. Graham, *Hispanic-American Material Culture*, 207–236; James W. Peyton, *La Cocina de la Frontera: Mexican-American Cooking from the Southwest*, 45–67.

12. *San Antonio Light*, "Cantu's Tex-Mex Not Playing Fare," D1, D11.

13. *Los Angeles Times*, "Fajitas," part 8, pp. 1, 28, 32.

14. John G. Bourke, "The Folk-Foods of the Rio Grande Valley and of Northern Mexico," 41–71.

15. Ibid., 60.

16. Arreola, "Mexican American Cultural Capital," 28.

17. Everett, *San Antonio: The Flavor of Its Past, 1845–1898*, 1–11; John L. Davis, *San Antonio: A Historical Portrait*, 75, 90.

18. Federal Writers' Project, *San Antonio*, 65; Arreola, "Mexican American Cultural Capital," 28–29.

19. G. Peyton, *San Antonio, City in the Sun*, 139–144.

20. *Picturesque San Antonio*, 28.

21. J. C. Sologaistoa, ed., *Guía general directorio mexicano de San Antonio, Texas*, 221–222.

22. Waverly Root and Richard de Rochemont, *Eating in America*, 281.

23. Helen Simons, "The Tex-Mex Menu," 136.

24. Richard Pillsbury, *No Foreign Food: The American Diet in Time and Place*, 160.

25. T. R. Fehrenbach, *The San Antonio Story*, 210–211; Landolt, *Mexican-American Workers of San Antonio*, 166.

26. *San Antonio Light*, *Viva* (supplement), "Sauce Wars," 19–23; Terrence W. Haverluk, "Chiles!"; J. W. Peyton, *La Cocina de la Frontera*, 112, 337.

27. Atlas Cultural de México, *Gastronomía*, 74; Joe S. Graham, "Mexican-American Traditional Foodways at La Junta de los Rios," 19–20.

28. *San Antonio Light*, "Chicharrón Vendors Fade Away," B1, B2; J. W. Peyton, *La Cocina de la Frontera*, 70, 335.

29. P. H. Carlson, *Texas Woollybacks: The Range Sheep and Goat Industry*, 62–63; Lehmann, *Forgotten Legions: Sheep in the Rio Grande Plain of Texas*, 133.

30. *Monitor* (McAllen), "Getting Your Goat," C1, C2.

31. J. W. Peyton, *La Cocina de la Frontera*, 303.

32. Mario Montaño, *The History of Mexican Folk Foodways of South Texas: Street Vendors, Offal Foods, and Barbacoa de Cabeza*, viii.

33. *San Antonio Express-News*, "Barbacoa a Weekend Tradition in S.A.," G12; *Laredo News*, "Barbacoa: Sunday Treat," A2; *Monitor* (McAllen), "Moo-choo Sabroso," D1, D2.

34. Montaño, *History of Mexican Folk Foodways of South Texas*, 258–260.

35. *San Antonio Express-News*, "Barbacoa a Weekend Tradition in S.A."

36. *Monitor* (McAllen), "Bakers Raise Bread to Art Form," B1, B2; *Monitor* (McAllen), "Bread Battle Continues Old Cooking Method," B1.

37. West, *Mexican-American Folklore*, 213; J. W. Peyton, *La Cocina de la Frontera*, 230–232; Malcolm L. Comeaux, "The Tortilla Industry in Arizona," 19, 21.

38. Brett Williams, "Why Migrant Women Feed Their Husbands Tamales: Foodways as a Basis for a Revisionist View of Tejano Family Life," 113.

39. Simons, "The Tex-Mex Menu," 135–136, illustration *La Tamalada* by Carmen Lomas Garza, 137.

40. Sophie D. Cole, *America's First Cuisines*, 113–114.

41. See Pilcher, "The Tortilla Discourse," in *¡Que Vivan los Tamales!*, 77–97, 153.

42. West and Augelli, *Middle America*, 305–307, 355–359; Miguel León-Portilla, "The Norteño Variety of Mexican Culture: An Ethnohistorical Approach," 109–114.

43. Atlas Cultura de México, *Gastronomía*, 29, 33, 37; J. W. Peyton, *La Cocina de la Frontera*, 57.

44. Arthur L. Campa, *Hispanic Culture in the Southwest*, 280.

45. See Pilcher, "Replacing the Aztec Blender," in *¡Que Vivan los Tamales!*, 99–106; Federal Writers' Project, *San Antonio*, 69.

46. Graham, "Mexican-American Traditional Foodways," 12; personal communication with four individuals who lived in San Antonio between 1930 and 1950: Oliver Pérez (b. San Antonio, 1905), Abelardo H. Cantú (b. Monterrey, 1925), Mary Louise T. Cantú (b. Nuevo Laredo, 1926), and Rose Marie de la Peña (b. Los Angeles, 1938).

47. Statistics reported by the Tortilla Association of America in the following stories: *San Antonio Express-News*, "Tortilla Market Booming and Profits Are Zooming," J1, J6; *Monitor* (McAllen), "Tortillas Catching up to Bread's Popularity," B1, B5; *Arizona Republic*, "A Flouring Industry," D1, D8.

48. *Monitor* (McAllen), "Feisty Queen of Fast Food Turns Ambition into a Tasty Valley Tradition," A1, A11.

49. Graham, "Mexican-American Traditional Foodways," 1–27.

50. Jordan, with Bean and Holmes, *Texas: A Geography*, 91, esp. Fig. 4.16.

51. Pillsbury, *No Foreign Food*, 215.

52. *Monitor* (McAllen), "Restaurant 'Taco Wars' Heat Up in Valley," C1, C2.

53. *San Antonio Express-News*, "Tasty Taco Town Tale: The Whole Enchilada," Sunday magazine, 8–9.

54. Rosario Torres-Raines, "The Mexican Origin of Rituals, Ceremonies, and Celebrations in South Texas," 131.

55. See, for example, Kyriakos S. Markides and Thomas Cole, "Change and Continuity in Mexican American Religious Behavior: A Three-Generation Study," 618–625.

56. Alberto L. Pulido, "Mexican American Catholicism in the Southwest: The Transformation of a Popular Religion," 93.

57. José Roberto Juárez, "La Iglesia Católica y el chicano en Sud Texas, 1836–1911," 217–255; Roberto R. Treviño, "Mexican Americans and Religion," 672–676.

58. Anita Brenner, *Idols behind Altars*; Mary Lee Nolan, "The Mexican Pilgrimage Tradition," 13–27.

59. Torres-Raines, "The Mexican Origin of Rituals," 139–140. Some recent recorded sightings listed by town follow. In Hidalgo: *Monitor* (McAllen), "Image on Tortilla Draws Crowds to Hidalgo Home," A1, A12; *Monitor*, "Hundreds See Tortilla; Faith Healing is Claimed," A1, A10. In Elsa: *Monitor*, "Faithful Still Flocking to Mary's Image on Auto," A1. In Rio Grande City: *Monitor*, "Our Lady of Guadalupe Replica Becomes Pilgrimage Focus," D2. In Brownsville: *Monitor*, "Crowd Gathers to View Apparition [in tree trunk]," A1.

60. Interview with Mark Glazer, director, Rio Grande Folklore Archive. See also Mark Glazer, ed., *Flour from Another Sack and Other Proverbs, Folk Beliefs, Tales, Riddles and Recipes*.

61. Stephen F. de Borhegyi and E. Boyd, *El Santuario de Chimayó*, 20–22; James S. Griffith, *Beliefs and Holy Places: A Spiritual Geography of the Pimería Alta*, 31–66.

62. William Curry Holden, *Teresita*; James S. Griffith, *A Shared Space: Folklife in the Arizona-Sonora Borderlands*, 72–86.

63. Ruth Dodson, "Don Pedrito Jaramillo: The Curandero of Los Olmos," 9–70; Octavio Ignacio Romano V., "Charismatic Medicine, Folk-Healing, and Folk-Sainthood," 1158–1159.

64. Dodson, "Don Pedrito Jaramillo," 18–68.

65. Romano V., "Charismatic Medicine, Folk-Healing, and Folk-Sainthood," 1163.

66. Dick J. Reavis, "The Saint of Falfurrias," 98–103; *Monitor* (McAllen), "Don Pedrito, Curandero without Peer," A13, A14.

67. Kay F. Turner, "'Because of This Photography': The Making of a Mexi-

can Folk Saint," in *Niño Fidencio: A Heart Thrown Open*, by Dore Gardner, 120–132; West, *Mexican-American Folklore*, 140.

68. Robert T. Trotter II and Juan Antonio Chavira, *Curanderismo, Mexican American Folk Healing*, 35, 78.

69. *Austin American-Statesman*, "Fiesta of Faith: Pilgrims on a Path of Pain, Joy Gather to Honor Mexican Healer," A1, A5; *Monitor* (McAllen), "The Lore and Legend of El Niño Fidencio," D1, D2; Dore Gardner, *Niño Fidencio: A Heart Thrown Open*, 9, 12, 38.

70. Joseph Azpiazu, O.M.I., "Virgen de San Juan del Valle Shrine," 760.

71. *Virgen de San Juan Shrine.*

72. Blanca M. Gutiérrez, "The Shrine of La Virgen de San Juan del Valle," 108.

73. Kay F. Turner, "Cultural Semiotics of Religious Icons: La Virgen de San Juan de Los Lagos," 350.

74. Ibid., 323, 325, 338.

75. Pat Jasper and Kay Turner, *Art among Us / Arte Entre Nosotros: Mexican American Folk Art of San Antonio*, 26–27; Arreola, "Mexican American Housescapes," 309; Kay F. Turner, "Mexican American Home Altars: Towards Their Interpretation," 318.

76. Jan Jarboe, "The Week of the Virgin," 216.

77. Gary Mounce, "Popular Culture and Politics: The Pelea de Gallo (Cockfight) in South Texas," 2; Kathleen Mullen Sands, *Charrería Mexicana: An Equestrian Folk Tradition*, 310.

78. Torres-Raines, "The Mexican Origins of Rituals," 135–136; West, *Mexican-American Folklore*, 174–180.

79. Richard R. Flores, *Los Pastores: History and Performance in the Mexican Shepherd's Play of South Texas*, 27, 46.

80. West, *Mexican-American Folklore*, 147.

81. Arreola, "Mexican Texas: A Distinctive Borderland," 7.

82. Brownsville, Texas, scrapbook of ephemera; "Charro Days Has Colorful History"; Ruby A. Wooldridge and Robert B. Vezzetti, *Brownsville: A Pictorial History*, 164–166, 174–175; Simons and Hoyt, *Hispanic Texas: A Historical Guide*, 235.

83. Fermina Guerra, *Mexican and Spanish Folklore and Incidents in Southwest Texas*, 48–59; De León, *The Tejano Community, 1836–1900*, 175–176.

84. Lionel G. García, *I Can Hear the Cowbells Ring*, 75–77.

85. Poncho Hernandez Jr., personal communication; Alfredo E. Cardenas, personal communication; Roque Salas, personal communication.

86. *San Antonio Express-News*, "'Fiesta del Rancho,' South Texas at Its Best," B1, B8; *San Antonio Express-News*, "Pan de Campo—Duval Style," B1, B8.

87. *Alice-Echo News*, "19th Annual Pan de Campo," 8.

88. Manuel Peña, *The Texas-Mexican Conjunto: History of a Working-Class Music*, 1.

89. Manuel Peña, "From *Ranchero* to *Jaitón*: Ethnicity and Class in Texas-Mexican Music (Two Styles in the Form of a Pair)," 152.

90. José R. Reyna, "Notes on Tejano Music," 93.

91. Evidence of the evolved nature of Tejano music is apparent in the Héctor Galán documentary *Songs of the Homeland* (1993), see John Mortland, "Border Music: A Veteran Filmmaker's New Documentary Looks at the Rich History of Tejano," 102–103; in the rise to stardom of Selena Quintanilla, whose life story is chronicled in Joe Nick Patoski, *Selena como la flor*; as well as in the promotion since 1980 of the Tejano Music Awards program, an annual event staged in San Antonio that draws more than 35,000 fans and is broadcast as a television special in the United States, Mexico, and 120 other countries. There is even a Tejano Music Hall of Fame whose primary goal is to collect, maintain, document, and preserve the history and development of Tejano music, its performers, recording artists, and composers.

92. Ramon Hernandez, personal communication. Hernandez lives in San Antonio, and he is the premier archivist of Tejano music, both *conjunto* and other popular styles. His collection includes records, cassettes, compact discs, a book and video library, still photos, files of ephemera and newspaper clippings, and other memorabilia.

93. *San Antonio Express-News*, "The Conjunto Connection: Accordion-Driven Music Rooted in South Texas Heartland," G1, G11; see also Manuel Peña, *Música Tejana*.

CHAPTER 9

1. *South Texas, the Proposed 49th State* (pamphlet, 1938).

2. Donald W. Whisenhunt, *The Five States of Texas: An Immodest Proposal*, 46, 72–74.

3. This section is drawn especially from Arreola, "Texas-Mexican Homeland," 63–69.

4. Jordan, with Bean and Holmes, *Texas: A Geography*, 142–144, 150; Anders, *Boss Rule in South Texas: The Progressive Era.*

5. Wilkinson, *Laredo and the Rio Grande Frontier*, 165–174.

6. James A. Sandos, *Rebellion in the Borderlands: Anarchism and the Plan of San Diego, 1904–1923*, 63–100.

7. Kibbe, *Latin Americans in Texas*; R. A. García, *Rise of the Mexican American Middle Class: San Antonio, 1929–1941*, 42–43, 253–299; Meier and Rivera, *Dictionary of Mexican American History*, 191.

8. John Staples Shockley, *Chicano Revolt in a Texas Town*; Douglas E. Foley et al., *From Peones to Políticos: Ethnic Relations in a South Texas Town, 1900 to 1970.*

9. Michael V. Miller, "Chicano Community Control in South Texas: Problems and Prospects," 70–89.

10. Ignacio M. García, *United We Win: The Rise and Fall of La Raza Unida Party*, 79, 128, 146–148; Jordan, with Bean and Holmes, *Texas: A Geography*, 140, 144.

11. Miller, "Chicano Community Control in South Texas," 86; I. M. García, *United We Win: The Rise and Fall of La Raza Unida*, 202, 219, 227.

12. Larry Hufford, "The Velásquez Legacy," 6–8; Robert R. Brischetto, "Electoral Empowerment: The Case for Tejanos," 71–90.

13. National Association of Latino Elected and Appointed Officials, *1990 National Roster of Hispanic Elected Officials*, vii, 67–87.

14. Clifton McCleskey and Bruce Merril, "Mexican-American Political Behavior in Texas," 789–792; Fred M. Shelly, J. Clark Archer, and G. Thomas Murauskas, "The Geography of Recent Presidential Elections in the Southwest," 9.

15. *Austin American-Statesman*, "How Texas Voted for President," A8.

16. Leonard Broom and Eshref Shevky, "Mexicans in the United States: A Problem of Social Differentiation," 150–158.

17. Fernando Peñalosa and Edward C. McDonagh, "Social Mobility in a Mexican-American Community," 498–505.

18. Manuel A. Machado, Jr., "The Mexican American: A Problem in Cross-Cultural Identity," 47–66.

19. Joan Moore and Raquel Pinderhughes, eds., *In the Barrios: Latinos and the Underclass Debate*, 101–128, 149–172, 173–194, 195–210; Américo Paredes, "The Problem of Identity in a Changing Culture along the Lower Río Grande Border," 68–94.

20. Arnoldo De León, "Texas Mexicans: Twentieth-Century Interpretations," 20–49.

21. Arreola, "Mexican Americans," 111–138.

22. Thomas D. Boswell and Timothy C. Jones, "A Regionalization of Mexican Americans in the United States," 88–98.

23. Haverluk, "A Descriptive Model," 19, 28, 29.

24. Arreola, "Mexican Americans," 111–116; Américo Paredes, "El folklore de los grupos de origen mexicano en los Estados Unidos," 146–163.

25. Adán Benavides, Jr., "Tejano," 238–239.

26. L. Cruz, *Developing South Texas*, 6.

27. Arreola, "Mexican Texas: A Distinctive Borderland," 5–6.

28. Christian and Christian, "Spanish Language and Culture in the Southwest," 280–317; Daniel Cardenas, "Mexican Spanish," 1–5; Jacob Ornstein-Galicia, "Varieties of Southwest Spanish: Some Neglected Basic Considerations," 19–38.

29. Galván and Teschner, *El diccionario del español de Tejas*.

30. *Arizona Republic*, "Texas Town Officially Speaks Spanish," A10; *Arizona Republic*, "Spanish-Only Border Town at Center of Storm," A31. El Cenizo is documented as a colonia in Ward, *Colonias and Public Policy in Texas and Mexico*, 39–45.

31. *San Diego Reader*, "Battle of the Tongues," 5, 8; *New York Times*, "Texas and California: 2 Views of Illegal Aliens," I-8.

32. Los Caminos del Rio Heritage Task Force, *Los Caminos del Rio: A Binational Heritage Project along the Lower Rio Grande*, 3.

33. Ibid., 6.

34. Sánchez, *A Shared Experience*, 6–8.

35. Ibid., 81, 84, 88.

36. Los Caminos del Rio Heritage Task Force, *Los Caminos del Rio*, quotation from back cover.

37. Meinig, "Shaping of America, 1850–1915," 7.

38. John Brinckerhoff Jackson, "Learning about Landscapes," 16–18.

References

Adler, Jerry, and Tim Padgett. "Mexamerica: Selena Country." *Newsweek* 126 (23 October 1995): 76–79.

Agnew, John A., John Mercer, and David E. Sopher, eds. *The City in Cultural Context*. Boston: Allen and Unwin, 1984.

Alarcón Cantú, Eduardo. *Interpretación de la estructura urbana de Laredo y Nuevo Laredo*. Tijuana: El Colegio de la Frontera Norte, 1997.

Alessio Robles, Vito. *Coahuila y Texas en la Epoca Colonial*. Mexico, D.F.: Editorial Cultura, 1938.

Alice Echo-News. "19th Annual Pan de Campo." August 1, 1996. 8.

Allen, James P., and Eugene Turner. *The Ethnic Quilt: Population Diversity in Southern California*. Northridge, Calif.: Center for Geographical Studies, California State University, 1997.

———. "The Most Ethnically Diverse Places in the United States." *Urban Geography* 10 (1989): 523–539.

Allhands, James L. *Gringo Builders*. Privately published, 1931.

Almonte, Juan N. "Statistical Report on Texas [1835]." Translated by Carlos E. Casteñeda. *Southwestern Historical Quarterly* 28 (January 1925): 177–222.

Alonzo, Armando C. "Change and Continuity in Tejano Ranches in the Trans-Nueces, 1848–1900." In *Ranching in South Texas: A Symposium*, edited by Joe S. Graham, 53–68. Kingsville, Tex.: John E. Conner Museum and Texas A&I University, 1994.

————. *Tejano Legacy: Rancheros and Settlers in South Texas, 1734–1900*. Albuquerque: University of New Mexico Press, 1998.

Anders, Evan. *Boss Rule in South Texas: The Progressive Era*. Austin: University of Texas Press, 1982.

Arbingast, Stanley A., L. G. Kennamer, R. H. Ryan, J. R. Buchanan, W. L. Hezlep, L. T. Ellis, T. G. Jordan, C. T. Granger, and C. P. Zlatkovich. *Atlas of Texas*. Austin: Bureau of Business Research, University of Texas, 1976.

Arizona Republic. "A Flouring Industry." December 30, 1999. D1, D8.

————. "'Spanish-Only' Border Town at Center of Storm." December 19, 1999. A31.

————. "Texas Town Officially Speaks Spanish." August 14, 1999. A10.

Arreola, Daniel D. "Across the Street Is Mexico: The Invention and Persistence of the Border Town Curio Landscape." *Yearbook of the Association of Pacific Coast Geographers*, vol. 61, 9–41. Northridge, Calif.: Association of Pacific Coast Geographers, 1999.

————. "Beyond the Nueces: The Early Geographical Identity of South Texas." *Río Bravo: A Journal of Research and Issues* 2 (spring 1993): 46–60.

————. "The Mexican American Cultural Capital." *Geographical Review* 77 (January 1987): 17–34.

————. "Mexican American Housescapes." *Geographical Review* 78 (July 1988): 299–315.

————. "Mexican Americans." In *Ethnicity in Contemporary America: Geographical Essays*, edited by Jesse O. McKee, 111–138. Lahman, Md.: Rowman and Littlefield, 2000.

————. "Mexican Texas: A Distinctive Borderland." In *A Geographic Glimpse of Central Texas and the Borderlands: Images and Encounters*, edited by James F. Petersen and Julie A. Tuason, 3–9. Indiana, Pa.: National Council for Geographic Education, 1995.

————. "Mexico Origins of South Texas Mexican Americans, 1930." *Journal of Historical Geography* 19 (1993): 43–63.

————. "Nineteenth-Century Townscapes of Eastern Mexico." *Geographical Review* 72 (January 1982): 1–19.

————. "Plazas of San Diego, Texas: Signatures of Mexican-American Place Identity." *Places: A Quarterly Journal of Environmental Design* 8 (spring 1993): 80–87.

————. "Plaza Towns of South Texas." *Geographical Review* 81 (January 1992): 56–73.

————. "Texas." In *Encyclopedia of American Social History*, edited by Mary K. Cayton, Elliot J. Gorn, and Peter W. Williams, vol. 2, 1069–1077. New York: Charles Scribner's Sons, 1993.

————. "The Texas-Mexican Homeland." *Journal of Cultural Geography* 13 (spring/summer 1993): 61–74.

————. "Urban Ethnic Landscape Identity." *Geographical Review* 85 (October 1995): 518–534.

————. "*La Tierra Tejana*: A South Texas Homeland." In *Homelands in the United States: A Geography of Culture and Place across America*, edited by Richard L. Nostrand and Lawrence E. Estaville Jr., 101–124. Baltimore: Johns Hopkins University Press, 2001.

Arreola, Daniel D., and James R. Curtis. *The Mexican Border Cities: Landscape Anatomy and Place Personality*. Tucson: University of Arizona Press, 1993.

Atlas Cultural de México. *Gastronomía*. Mexico, D.F.: Secretaría de Educación Pública, Instituto Nacional de Antropología e Historia, Grupo Editorial Planeta, 1988.

Austin American-Statesman. "Boom on Border: Flood of Students Washes across Rio Grande Valley." October 2, 1989. A1, A5.

———. "Fiesta of Faith: Pilgrims on a Path of Pain, Joy Gather to Honor Mexican Healer." March 19, 1990. A1, A5.

———. "How Texas Voted for President." November 6, 1996. A8.

Azpiazu, Joseph, O.M.I. "Virgen de San Juan del Valle Shrine." In *The New Handbook of Texas*, edited by Ron Tyler, vol. 6, 760. Austin: Texas State Historical Association, 1996.

Bacon, Robert Sargent. "The Factorial Ecology of the Mexican-American Barrio." Ph.D. diss., University of Colorado, Boulder, 1975.

Barbee, William Clayton. "A Historical and Architectural Investigation of San Ygnacio, Texas." Master's thesis, University of Texas, Austin, 1981.

Barnes, Trevor, and Derek Gregory. "Place and Landscape." In *Reading Human Geography: The Poetics and Politics of Inquiry*, edited by Trevor Barnes and Derek Gregory, 292–298. London: Edward Arnold, 1997.

Bartlett, John Russell. *Personal Narrative of Explorations and Incidents in Texas, New Mexico, California, Sonora and Chihuahua, 1850–1853*. 2 vols. New York: D. Appleton, 1854.

Bean, Frank D., and Marta Tienda. *The Hispanic Population of the United States*. New York: Russell Sage Foundation, 1988.

Beard, J. R. *Map 17, City of McAllen, Hidalgo County Texas, 1946* and *Map 17, City of McAllen, Hidalgo County, Texas, 1960*. Rio Grande Valley Historical Collection. University of Texas, Pan American, Edinburg.

Beezley, William H., Cheryl English Martin, and William E. French, eds. *Rituals of Rule, Rituals of Resistance: Public Celebrations and Popular Culture in Mexico*. Wilmington, Del.: Scholarly Resources, 1994.

Benavides, Adán, Jr. "Tejano." In *The New Handbook of Texas*, edited by Ron Tyler, vol. 6, 238–239. Austin: Texas State Historical Association, 1996.

Berlandier, Jean Louis. *Journey to Mexico during the Years 1826 to 1834*. 2 vols. Translated by Sheila M. Ohlendorf, Josette M. Bigelow, and Mary M. Standifer. Austin: Texas State Historical Association, 1980.

Bernal, Joe. Personal communication, San Antonio, Texas, May 16, 1997.

Bilbao, Elena, and María Antonieta Gallart. *Los chicanos: segregación y educación*. Mexico, D.F.: Editorial Nueva Imagen, 1981.

Binkley, William Campbell. *The Expansionist Movement in Texas, 1836–1850*. University of California Publications in History, vol. 13. Berkeley: University of California Press, 1925.

Blair, W. Frank. "The Biotic Provinces of Texas." *Texas Journal of Science* 2 (1950): 93–117.

Blanton, Burt C. *Industrial and Economic Survey of the City of Laredo and Webb County, Texas*. Dallas: San Antonio Central Power and Light Co., 1928.

Bolton, Herbert Eugene. *Guide to Materials for the History of the United States in the Principal Archives of Mexico*. Washington, D.C.: Carnegie Institution, 1913.

———. "The Spanish Occupation of Texas, 1519–1690." *Southwestern Historical Quarterly* 16 (July 1912): 1–26.

———. *Texas in the Middle Eighteenth Century: Studies in Spanish Colonial History and Administration.* University of California Publications in History, vol. 3. Berkeley: University of California, 1915.

Boswell, Thomas D. "The Growth and Proportional Redistribution of the Mexican Stock Population in the United States, 1900–1970." *Mississippi Geographer* 6 (spring 1979): 57–76.

Boswell, Thomas D., and Timothy C. Jones. "A Regionalization of Mexican Americans in the United States." *Geographical Review* 70 (January 1980): 88–98.

Bourke, John G. "The American Congo." *Scribner's Magazine* 15 (May 1894): 590–610.

———. "The Folk-Foods of the Rio Grande Valley and of Northern Mexico." *Journal of American Folk-lore* 8 (January–March 1895): 41–71.

Brenner, Anita. *Idols behind Altars.* New York: Payson and Clark, 1929.

———. *Your Mexican Holiday: A Modern Guide.* Rev. ed. with motor maps and directory. New York: G. P. Putnam's Sons, 1947.

Brischetto, Robert R. "Electoral Empowerment: The Case for Tejanos." In *Latino Empowerment: Progress, Problems, and Prospects,* edited by Roberto E. Villareal, Norma G. Hernandez, and Howard D. Neighbor, 71–90. New York: Greenwood Press, 1988.

Brischetto, Robert, Charles L. Cotrell, and R. Michael Stevens. "Conflict and Change in the Political Culture of San Antonio in the 1970s." In *The Politics of San Antonio: Community, Progress, and Power,* edited by David R. Johnson, John A. Booth, and Richard J. Harris, 75–94. Lincoln: University of Nebraska Press, 1983.

"Britton Avenue, Rio Grande City." Photograph. Archive, Hidalgo County Historical Museum, Edinburg, Tex.

Broadbent, Elizabeth. *The Distribution of Mexican Population in the United States.* Originally published, Chicago: University of Chicago, 1941. Reprint, San Francisco: R and E Research Associates, 1972.

Broek, Jan O. M., and John W. Webb. *A Geography of Mankind.* 3d ed. New York: McGraw-Hill, 1978.

Broom, Leonard, and Eshref Shevky. "Mexicans in the United States: A Problem in Social Differentiation." *Sociology and Social Research* 36 (January–February 1952): 150–158.

Brown, Harold Owen. *The Building of the Texas-Mexican Railroad.* Master's thesis, Texas A&I College, 1937.

Brown, L. F., Jr., J. L. Brewton, T. J. Evans, J. H. McGowen, W. A. White, C. G. Groat, and W. L. Fisher. *Environmental Geologic Atlas of the Texas Coastal Zone—Brownsville-Harlingen Area.* Austin: University of Texas, Bureau of Economic Geology, 1980.

Brown, Linda Keller, and Kay Mussell, eds. *Ethnic and Regional Foodways in the United States: The Performance of Group Identity.* Knoxville: University of Tennessee Press, 1984.

Brownsville Herald. "San Ygnacio Has Ghost-Like Quality." January 3, 1982. 1C.

Brownsville, Texas. Scrapbook of ephemera. Archives, Center for American History, University of Texas, Austin.

Bryan–College Station Eagle. "Lawyer Wants Mexican Flag Out of City Hall." May 10, 1986. A3.

Byfield, Patsy Jeanne. *Falcon Dam and the Lost Towns of Zapata.* Miscellaneous Papers, no. 2. Austin: University of Texas Press, 1966.

Campa, Arthur L. *Hispanic Culture in the Southwest.* Norman: University of Oklahoma Press, 1979.

Campbell, Thomas N. *The Indians of Southern Texas and Northeastern Mexico.* Austin: Texas Archeological Research Laboratory, University of Texas, 1988.

Canseco Botello, José Raúl. *Historia de Matamoros.* 2d ed. Matamoros, Mex.: Tipográficos de Litográfica Jardín, 1981.

Cantú, Abelardo H. Personal communication, June 1986.

Cantú, Mary Louise T. Personal communication, June 1986.

Cantú, Norma Elia. *Canícula: Snapshots of a Girlhood en La Frontera.* Albuquerque: University of New Mexico Press, 1995.

Cardenas, Alfredo E. "A Brief History of Duval County." Duval County Courthouse, San Diego, Texas, 1983. Typescript.

———. [mayor of San Diego; editor of *Duval County Picture*]. Personal communication, San Diego, Texas, April 21, 1993, and January 30, 1997.

Cardenas, Daniel. "Mexican Spanish." In *El Lenguage de los Chicanos: Regional and Social Characteristics Used by Mexican Americans*, edited by Eduardo Hernández-Chavez, Andrew D. Cohen, and Anthony F. Beltramo, 1–5. Arlington, Va.: Center for Applied Linguistics, 1975.

Carlson, Alvar W. *The Spanish-American Homeland: Four Centuries in New Mexico's Río Arriba.* Baltimore: Johns Hopkins University Press, 1991.

Carlson, Paul H. *Texas Woollybacks: The Range Sheep and Goat Industry.* College Station: Texas A&M University Press, 1982.

Carson, Chris, and William McDonald, eds. *A Guide to San Antonio Architecture.* San Antonio: San Antonio Chapter of the American Institute of Architects, 1986.

Carver, Craig M. *American Regional Dialects: A Word Geography.* Ann Arbor: University of Michigan Press, 1987.

Casstevens, Mary Anna. "Randado: The Built Environment of a Texas-Mexican Ranch." In *Hecho en Tejas: Texas-Mexican Folk Arts and Crafts*, edited by Joe S. Graham, 309–334. Texas Folklore Society Publication no. 50. Denton, Tex.: University of North Texas Press, 1991.

Castañeda, Carlos E. *Our Catholic Heritage in Texas, 1519–1936.* 7 vols. Austin: Von Boeckmann-Jones, 1936.

Caudill-Rowlett-Scott. *Area Development Plan: Laredo and Webb County, Texas. Report 1: Community Inventory and Development Concepts.* Houston: Caudill-Rowlett-Scott Architects, Engineers, Planners, 1964.

Chambers, William T. "Geographic Regions of Texas." *Texas Geographical Magazine* 12 (1948): 9–11.

———. "San Antonio, Texas." *Economic Geography* 16 (July 1940): 291–298.

"Charro Days Has Colorful History." Local History File. McAllen Memorial Library, McAllen, Texas.

Chatfield, W. H. *The Twin Cities of the Border and the Country of the Rio Grande.* New Orleans: E. P. Brandao, 1893.

Chávez, John R. *The Lost Land: The Chicano Image of the Southwest.* Albuquerque: University of New Mexico Press, 1984.

Chevalier, Francois. *Land and Society in Colonial Mexico: The Great Hacienda.* Berkeley: University of California Press, 1963.

Chipman, Donald E. *Nuño de Guzmán and the Province of Pánuco in New Spain, 1518–1533.* Glendale, Calif.: A. H. Clark, 1967.

Christian, Jane MacNab, and Chester C. Christian, Jr. "Spanish Language and Culture in the Southwest." In *Language Loyalty in the United States: The Maintenance and*

Perpetuation of Non-English Mother Tongues by American Ethnic and Religious Groups, edited by Joshua A. Fishman, 280–317. The Hague: Mouton, 1966.

Christian Science Monitor. "*Colonia* Families Put Up with Much to Own Land." August 4, 1986. 1, 32.

Cisneros, Sandra. "Purple Casa (Casa Violeta)." *Aula: Architecture and Urbanism in Las Américas / Arquitectura y urbanismo en Las Américas* 1 (spring/primavera 1999): 32–38.

Clark, John W., Jr., and Ana Maria Juárez. *Urban Archaeology: A Culture History of a Mexican-American Barrio in Laredo, Webb County, Texas*. Austin: Texas State Department of Highways and Public Transportation, 1986.

Clarke, W. P. *Map of San Antonio, 1924*. San Antonio, Tex.: Institute of Texan Cultures, n.d.

Coe, Sophie D. *America's First Cuisines*. Austin: University of Texas Press, 1994.

Comeaux, Malcolm L. "The Tortilla Industry in Arizona." *North American Culture* 2 (1985): 15–23.

Corner, William. *San Antonio de Bexar: A Guide and History*. San Antonio: Bainbridge and Corner, 1890.

Corpus Christi Caller-Times. "San Diego Gets Lots of Notice for Town of Only 5,000 People." June 27, 1954. D16.

Cosgrove, Denis. "Prospect, Perspective, and the Evolution of the Landscape Idea." *Transactions, Institute of British Geographers*, n.s., 10 (1985): 45–62.

Cotulla, Texas. *Map of the Town of Cotulla Located on the International and Great Northern Railroad. La Salle, County, Texas. Ca. 1881*. San Antonio, Tex.: Institute of Texan Cultures, n.d.

Cox, I. J. "The Southwest Boundary of Texas." *Quarterly of the Texas State Historical Association* 6 (October 1902): 81–102.

Crang, Mike. *Cultural Geography*. London: Routledge, 1998.

Crook, Carland Elaine. *San Antonio, Texas, 1846–1861*. Master's thesis, Rice University, 1964.

Crouch, Dora P., Daniel J. Garr, and Axel I. Mundigo. *Spanish City Planning in North America*. Cambridge, Mass.: MIT Press, 1982.

Cruz, Gilbert R. *Let There Be Towns: Spanish Municipal Origins in the American Southwest, 1610–1810*. College Station: Texas A&M University Press, 1988.

Cruz, Lauro. *Developing South Texas: A Report to the Governor and Legislature—Executive Summary*. Austin: Office of the Governor, 1977.

Cunninghame [Graham], R. B. *The North American Sketches of R. B. Cunninghame Graham*. Edited with introduction by John Walker. Edinburgh: Scottish Academic Press, 1986.

Curtis, James R. "Central Business Districts of the Two Laredos." *Geographical Review* 83 (January 1993): 54–65.

Dabbs, J. Autrey. *The French Army in Mexico, 1861–1867: A Study in Military Government*. The Hague: Mouton, 1963.

Da Cámara, Kathleen. *Laredo on the Rio Grande*. San Antonio: Naylor Co., 1949.

Daddysman, James W. *The Matamoros Trade: Confederate Commerce, Diplomacy and Intrigue*. Newark: University of Delaware Press, 1984.

Davies, Christopher S., and Robert K. Holtz. "Settlement Evolution of 'Colonias' along the US-Mexico Border: The Case of the Lower Rio Grande Valley of Texas." *Habitat International* 16 (1992): 119–142.

Davis, John L. *San Antonio: A Historical Portrait*. Austin: Encino Press, 1978.

de Borhegyi, Stephen, and E. Boyd. *El santuario de Chimayó*. Santa Fe: Spanish Colonial Arts Society, 1956.

de La Fora, Nicolás. *See* La Fora, Nicolás de.

de la Peña, Rose Marie. Personal communication, June 1986.

de la Teja, Jesús F., and John Wheat. "Béxar: Profile of a Tejano Community, 1820–1832." *Southwestern Historical Quarterly* 89 (July 1985): 7–34.

De León, Arnoldo. *Benavides: The Town and Its Founder, 1880*. Duval County, Tex.: Office of Economic Development, 1980.

———. "A Social History of Mexican Americans in Nineteenth-Century Duval County." Copy of typescript in Daniel Arreola's possession.

———. *The Tejano Community, 1836–1900*. Albuquerque: University of New Mexico Press, 1982.

———. "Texas Mexicans: Twentieth-Century Interpretations." In *Texas through Time: Evolving Interpretations*, edited by Walter L. Buenger and Robert A. Calvert, 20–49. College Station: Texas A&M University Press, 1991.

De León, Arnoldo, and Kenneth L. Stewart. *Tejanos and the Numbers Game: A Socio-Historical Interpretation from the Federal Censuses, 1850–1900*. Albuquerque: University of New Mexico Press, 1989.

del Hoyo, Eugenio. *Historia del nuevo reino de León (1577–1723)*. 2 vols. Monterrey: Publicaciones del Instituto Tecnológico Estudios Superiores de Monterrey, 1972.

Dicken, Samuel N. "Cotton Regions of Mexico." *Economic Geography* 14 (October 1938): 363–371.

———. "Galeana: A Mexican Highland Community." *Journal of Geography* 34 (April 1935): 140–147.

Dodson, Ruth. "Don Pedrito Jaramillo: The Curandero of Los Olmos." In *The Healer of Los Olmos and Other Mexican Lore*, edited by Wilson M. Hudson, 9–70. Publications of the Texas Folklore Society, no. 24. Dallas: Southern Methodist University, 1951.

Duncan, James S. *The City as Text: The Politics of Landscape Interpretation in the Kandyan Kingdom*. Cambridge: Cambridge University Press, 1990.

———. "Landscape and the Communication of Social Identity." In *The Mutual Interaction of People and Their Built Environment: A Cross-Cultural Perspective*, edited by Amos Rapoport, 391–401. The Hague: Mouton, 1976.

———. "Landscape Taste as a Symbol of Group Identity: A Westchester County Village." *Geographical Review* 63 (July 1973): 334–355.

Duncan, James S., and David Ley, eds. *Place / Culture / Representation*. London: Routledge, 1993.

Dunson. Jack, ed. *The Gateway*. San Antonio: Graphic Arts Engraving Co., 1931.

Emory, William H. *Report on the United States and Mexican Boundary Survey*. 3 vols. Originally published, Washington, D.C.: H. Exec. Doc. 135, 34th Cong., 1st sess., 1857–1859. Reprint, Austin: Texas State Historical Association, 1987.

Entrikin, J. Nicholas. *The Betweeness of Place: Towards a Geography of Modernity*. London: Macmillan, 1991.

Espinosa Rescala, Juan Carlos, Rob Harrison, and B. F. McCullough. *Effect of the North American Free Trade Agreement on the Transportation Infrastructure in the Laredo–Nuevo Laredo Area*. Research report 1312–2. Austin: Center for Transportation Research, University of Texas, 1993.

Estado general de las fundaciones hechas por D. José de Escandón en la colonia del Nuevo

Santander, costa del Seno Mexicano. 2 vols. Mexico, D.F.: Talleres Gráficos de la Nación, 1929–1930.

Everett, Donald E. *San Antonio: The Flavor of Its Past, 1845–1898.* San Antonio: Trinity University Press, 1975.

Falvella, J.W. *A Souvenir Album of Laredo the Gateway to Mexico.* Privately published, 1917.

Faulk, Odie B. *The Last Years of Spanish Texas, 1778–1821.* The Hague: Mouton, 1964.

Federal Writers' Project, Texas. *San Antonio: An Authoritative Guide to the City and Its Environs.* San Antonio: Clegg Co., 1938.

———. *The WPA Guide to Texas.* Originally published, *Texas: A Guide to the Lone Star State.* New York: Hastings House, 1940. Reprint, Austin: Texas Monthly Press, 1986.

Fehrenbach, T. R. *The San Antonio Story.* Tulsa, Okla.: Continental Heritage, 1979.

Ferguson, Walter Keene, and Barbara Hartman. *The Geographical Provinces of Texas.* Map. N.p., n.d.

Fish, Jean Y. *José Vásquez Borrego and La Hacienda de Nuestra Señora de Dolores.* Zapata, Tex.: Zapata County Historical Society, 1991.

———. *Zapata County Roots Revisited.* Edinburg, Tex.: New Santander Press, 1990.

Flandrau, Charles Malcolm. *¡Viva Mexico!* Edited and with an Introduction by C. Harvey Gardiner. Originally published, New York: D. Appleton, 1908. Reprint, Urbana: University of Illinois Press, 1964.

Flores, Richard R. *Los Pastores: History and Performance in the Mexican Shepherd's Play of South Texas.* Washington: Smithsonian Institution Press, 1995.

Foik, Paul J. "Captain Don Domingo Ramón's Diary of His Expedition into Texas in 1716." *Preliminary Studies of the Texas Catholic Historical Society* 2 (1933): 3–23.

Foley, Douglas E., and Clarice Mota, Donald E. Post, and Ignacio Lozano. *From Peones to Políticos: Ethnic Relations in a South Texas Town, 1900–1977.* Austin: Center for Mexican American Studies, University of Texas, 1977.

Foley, Neil. "Mexican Migrant and Tenant Labor in Central Texas Cotton Counties, 1880–1930: Social and Economic Transformation in a Multicultural Society." *Wooster Review* 9 (spring 1989): 95–99.

———. *White Scourge: Mexicans, Blacks and Poor Whites in Texas Cotton Culture.* Berkeley: University of California Press, 1997.

Foote, Kenneth E., Peter J. Hugill, Kent Mathewson, and Jonathan M. Smith, eds. *Re-Reading Cultural Geography.* Austin: University of Texas Press, 1994.

Foscue, Edwin J. "Land Utilization in the Lower Rio Grande Valley of Texas." *Economic Geography* 8 (January 1932): 1–11.

Foster, George M. *Culture and Conquest: America's Spanish Heritage.* Viking Fund Publications in Anthropology, no. 27. New York: Wenner-Gren Foundation, 1960.

Fowler, Sheri. "Tested by Fire: A South Texas Town Rebuilds Its Church with Faith, Hope, and Lots of Charity." *Texas Monthly* (August 1993): 72–73.

Frantz, Joe B., and Mike Cox. *Lure of the Land: Texas County Maps and the History of Settlement.* College Station: Texas A&M University Press, 1988.

Frary, I. T. "Picturesque Towns of the Borderland." *Architectural Record* 44 (April 1919): 382–384.

Freisleben, G. *San Antonio and Its Ancient Wards.* Map, 1845. Archives, Center for American History, University of Texas, Austin.

Galván, Roberto A., and Richard V. Teschner. *El diccionario del español de Tejas / The Dictionary of the Spanish of Texas.* Silver Spring, Md.: Institute of Modern Languages, 1975.

Gamio, Manuel. *The Life Story of the Mexican Immigrant*. Chicago: University of Chicago Press, 1931. Reprint, New York: Dover Publications, 1971.

————. *Mexican Immigration to the United States: A Study of Human Migration and Adjustment*. Chicago: University of Chicago Press, 1930. Reprint, New York: Dover Publications, 1971.

García, Ignacio M. *United We Win: The Rise and Fall of La Raza Unida Party*. Tucson: University of Arizona Press, 1989.

García, Lionel G. *I Can Hear the Cowbells Ring*. Houston: Arte Público Press, 1994.

García, Mario T. *Desert Immigrants: The Mexicans of El Paso, 1880–1920*. New Haven: Yale University Press, 1981.

García, Richard A. *Rise of the Mexican American Middle Class: San Antonio, 1929–1941*. College Station: Texas A&M University Press, 1990.

García Cubas, Antonio. *Atlas geográfico, estadístico e histórico de la República Mexicana*. Mexico, D.F.: 1858.

García de Miranda, Enriqueta. *Nuevo atlas Porrúa de la República Mexicana*. Mexico, D.F.: Editorial Porrúa, 1989.

Gardner, Dore. *Niño Fidencio: A Heart Thrown Open*. Photographs and interviews by Dore Gardner, with an essay by Kay F. Turner. Santa Fe: Museum of New Mexico Press, 1992.

Garreau, Joel. *The Nine Nations of North America*. Boston: Houghton Mifflin, 1981.

Garrett, Wilbur E., ed. "A Grand Fiesta Called Hispanics." In *Historical Atlas of the United States*, edited by Wilbur E. Garrett, 72–73. Washington, D.C.: National Geographic Society, 1988.

Geertz, Clifford. "Thick Description: Toward an Interpretive Theory of Culture." In *The Interpretation of Cultures*, by Clifford Geertz, 3–30. New York: Basic Books, 1973.

Gehlbach, Frederick R. *Mountain Islands and Desert Seas: A Natural History of the U.S.-Mexican Borderlands*. College Station: Texas A&M University Press, 1981.

George, Eugene. *Historic Architecture of Texas: The Falcon Reservoir*. Austin: Texas Historical Commission and Texas Historical Foundation, 1975.

Gerhard, Peter. *The North Frontier of New Spain*. Princeton: Princeton University Press, 1982.

Gilmore, Kathleen. "Spanish Colonial Settlements in Texas." In *Texas Archeology: Essays Honoring R. King Harris*, edited by Kurt D. House, 132–145. Dallas: Southern Methodist University Press, 1978.

Glassie, Henry. *Passing Time in Ballymenone: Culture and History of an Ulster Community*. Philadelphia: University of Pennsylvania Press, 1982.

Glazer, Mark. [director, Rio Grande Folklore Archive, University of Texas, Pan-American, Edinburg]. Personal communication, January 27, 1997.

————, ed. *Flour from Another Sack and Other Proverbs, Folk Beliefs, Tales, Riddles, and Recipes*. Edinburg, Tex.: University of Texas–Pan American Press, 1994.

Godfrey, Brian J. *Neighborhoods in Transition: The Making of San Francisco's Ethnic and Nonconformist Communities*. University of California Publications in Geography, no. 27. Berkeley: University of California Press, 1988.

González, Jorge. [former curator, Nuevo Santander Museum, Laredo State University, Laredo, Texas]. Personal communication, January 9, 1991.

González, Jovita. "America Invades the Border Towns." *Southwest Review* 15 (summer 1930): 469–477.

————. *Social Life in Cameron, Starr, and Zapata Counties*. Master's thesis, University of Texas, Austin, 1930.

Graf, Leroy P. "Colonizing Projects in Texas South of the Nueces, 1820–1845." *Southwestern Historical Quarterly* 50 (April 1947): 431–448.

Graham, Joe S. "The Built Environment in South Texas: The Hispanic Legacy." In *Hispanic Texas: A Historical Guide*, edited by Helen Simons and Cathryn A. Hoyt, 58–75. Austin: University of Texas Press, 1992.

————. "Folk Medicine and Intercultural Diversity among West Texas Mexican Americans." *Western Folklore* 44 (July 1985): 168–193.

————. *Hispanic-American Material Culture: An Annotated Directory of Collections, Sites, Archives, and Festivals in the United States*. New York: Greenwood Publishers, 1989.

————. "The *Jacal* in South Texas: The Origins and Forms of a Folk House." In *Hecho en Tejas: Texas-Mexican Folk Arts and Crafts*, edited by Joe S. Graham, 293–308. Texas Folklore Society Publication 50. Denton, Tex.: University of North Texas Press, 1991.

————. "Mexican-American Traditional Foodways at La Junta de los Rios." *Journal of Big Bend Studies* 2 (January 1990): 1–27.

————. *El Rancho in South Texas: Continuity and Change from 1750*. Denton, Tex.: University of North Texas Press, 1994.

Granneberg, Audrey. "Maury Maverick's San Antonio." *Survey Graphic: Magazine of Social Interpretation* 28 (July 1939): 421–426.

Grebler, Leo, Joan W. Moore, and Ralph C. Guzman. *The Mexican-American People: The Nation's Second-Largest Minority*. New York: Free Press, 1970.

Griffith, James S. *Beliefs and Holy Places: A Spiritual Geography of the Pimería Alta*. Tucson: University of Arizona Press, 1992.

————. *A Shared Space: Folklife in the Arizona-Sonora Borderlands*. Logan: Utah State University Press, 1995.

Grimm, Agnes G. *Llanos Mesteñas: Mustang Plains*. Waco: Texian Press, 1968.

Griswold del Castillo, Richard. *La Familia: Chicano Families in the Urban Southwest, 1848 to Present*. Notre Dame: University of Notre Dame Press, 1984.

————. "Tejanos and California Chicanos: Regional Variations in Mexican American History." *Mexican Studies/Estudios Mexicanos* 1 (1985): 134–139.

Groth, Paul, and Todd W. Bressi, eds. *Understanding Ordinary Landscapes*. New Haven: Yale University Press, 1997.

Guajardo, Luciano. [director, Historical Collection, Laredo Public Library, Laredo, Texas]. Personal communication, January 9, 1991.

Guerra, Fermina. *Mexican and Spanish Folklore and Incidents in Southwest Texas*. San Antonio: San Antonio Press, 1979.

Guerra, Mary Ann Noonan. *The History of San Antonio's Market Square*. San Antonio: Alamo Press, 1988.

Guide to Spanish and Mexican Land Grants in South Texas. Austin: Texas General Land Office, 1988.

Gutiérrez, Blanca M. "The Shrine of La Virgen de San Juan del Valle." In *Border Life in the Rio Grande Valley: Essays of Remembrance and Research*, edited by Hal Kopel, 105–109. Edinburg, Tex.: Hidalgo County Historical Society, 1996.

Hammett, A. B. J. *The Empresario Don Martin De León*. Waco: Texian Press, 1973.

Handman, Max Sylvius. "The Mexican Immigrant in Texas." *Southwestern Political and Social Science Quarterly* 7 (June 1926): 33–41.

———. "San Antonio: The Old Capital City of Mexican Life and Influence." *Survey* 66 (1 May 1931): 163–166.

Hardoy, Jorge E. "La forma de las ciudades coloniales en la América Española." In *Estudios sobre la ciudad iberoamericana*, edited by Francisco de Solano, 315–344. Madrid: Consejo Superior de Investigaciones Científicas, Instituto Gonzalo Fernández de Oviedo, 1975.

Harris, Charles H., III. *A Mexican Family Empire: The Latifundio of the Sánchez Navarro Family, 1765–1867*. Austin: University of Texas Press, 1975.

Havard, V. "Report on the Flora of Western and Southern Texas." *Proceedings of United States National Museum* 8 (1885): 449–533.

Haverluk, Terrence William. "Chiles!" Paper presented to the Conference of Latin Americanist Geographers, Santa Fe, 1998.

———. "Hispanic Community Types and Assimilation in Mex-America." *Professional Geographer* 50 (November 1998): 465–480.

———. "A Descriptive Model for Understanding the Wider Distribution and Increasing Influence of Hispanics in the American West." Working Paper WP-04. San Antonio: Hispanic Research Center, University of Texas, 1994.

Haynes, Kingsley E. *Colonias in the Lower Rio Grande Valley of South Texas: A Summary Report*. Lyndon B. Johnson School of Public Affairs, Policy Research Report 18. Austin: University of Texas, 1977.

Heller, Dick D., Jr. "San Ygnacio, Texas." In *The New Handbook of Texas*, edited by Ron Tyler, vol. 5, 894. Austin: Texas State Historical Association, 1996.

Henderson, Floyd M. "Foodways." In *This Remarkable Continent: An Atlas of United States and Canadian Society and Cultures*, edited by John F. Rooney, Jr., Wilbur Zelinsky, and Dean R. Louder, 225–233. College Station: Texas A&M University Press, 1982.

Hernandez, Poncho, Jr. [former director, Fiesta Benavides]. Personal communication, Benavides, Texas, January 30, 1997.

Hernandez, Ramon. [Tejano music archivist]. Personal communication, San Antonio, May 15, 1997.

Herzog, Lawrence A. "Mexican-Americans and the Evolution of the San Diego, California, Built Environment." *Crítica, A Journal of Critical Essays* 1 (fall 1986): 115–134.

Hester, Thomas R. *Digging into South Texas Prehistory*. San Antonio: Corona Publishing, 1980.

Hewes, Leslie. "Huepac: An Agricultural Village of Sonora, Mexico." *Economic Geography* 11 (July 1935): 284–292.

Hill, Lawrence Francis. *José de Escandón and the Founding of Nuevo Santander: A Study in Spanish Colonization*. Columbus: Ohio State University Press, 1926.

Hinojosa, Gilberto Miguel. *A Borderlands Town in Transition: Laredo, 1755–1870*. College Station: Texas A&M University Press, 1983.

Hoffman, David. *Roma*. Austin: School of Architecture, University of Texas, 1971.

Holden, William Curry. *Teresita*. Owings Mills, Md.: Stemmer House, 1978.

Hollon, W. Eugene, and Ruth Lapham Butler. *William Bollaert's Texas*. Norman: University of Oklahoma Press, 1956.

Holm, Stanley H. La Salle County scrapbook. Editorial field copy, La Salle County, District 15, 1937 (ephemera). Archives, Center for American History, University of Texas, Austin.

Houston Chronicle. "Perpetual City" (San Diego, Tex.). July 31, 1960.

Hufford, Larry. "The Velásquez Legacy." *Texas Observer.* July 29, 1988, 6–8.

Hugill, Peter J. "The Macro-Landscape of the Wallerstein World-Economy: 'King Cotton' and the American South." In *The American South,* edited by Richard L. Nostrand and Sam B. Hilliard, 77–84. Baton Rouge: Louisiana State University, 1988.

Humboldt, Alejandro de. *Ensayo político sobre el reino de la Nueva España.* 5 vols. With an introduction and notes by Vito Alessio Robles. Mexico, D.F.: Robredo, 1941.

Huson, Hobart. *Refugio: A Comprehensive History of Refugio County.* 2 vols. Woodsboro, Tex.: Rooke Foundation, 1953–1955.

Inglis, Jack M. *A History of Vegetation on the Rio Grande Plain.* Texas Parks and Wildlife Department Bulletin 45. Austin: Texas Parks and Wildlife Department, 1964.

Isbell, Frances W., ed. *Hidalgo County Ranch Histories.* Edinburg, Tex.: Hidalgo County Historical Society, 1994.

Issac, Eric. "The Act and the Covenant." *Landscape* 11 (winter 1961–1962): 12–17.

Jackson, Jack. *Los Mesteños: Spanish Ranching in Texas, 1721–1821.* College Station: Texas A&M University Press, 1986.

Jackson, John Brinckerhoff. "Learning about Landscapes." In *The Necessity for Ruins and Other Topics,* J. B. Jackson, 1–18. Amherst: University of Massachusetts Press, 1980.

Jackson, Peter. *Maps of Meaning: An Introduction to Cultural Geography.* Originally published, Unwin Hyman, 1989. Reprint, London: Routledge, 1992.

Jarboe, Jan. "The Week of the Virgin." *Texas Monthly* 13 (December 1985): 138–145.

Jasper, Pat and Kay Turner. *Art among Us / Arte Entre Nosotros: Mexican American Folk Art of San Antonio.* San Antonio: San Antonio Museum Association, 1986.

Jenkins, John H. *Basic Texas Books: An Annotated Bibliography of Selected Works for a Research Library.* Rev. ed. Austin: Texas State Historical Association, 1988.

John, Elizabeth A. H. *Storms Brewed in Other Men's Worlds: The Confrontation of Indians, Spanish, and French in the Southwest, 1540–1795.* College Station: Texas A&M University Press, 1975.

Johnson, A. P. *Map of Carrizo Springs, Dimmit County, 1914.* Carrizo Springs Public Library, Carrizo Springs, Texas.

Johnson, Elmer H. *The Natural Regions of Texas.* University of Texas Bulletin 3113. Austin: University of Texas, 1931.

Johnston, Marshall C. "Past and Present Grasslands of Southern Texas and Northeastern Mexico." *Ecology* 44 (1963): 456–466.

Jones, John M., ed. *La Hacienda: Spirit of Val Verde.* Del Rio, Tex.: Whitehead Museum and Val Verde County Historical Commission, 1990.

Jones, Oakah L. *Los Paisanos: Spanish Settlers on the Northern Frontier of New Spain.* Norman: University of Oklahoma Press, 1979.

Jones, Richard C. "Changing Patterns of Undocumented Mexican Migration to South Texas." *Social Science Quarterly* 65 (1984): 465–481.

Jordan, Terry G. "The Anglo-Texan Homeland." *Journal of Cultural Geography* 13 (spring/summer 1993): 75–86.

———. "A Century and a Half of Ethnic Change in Texas, 1836–1986." *Southwestern Historical Quarterly* 89 (April 1986): 385–422.

———. "The Concept and Method." In *Regional Studies: The Interplay of Land and People,* edited by Glen E. Lich, 8–24. College Station: Texas A&M University Press, 1992.

————. *North American Cattle-Ranching Frontiers: Origins, Diffusion, and Differentiation.* Albuquerque: University of New Mexico Press, 1993.

————. "Perceptual Regions in Texas." *Geographical Review* 68 (July 1978): 293–307.

Jordan, Terry G., with John L. Bean Jr. and William M. Holmes. *Texas: A Geography.* Boulder: Westview Press, 1984.

Jordan-Bychkov, Terry, and Mona Domash. *The Human Mosaic: A Thematic Introduction to Cultural Geography,* 8th ed. New York: Longman, 1999.

Juárez, José Roberto. "La Iglesia Católica y el chicano en Sud Texas, 1836–1911." *Aztlán* 4 (fall 1973): 217–255.

Kanellos, Nicolás. *A History of Hispanic Theatre in the United States: Origins to 1940.* Austin: University of Texas Press, 1990.

Kaplan, Anne R., Marjorie A. Hoover, and Willard B. Moore. "Introduction: On Ethnic Foodways." In *The Taste of American Place: A Reader on Regional and Ethnic Foods,* edited by Barbara G. Shortridge and James R. Shortridge, 121–133. Lanham, Md.: Rowman and Littlefield, 1998.

Kearney, Milo, and Anthony Knopp. *Border Cuates: A History of the U.S.-Mexican Twin Cities.* Austin: Eakin Press, 1995.

Kelley, Pat. *River of Lost Dreams: Navigation on the Rio Grande.* Lincoln: University of Nebraska Press, 1986.

Kell-Muñoz-Wigodsky, Architects. "*Mestizo* Regionalism: Cultural Activism in the Built Environment along the Texas-Mexico Border." Kell-Muñoz-Wigodsky, San Antonio, Texas, n.d. Typescript.

Kendall, Dorothy Steinbomer, and Carmen Perry. *Gentilz: Artist of the Old Southwest.* Austin: University of Texas Press, 1974.

Kerr, Homer L. *Migration into Texas, 1865–1880.* Ph.D. diss., University of Texas, Austin, 1953.

Kibbe, Pauline R. *Latin Americans in Texas.* Albuquerque: University of New Mexico Press, 1946.

Kingston, Mike, ed. *1990–91 Texas Almanac and State Industrial Guide.* Dallas: A. H. Belo, 1989.

Kinnaird, Lawrence. *The Frontiers of New Spain: Nicolás de Lafora's Description, 1766–1768.* Berkeley: Quivira Society, 1958.

Klein, Alan M. *Baseball on the Border: A Tale of Two Laredos.* Princeton: Princeton University Press, 1997.

Kohout, Martin Donell. "San Diego, Texas." In *The New Handbook of Texas,* edited by Ron Tyler, vol. 5, 832–834. Austin: Texas State Historical Association, 1996.

Kruszewski, Z. Anthony. "Territorial Minorities: Some Sociopolitical and International Aspects and Their Possible Implications." In *Politics and Society in the Southwest: Ethnicity and Chicano Pluralism,* edited by Z. Anthony Kruszewski, Richard L. Hough, and Jacob Ornstein-Galicia, 268–275. Boulder, Colo.: Westview Press, 1982.

Labastida, Ygnacio de. *Plano de la Ciudad de Béjar y fortificación del Alamo.* Map, 1836. Archives, Center for American History, University of Texas, Austin.

La Fora, Nicolás de. *Relación del viaje que hizo a los presidios internos situados en la frontera de la América Septentrional perteneciente al rey de España.* Mexico, D.F.: P. Robredo, 1939.

Landolt, Robert Garland. *The Mexican-American Workers of San Antonio, Texas.* New York: Arno Press, 1976. Originally, Ph.D. diss., University of Texas, Austin, 1965.

Laredo Chamber of Commerce. *The Gateway to Mexico: Laredo, South Texas.* 1926. Luciano Guajardo Historical Collection, Laredo Public Library, Laredo, Texas.

Laredo, City of. *Historic Preservation Plan*. Laredo: City of Laredo, 1996.

Laredo News. "Barbacoa: Sunday Treat." November 30, 1980. A2.

————. "Old San Ygnacio Customhouse 'Made It Legal Two Days a Week.'" July 18, 1982.

————. "Uribe Event Sets Record." October 9, 1983. A1, A6.

Laredo Times. "Holiday Excursionists See Typical Border Community." July 6, 1961. 5.

————. "Hundreds Gather to Honor Virgen de San Juan." June 28, 1981. C10.

————. "San Ygnacio: Sleepy South Texas Town Is Rich in History, Tradition." July 15, 1979.

————. "There Was a Homecoming in San Ygnacio." June 25, 1978.

————. "Tourists Favor San Ygnacio." May 25, 1975. D2, D23.

Lasater, Dale. *Falfurrias: Ed C. Lasater and the Development of South Texas*. College Station: Texas A&M University Press, 1985.

Lea, Tom. *The King Ranch*. 2 vols. Boston: Little, Brown, 1957.

Lehmann, V. W. *Forgotten Legions: Sheep in the Rio Grande Plain of Texas*. El Paso: Texas Western Press, 1969.

León-Portilla, Miguel. "The Norteño Variety of Mexican Culture: An Ethno-historical Approach." In *Plural Society in the Southwest*, edited by Edward M. Spicer and Raymond H. Thompson, 77–114. Albuquerque: University of New Mexico Press, 1972.

Lewis, Peirce F. "Axioms for Reading the Landscape: Some Guides to the American Scene." In *The Interpretation of Ordinary Landscapes: Geographical Essays*, edited by D. W. Meinig, 11–32. New York: Oxford University Press, 1979.

Lochbaum, Jerry. *Old San Antonio: History in Pictures*. San Antonio: Express Publishing Co., 1965.

Los Angeles Times. "A Cultural Diamond in the Rough. San Antonio Has Emerged as an Artistic and Political Mecca for Latinos." August 2, 1999. A1.

————. "Fajitas." May 9, 1985. Part VIII, 1, 28, 32.

————. "Purple Passions Swirl about Texas Abode." August 11, 1997. A1, A13.

Los Caminos del Rio Heritage Task Force. *Los Caminos del Rio: A Binational Heritage Project along the Lower Rio Grande*. Austin: Texas Historical Commission, 1994.

Lott, Virgil N., and Mercurio Martínez. *The Kingdom of Zapata*. San Antonio: Naylor Co., 1953.

Ludeman, Annette Martin. *La Salle: A History of La Salle County, 1856–1975*. Quanah, Tex.: Nortex Press, 1975.

Lundy, Benjamin. *Life, Travels, and Opinions of Benjamin Lundy, Including His Journeys to Texas and Mexico*. Philadelphia: William D. Parrish, 1847.

Machado, Manuel A. "The Mexican American: A Problem in Cross-Cultural Identity." In *Politics and Society in the Southwest: Ethnicity and Chicano Pluralism*, edited by Z. Anthony Kruszewski, Richard L. Hough, and Jacob Ornstein-Galicia, 47–66. Boulder, Colo.: Westview Press, 1982.

Madsen, William. *The Mexican-Americans of South Texas*. New York: Holt, Rinehart and Winston, 1964.

Markides, Kyriakos S., and Thomas Cole. "Change and Continuity in Mexican-American Religious Behavior: A Three-Generation Study." *Social Science Quarterly* 65 (June 1984): 618–625.

Martínez, Adrián, with Felix García. *Adrián: An Autobiography*. Austin: Morgan Printing, 1986.

Martínez, Higinio, Jr. [manager, City of Cotulla]. Personal communication, March 20, 1997.

Martínez, Marcos. [priest, St. John Neumann Church]. Personal communication, January 10, 1991.

Mason, H. M., Jr. *A Century on Main Plaza: A History of the Frost National Bank*. San Antonio: Frost National Bank, 1968.

Maverick, Samuel A. *Plat of Grand Plaza*. Map, 1860. Maverick Papers, Archives, Center for American History, University of Texas, Austin.

McCleskey, Clifton, and Bruce Merrill. "Mexican-American Political Behavior in Texas." *Social Science Quarterly* 53 (1973): 785–799.

McKay, Robert R. "Mexican Americans and Repatriation." In *The New Handbook of Texas*, edited by Ron Tyler, vol. 4, 676–679. Austin: Texas State Historical Association, 1996.

McVey, Lori Brown. *Guerrero Viejo: A Photographic Essay*. Occasional Papers 3. Laredo: Nuevo Santander Museum, 1988.

McWilliams, Carey. *Ill Fares the Land: Migrants and Migratory Labor in the United States*. Boston: Little, Brown, 1942.

———. "Mexicans to Michigan." *Common Ground* 2 (1941): 5–17.

———. *North from Mexico: The Spanish-Speaking People of the United States*. Originally published 1948. Reprint, New York: Greenwood Press, 1968.

Meier, Matt S., and Feliciano Rivera. *Dictionary of Mexican American History*. Westport, Conn.: Greenwood Press, 1981.

Meinig, D. W. "The Beholding Eye: Ten Versions of the Same Scene." In *The Interpretation of Ordinary Landscapes: Geographical Essays*, edited by D. W. Meinig, 33–48. New York: Oxford University Press, 1979.

———. "Environmental Appreciation: Localities as a Humane Art." *Western Humanities Review* 25 (1971): 1–11.

———. *Imperial Texas: An Interpretive Essay in Cultural Geography*. Austin: University of Texas Press, 1969.

———. "The Mormon Culture Region: Strategies and Patterns in the Geography of the American West, 1847–1964." *Annals of the Association of American Geographers* 55 (June 1965): 191–220.

———. "The Shaping of America, 1850–1915." *Journal of Historical Geography* 25 (1999): 1–16.

———. *Southwest: Three Peoples in Geographical Change, 1600–1970*. New York: Oxford University Press, 1971.

———., ed. *The Interpretation of Ordinary Landscapes: Geographical Essays*. New York: Oxford University Press, 1979.

Melville, Margarita B. "The Mexican-American and the Celebration of the *Fiestas Patrias*: An Ethnohistorical Analysis." *Grito del Sol: A Chicano Quarterly* 3 (January–March 1978): 107–116.

Menefee, Sheldon C. *Mexican Migratory Workers of South Texas*. Washington, D.C.: Works Progress Administration, 1941.

México. Comisión Pesquisidora de la Frontera Norte. *Reports of the Committee of Investigation, Sent in 1873 by the Mexican Government to the Frontier of Texas*. Translated from the official edition. New York: Baker and Godwin, 1875.

México en cifras (Atlas estadístico), 1934. Mexico, D.F.: Secretaría de la Economía Nacional, Dirección General de Estadística.

Miller, Michael V. "Chicano Community Control in South Texas: Problems and Prospects." *Journal of Ethnic Studies* 3 (fall 1975): 70–89.

Miller, Ray. *The Eyes of Texas Travel Guide. San Antonio/Border Edition.* Houston: Cordovan Corporation Publishers, 1979.

Mitchell, Don. *Cultural Geography: A Critical Introduction.* Oxford: Blackwell Publishers, 2000.

Mitchell, Q. *50th Anniversary, Jim Hogg County: 1913–1963.* Hebbronville, Tex.: Chamber of Commerce, 1963.

Monitor. [McAllen, Texas]. "Bakers Raise Bread to Art Form." November 7, 1993. B1, B2.

———. "Bread Battle Continues Old Cooking Method: Two Compete to Make the Best Mexican Pastry over Coals." January 22, 1995. B1.

———. "Crowd Gathers to View Apparition." August 10, 1993. A1, A10.

———. "Don Pedrito, Curandero without Peer." May 19, 1991. A13, A14.

———. "Faithful Still Flocking to Mary's Image on Auto." October 5, 1993. A1.

———. "Feisty Queen of Fast Food Turns Ambition into Tasty Valley Tradition." June 18, 1995. A1, A11.

———. "Getting Your Goat." February 26, 1992. C1, C2.

———. "Hundreds See Tortilla; Faith Healing is Claimed." March 10, 1983. A1, A10.

———. "Image on Tortilla Draws Crowds to Hidalgo Home." March 4, 1983. A1, A12.

———. "Lack of Standards: Helter-skelter Housing." May 3, 1994. A1, A6.

———. "The Lore and Legend of El Niño Fidencio." October 22, 1995. D1, D2.

———. "Moo-choo Sabroso. Barbacoa, or Cow's Head Barbecue, Is a Weekend Delicacy for Those Raised in the Mexican Culture." April 22, 1992. D1, D2.

———. "New Type of Development: Much Like Old." May 1, 1994. A1, A14.

———. "Old San Isidro." July 31, 1983.

———. "Our Lady of Guadalupe Replica Becomes Pilgrimage Focus." June 17, 1995. D2.

———. "Restaurant 'Taco Wars' Heat Up in Valley." May 20, 1993. C1, C2.

———. "El Sauz Folks Relish Small-Town Life." March 8, 1992. A17, A18.

———. "Tortillas Catching Up to Bread's Popularity." September 16, 1993. B1, B5.

———. "Town inside a Town Has a Long Way to Go." January 14, 1996. A1, A8.

Montaño, Mario. *The History of Mexican Folk Foodways of South Texas: Street Vendors, Offal Foods, and Barbacoa de Cabeza.* Ph.D. diss., University of Pennsylvania, 1992.

Montejano, David. *Anglos and Mexicans in the Making of Texas, 1836–1986.* Austin: University of Texas Press, 1987.

Moore, Joan, and Raquel Pinderhughes, eds. *In the Barrios: Latinos and the Underclass Debate.* New York: Russell Sage Foundation, 1993.

Mortland, John. "Border Music: A Veteran Filmmaker's New Documentary Looks at the Rich History of Tejano." *Texas Monthly* (September 1993): 98, 103.

Mounce, Gary. "Popular Culture and Politics: The Pelea de Gallo (Cockfight) in South Texas." In *South Texas Studies*, vol. 1, 1–36. Victoria, Tex.: Victoria College Press, 1990.

Myres, Sandra L. *The Ranch in Spanish Texas, 1691–1800.* El Paso: Texas Western Press, 1969.

National Association of Latino Elected and Appointed Officials. *1990 National Roster of Hispanic Elected Officials.* Washington, D.C.: NALEO Education Fund, 1991.

Newcomb, Pearson. *The Alamo City*. San Antonio: Standard Printing Co., 1926.

Newcomb, William W., Jr. *The Indians of Texas: From Prehistoric to Modern Times*. Austin: University of Texas Press, 1961.

New York Times. "Novelist's Purple Palette Is Not to Everyone's Taste." July 13, 1998. A14.

———. "Texas and California: 2 Views of Illegal Aliens." June 26, 1994, I-8.

Nolan, Mary Lee. "The Mexican Pilgrimage Tradition." *Pioneer America* 1 (July 1973): 13–27.

Norton, William. *Cultural Geography: Themes, Concepts, Analyses*. Oxford: Oxford University Press, 2000.

———. *Explorations in the Understanding of Landscape: A Cultural Geography*. New York: Greenwood Press, 1989.

Norwine, Jim, and Ralph Bingham. "Frequency and Severity of Droughts in South Texas: 1900–1983." In *Livestock and Wildlife Management during Drought*, edited by R. Braun, 1–17. Kingsville, Tex.: Caesar Kleberg Wildlife Research Institute, Texas A&I University, 1985.

Nostrand, Richard L. "A Changing Culture Region." In *Borderlands Sourcebook: A Guide to the Literature of Northern Mexico and the American Southwest*, edited by Ellwyn R. Stoddard, Richard L. Nostrand, and Jonathan P. West, 6–15. Norman: University of Oklahoma Press, 1983.

———. "The Hispanic-American Borderland: Delimitation of an American Culture Region." *Annals of the Association of American Geographers* 60 (December 1970): 638–661.

———. *The Hispano Homeland*. Norman: University of Oklahoma Press, 1992.

———. "The Hispano Homeland in 1900." *Annals of the Association of American Geographers* 70 (September 1980): 382–396.

———. "Mexican Americans circa 1850." *Annals of the Association of American Geographers* 65 (September 1975): 378–390.

Oberste, William H. *Texas Irish Empresarios and Their Colonies*. Austin: Von Boeckmann-Jones, 1953.

Oblate map, 1918. Lower Rio Grande Valley Archives, University of Texas, Pan American, Edinburg, Texas.

O'Conner, Kathleen Stoner. *The Presidio La Bahía del Espíritu Santo de Zúñiga, 1721 to 1846*. Austin: Von Boeckmann-Jones, 1966.

Olmsted, Frederick Law. *A Journey through Texas; or, A Saddle-Trip on the Southwestern Frontier*. Originally published, New York: Dix, Edwards, 1857. Reprint, Austin: University of Texas Press, 1978.

La Onda de Corpus Christi. "San Diego Celebrates Annual Pan de Campo Fiesta." August 1996.

Ornstein-Galicia, Jacob. "Varieties of Southwest Spanish: Some Neglected Basic Considerations." In *Latino Language and Communicative Behavior*, edited by Richard P. Duran, 19–38. Norwood, N.J.: Ablex Publishing, 1981.

O'Shea, Elena Zamora. *El Mesquite, A Story of the Early Spanish Settlements between the Nueces and the Rio Grande as Told by "La Posta del Palo Alto."* Dallas: Mathis Publishing, 1935.

Paredes, Américo. *Folklore and Culture on the Texas-Mexican Border*. Edited by Richard Bauman. Austin: Center for Mexican American Studies, University of Texas, 1993.

————. "El folklore de los grupos de origen mexicano en los Estados Unidos." *Folklore Americano* 14 (1966): 146–163.

————. "The Problem of Identity in a Changing Culture along the Lower Río Grande Border." In *Views across the Border: The United States and Mexico*, edited by Stanley R. Ross, 68–94. Albuquerque: University of New Mexico Press, 1978.

Patoski, Joe Nick. *Selena como la flor.* New York: Boulevard Books, 1996.

Pattan, M. *Town of San Antonio de Bejar.* Map, 1836. Archives, Center for American History, University of Texas, Austin.

Peña, Manuel H. "From *Ranchero* to *Jaitón*: Ethnicity and Class in Texas-Mexican Music (Two Styles in the Form of a Pair)." In *Between Two Worlds: Mexican Immigrants in the United States*, edited by David G. Gutiérrez, 149–174. Wilmington, Del.: Scholarly Resources, 1996.

————. *Música Tejana: The Cultural Economy of Artistic Transformation.* College Station: Texas A&M University Press, 1999.

————. *The Texas-Mexican Conjunto: History of a Working-Class Music.* Austin: Center for Mexican American Studies, University of Texas Press, 1985.

Peñalosa, Fernando, and Edward C. McDonagh. "Social Mobility in a Mexican-American Community." *Social Forces* 44 (June 1966): 498–505.

Pérez, Oliver. Personal communication, June 1986.

Peyton, Green [Wertebaker]. *San Antonio, City in the Sun.* New York: McGraw Hill and Whittlesey House, 1946.

Peyton, James W. *La Cocina de la Frontera: Mexican-American Cooking from the Southwest.* Santa Fe: Red Crane Books, 1994.

Picturesque San Antonio. San Antonio: Sigmund Press, 1910.

Pierce, Frank G. *A Brief History of the Lower Rio Grande Valley.* Menasha, Wis.: George Banta Publishing, 1917.

Pilcher, Jeffrey M. *¡Que Vivan los Tamales! Food and the Making of Mexican Identity.* Albuquerque: University of New Mexico Press, 1998.

Pillsbury, Richard. *No Foreign Food: The American Diet in Time and Place.* Boulder, Colo.: Westview Press, 1998.

Pletcher, David M. *The Diplomacy of Annexation: Texas, Oregon, and the Mexican War.* Columbia: University of Missouri Press, 1973.

Poyo, Gerald E. "Immigrants and Integration in Late-Eighteenth-Century Béxar." In *Tejano Origins in Eighteenth-Century San Antonio*, edited by Gerald E. Poyo and Gilberto M. Hinojosa, 85–104. Austin: University of Texas Press, 1991.

Poyo, Gerald E., and Gilberto M. Hinojosa, eds. *Tejano Origins in Eighteenth-Century San Antonio.* Austin: University of Texas Press, 1991.

Pulido, Alberto L. "Mexican American Catholicism in the Southwest: The Transformation of a Popular Religion." In *Emerging Themes in Mexican American Research*, edited by Juan R. García, 93–108. Perspectives in Mexican American Studies 4. Tucson: Mexican American Studies and Research Center, University of Arizona, 1993.

"Quiosco." In *Enciclopedia universal ilustrada europeo-americana*, vol. 48, 1416. Madrid: Espasa-Calfe, 1922.

Rafferty, Robert R. *Texas: The Newest, the Biggest, the Most Complete Guide to All of Texas.* Rev. 2d ed. Austin: Texas Monthly Press, 1989.

Raisz, Erwin. *Landforms of the United States.* 1957 map. Danvers, Mass.: Geoplus, 1998.

Reavis, Dick J. "The Saint of Falfurrias." *Texas Monthly* 10 (January 1982): 98–103.

Reddy, Martha A., ed. *Statistical Record of Hispanic Americans.* Detroit: Gale Research, 1993.

Reinhartz, Dennis. "Two Manuscript Maps of *Nuevo Santander* in Northern New Spain from the Eighteenth Century." In *Images & Icons of the New World*, edited by Karen Severud Cook, 55–65. Cambridge: Cambridge University Press, 1996.

Reisler, Mark. *By the Sweat of Their Brow: Mexican Immigrant Labor in the United States, 1900–1940.* Westport, Conn.: Greenwood Press, 1976.

Reps, John W. *Cities of the American West: A History of Frontier Urban Planning.* Princeton: Princeton University Press, 1979.

Reyna, José R. "Notes on Tejano Music." *Aztlán* 13 (spring/fall 1982): 81–94.

Rio Grande City. Map, December 1910. Map Archives, State Library, Austin, Texas.

Roads of Texas. Prepared by Texas A&M University, Cartographics Laboratory. Fredericksburg, Tex.: Shearer Publishing, 1988.

Robertson, Douglas Lee. *A Behavioral Portrait of the Mexican Plaza.* Ph.D. diss., Syracuse University, 1978.

Robinson, Willard B. "Colonial Ranch Architecture in the Spanish-Mexican Tradition." *Southwestern Historical Quarterly* 83 (October 1979): 123–150.

Roemer, Ferdinand. *Roemer's Texas: 1845 to 1847.* Translated by Oswald Mueller. Originally published, San Antonio: Standard Printing, 1935. Reprint, Waco: Texian Press, 1983.

Rogers, Thomas Guy. *The Housing Situation of the Mexicans in San Antonio, Texas.* Master's thesis, University of Texas, 1927.

Romano V., Octavio Ignacio. "Charismatic Medicine, Folk-Healing, and Folk-Sainthood." *American Anthropologist* 67 (1965): 1151–1173.

Root, Waverly, and Richard de Rochemont. *Eating in America: A History.* New York: Morrow, 1976.

Rowntree, Lester B. "The Cultural Landscape Concept in American Human Geography." In *Concepts in Human Geography*, edited by Carville Earle, Kent Mathewson, and Martin S. Kenzer, 127–159. Lanham, Md.: Rowman and Littlefield, 1996.

Rubel, Arthur J. *Across the Tracks: Mexican-Americans in a Texas City.* Austin: University of Texas Press, 1966.

Russell, Richard Joel. "Climates of Texas." *Annals, Association of American Geographers* 35 (1945): 37–52.

Salas, Roque. [director, Fiesta del Rancho]. Personal communication, Concepción, Texas, January 30, 1997.

Salinas, Martín. *Indians of the Rio Grande Delta: Their Role in the History of Southern Texas and Northeastern Mexico.* Austin: University of Texas Press, 1990.

Salter, Christopher L. *The Cultural Landscape.* Belmont, Calif.: Duxbury Press, 1971.

San Antonio Express. "San Diego Has Romantic Past, Bright Future." October 18, 1954. C1.

San Antonio Express-News. "Barbacoa a Weekend Tradition in S.A." October 22, 1997. G12.

———. [by Mike Greenberg]. "Chicano Architecture Shows Off New Takes on Hispanic Tradition." July 16, 1996. E2.

———. [by Ramiro Burr]. "The Conjunto Connection: Accordion-Driven Music Rooted in South Texas Heartland." May 11, 1997. G1, G11.

————. "'Fiesta del Rancho,' South Texas at Its Best." November 18, 1978. B1, B8.

————. [by Mike Greenberg]. "'Mestizo' Style's Roots Too Short." February 26, 1995. G1.

————. "Pan de Campo—Duval Style." August 18, 1979. B1, B8.

————. "Purple Politics." August 17, 1997. J1, J5.

————. "Tasty Taco Town Tale: The Whole Enchilada." September 7, 1986. Sunday magazine, 8–9.

————. "Tortilla Market Booming and Profits Are Zooming." November 1, 1992. J1, J6.

San Antonio Light. "Cantu's Tex-Mex Not Playing Fare." June 1, 1986. D1, D11.

————. "Chicharrón Vendors Fade Away." July 15, 1985. B1, B2.

————. "Famed S.A. Surgeon Is Dead: Urrutia, 103, a 'Legend.'" August 15, 1975. 1, 20.

————. Viva (supplement). "Sauce Wars." January 13, 1985. 19–23.

————. "Weather." January 9, 1990. E8.

Sanborn Map Co. Cotulla, La Salle County, Texas. New York: Sanborn Map Co., 1933.

————. Del Rio, Val Verde County, Texas. New York: Sanborn Map Co., 1924.

————. San Antonio, Bexar County, Texas. New York: Sanborn Map Co., 1888.

————. San Antonio, Bexar County, Texas. New York: Sanborn Map Co., 1904.

————. San Diego, Duval County, Texas. New York: Sanborn Map Co., 1885.

————. San Diego, Duval County, Texas. New York: Sanborn Map Co., 1910.

————. San Diego, Duval County, Texas. New York: Sanborn Map Co., 1922.

————. San Diego, Duval and Jim Wells Counties, Texas. New York: Sanborn Map Co., 1932.

Sanborn-Perris Map Co. Laredo, Webb County, Texas. New York: Sanborn-Perris Map Co., 1905.

————. Rio Grande City, Starr County, Texas. New York: Sanborn-Perris Map Co., 1894.

————. Roma, Starr County, Texas. New York: Sanborn-Perris Map Co., 1894.

————. San Antonio, Bexar County, Texas. New York: Sanborn-Perris Map Co., 1892.

————. San Antonio, Bexar County, Texas. New York: Sanborn-Perris Map Co., 1896.

Sánchez, George J. Becoming Mexican American: Ethnicity, Culture, and Identity in Chicano Los Angeles, 1900–1945. New York: Oxford University Press, 1993.

Sánchez, Mario L., ed. A Shared Experience: The History, Architecture and Historic Designations of the Lower Rio Grande Heritage Corridor. Austin: Los Caminos del Rio Heritage Project and the Texas Historical Commission, 1991.

San Diego Reader. "Battle of the Tongues." April 27, 2000. 5, 8.

Sandos, James A. Rebellion in the Borderlands: Anarchism and the Plan of San Diego, 1904–1923. Norman: University of Oklahoma Press, 1992.

Sands, Kathleen Mullen. Charrería Mexicana: An Equestrian Folk Tradition. Tucson: University of Arizona Press, 1993.

Santos, John Phillip. Places Left Unfinished at the Time of Creation. New York: Penguin Books, 1999.

San Ygnacio, Texas. Historic American Building Survey, Zapata County, 1936. Prints and Photos Collection, Archives Center for American History, University of Texas, Austin.

————. Mapa: terreno especial y pueblo de San Ygnacio, Tex., 1917. Colonel José Antonio Zapata Museum, Zapata, Texas.

————. *Plano de Rancho San Ignacio, Zapata Co., Texas, 1874*, by Felix A. Blucher. Map. Archives, Center for American History, University of Texas, Austin.

Sauer, Carl O. "The Personality of Mexico." *Geographical Review* 31 (July 1941): 353–364.

Saunders, Lyle, and Olen E. Leonard. *The Wetback in the Lower Rio Grande Valley of Texas*. In *Mexican Migration to the United States*, edited by Carlos E. Cortes, 3–92. Originally published, 1951. Reprint, New York: Arno Press, 1976.

Scott, Florence Johnson. "Early History of Starr County." In *Gift of the Rio: Story of Texas' Tropical Borderland*, sponsored by Valley-By-Liners, 27–40. Mission, Tex.: Border Kingdom Press, 1975.

————. "The Colonial Period: Spanish Colonization of the Lower Rio Grande, 1747–1767." In *Essays in Mexican History: The Charles Wilson Hackett Memorial Volume*, edited by Thomas E. Cotner and Carlos E. Castañeda, 3–20. Austin: University of Texas Press, 1958.

————. *Historical Heritage of the Lower Rio Grande*. Rev. ed. Waco: Texian Press, 1966.

————. *Royal Land Grants North of the Río Grande, 1777–1821*. Waco: Texian Press, 1969.

Shapiro, Harold A. "The Pecan Shellers of San Antonio, Texas." *Southwestern Social Science Quarterly* 32 (March 1952): 229–244.

Shelly, Fred M., J. Clark Archer, and G. Thomas Murauskas. "The Geography of Recent Presidential Elections in the Southwest." *Arkansas Journal of Geography* 2 (1986): 1–11.

Sheridan, Thomas E. *Los Tucsonenses: The Mexican Community in Tucson, 1854–1941*. Tucson: University of Arizona Press, 1986.

Shockley, John Staples. *Chicano Revolt in a Texas Town*. Notre Dame: University of Notre Dame Press, 1974.

Shortridge, Barbara G., and James R. Shortridge, eds. *The Taste of American Place: A Reader on Regional and Ethnic Foods*. Lanham, Md.: Rowman and Littlefield, 1998.

Simmons, Ozzie G. *Anglo Americans and Mexican Americans in South Texas*. Originally published 1952. Reprint, New York: Arno Press, 1974.

Simonds, Frederic William. *The Geography of Texas, Physical and Political*. Boston: Ginn, 1905.

Simons, Helen. "The Tex-Mex Menu." In *Hispanic Texas: A Historical Guide*, edited by Helen Simons and Cathryn A. Hoyt, 131–139. Austin: University of Texas Press, 1992.

Simons, Helen, and Cathryn A. Hoyt, eds. *Hispanic Texas: A Historical Guide*. Austin: University of Texas Press, 1992.

Sloan, John W., and Jonathan P. West. "Community Integration and Policies among Elites in Two Border Cities: Los Dos Laredos." *Journal of Inter-American and World Affairs* 18 (November 1976): 451–474.

Smith, Everett G. "Decent Places Off the Beaten Path: A Look at the Attraction of Small Communities in the United States." *Small Town* 26 (March–April 1996): 16–29.

Smith, Jeffrey S. "Spanish-American Village Anatomy." *Geographical Review* 88 (July 1998): 440–443.

Smith, Michael M. "Beyond the Borderlands: Mexican Labor in the Central Plains, 1900–1930." *Great Plains Quarterly* 1 (fall 1981): 239–251.

Sologaistoa, J. C., ed. *Guía general y directorio mexicano de San Antonio, Texas*. San Antonio: San Antonio Paper Co., 1924.

Sopher, David E. "Place and Location: Notes on the Spatial Patterning of Culture." *Social Science Quarterly* 53 (1972): 321–337.

South Texan. "Laredo Offers Hospitality to Centennial Tourists: Gateway to Mexico Affords Varied Services and Modern Accommodations." 6 (August 1936): 1–4.

South Texas Development Council. *Regional Historic Sites Survey and Development Plan.* Laredo: South Texas Development Council, 1973.

South Texas People. "70-year Traditional Religious Procession Practiced." April 25, 1984. 1.

South Texas, the Proposed 49th State. Pamphlet, 1938. Archives, Center for American History, University of Texas, Austin.

Spillman, Robert C. *A Historical Geography of Mexican American Population Patterns in the South Texas Hispanic Borderland.* Master's thesis, University of Southern Mississippi, 1977.

Spofford, Harriet Prescott. "San Antonio de Bexar." *Harper's New Monthly Magazine* 55 (November 1877): 831–850.

Spreiregen, Paul D. *Urban Design: The Architecture of Towns and Cities.* New York: McGraw-Hill, 1965.

Stambaugh, J. Lee, and Lillian J. Stambaugh. *The Lower Rio Grande Valley of Texas: Its Colonization and Industrialization, 1518–1953.* Austin: Jenkins Publishing and San Felipe Press, 1974.

Stanislawski, Dan. *The Anatomy of Eleven Towns in Michoacán.* Institute of Latin American Studies 10. Austin: University of Texas Press, 1950.

Steinfeldt, Cecilia. *San Antonio Was: Seen Through a Magic Lantern, Views from the Slide Collection of Albert Steves, Sr.* San Antonio: San Antonio Museum Association, 1978.

Talbert, Robert H. *Spanish-Name People in the Southwest and West.* Ft. Worth: Leo Potishman Foundation, Texas Christian University, 1955.

Tangum, Richard, and Dixie Watkins. *San Diego: Economic and Environmental Design Analysis.* San Antonio: Center for Economic Development, University of Texas, 1981.

Tarver, E. R. *Laredo the Gate Way between the United States and Mexico: An Illustrated Description of the Future City of the Great Southwest.* Laredo: Daily Times Print, 1889.

Taylor, Paul S. *An American-Mexican Frontier: Nueces County, Texas.* Chapel Hill: University of North Carolina Press, 1934.

————. *Mexican Labor in the United States: Dimmit County, Winter Garden District, South Texas.* University of California Publications in Economics, vol. 6, no. 5, 293–464. Berkeley: University of California Press, 1930.

Texas Center for Border Economic and Enterprise Development. "Texas Truck Crossing Information, Monthly/Yearly." Border Business Indicators. <www.tamiu.edu/coba/txcntr/>. 1999.

Texas Department of Parks and Wildlife. *San Ygnacio: A Proposal to Preserve an Hispanic Borderlands Settlement.* Austin: Texas Department of Parks and Wildlife, 1991.

Texas Water Development Board. *Water and Wastewater Needs of Texas Colonias.* Austin: Texas Water Development Board, 1992.

Thielepape, W. C. A. *Map of Land Lying within the Corporation Limits of the City of San Antonio, Surveyed and Divided in 1852.* Map, 1855. Archives, Center for American History, University of Texas, Austin.

Thompson, Jerry. *Laredo: A Pictorial History.* Norfolk, Va.: Donning Co., 1986.

Thonhoff, Robert H. *San Antonio Stage Lines, 1847–1881.* Southwestern Studies Monograph 29. El Paso: Texas Western Press, 1971.

Tijerina, Andrés. *Tejano Empire: Life on the South Texas Ranchos.* College Station: Texas A&M University Press, 1998.

Tjarks, Alicia V. "Comparative Demographic Analysis of Texas, 1777–1793." *Southwestern Historical Quarterly* 77 (January 1974): 291–338.

Toor, Frances. *Frances Toor's Motor Guide to Mexico.* Mexico City: Frances Toor Studios, 1938.

Torres-Raines, Rosario. "The Mexican Origin of Rituals, Ceremonies, and Celebrations in South Texas." *South Texas Studies*, vol. 7, 131–163. Victoria, Tex.: Victoria College Press, 1996.

Trautman, Wolfgang. "Geographical Aspects of Hispanic Colonization on the Northern Frontier of New Spain." *Erkunde* 40 (December 1986): 241–250.

Treviño, Roberto R. "Mexican Americans and Religion." In *The New Handbook of Texas*, edited by Ron Tyler, vol. 4, 672–676. Austin: Texas State Historical Association, 1996.

Trotter, Robert T., II, and Juan Antonio Chavira. *Curanderismo: Mexican American Folk Healing.* Athens, Ga.: University of Georgia Press, 1981.

Turner, Kay F. "'Because of This Photography': The Making of a Mexican Folk Saint." In *Niño Fidencio: A Heart Thrown Open*, by Dore Gardner, 120–132. Santa Fe: Museum of New Mexico Press, 1992.

———. "The Cultural Semiotics of Religious Icons: La Virgen de San Juan de Los Lagos." *Semiotica* 47 (1983): 317–361.

———. "Mexican American Home Altars: Toward Their Interpretation." *Aztlán* 13 (spring/fall 1982): 309–326.

A Twentieth Century History of Southwest Texas, Illustrated. 2 vols. Chicago: Lewis Publishing, 1907.

Tyler, Ron. ed. *The New Handbook of Texas.* 6 vols. Austin: Texas State Historical Association, 1996.

Uribe, Joel. Personal communication, Laredo, Texas, May 14, 1997.

U.S. Bureau of the Census. *Census of Population: 1950, Special Reports, Persons of Spanish Surname.* Washington D.C.: Government Printing Office, 1953.

———. *Census of Population: 1960, Subject Reports, Persons of Spanish Surname.* Washington D.C.: Government Printing Office, 1961.

———. *Census of Population: 1970, Subject Reports, Persons of Spanish Origin.* Washington D.C.: Government Printing Office, 1973.

———. *Census of Population: 1980, General Population Characteristics, Texas.* Washington D.C.: Government Printing Office, 1981.

———. *Census of Population and Housing: 1970, Census Tracts, Laredo, Tex. SMSA.* Washington, D.C.: Government Printing Office, 1972.

———. *Fifteenth Census of the United States: 1930.* Washington, D.C.: Government Printing Office, 1932.

———. *1950 U.S. Census of Population.* Washington, D.C.: Government Printing Office, 1953.

———. *1990 Census of Population.* Washington, D.C.: Government Printing Office, 1992.

———. *1990 Census of Population: General Population Characteristics, Texas.* Washington D.C.: Government Printing Office, 1992.

———. *1990 Census of Population and Housing, Texas.* Summary Tape File 3A, 1991.

———. *1990 Census of Population and Housing, Texas.* Summary Tape File 3C, 1991.

————. *Special Report, Population Mobility, States and Economic Areas.* Washington D.C.: Government Printing Office, 1956.

————. *Thirteenth Census of the United States.* Washington: Government Printing Office, 1913.

————. *2000 Census of Population and Housing.*

Valdez, Avelardo. "Persistent Poverty, Crime, and Drugs: U.S.-Mexican Border Region." In *In the Barrios: Latinos and the Underclass Debate,* edited by Joan Moore and Raquel Pinderhughes, 173–194. New York: Russell Sage Foundation, 1993.

Vidaurreta, Alicia. "Evolución urbana de Texas durante el siglo XVIII." *Revista de Indias* 131-138 (1973-1974): 605-636.

Vigness, David M. "Indian Raids on the Lower Rio Grande, 1836–1837." *Southwestern Historical Quarterly* 59 (July 1955): 14–23.

————, trans. "Nuevo Santander in 1795: A Provincial Inspection by Félix Calleja." *Southwestern Historical Quarterly* 75 (April 1992): 461–506.

Virgen de San Juan Shrine, San Juan, Texas. 2d ed. Hackensack, N.J.: Custombook, 1980.

Vizcaya Canales, Isidro. *Los orígines de la industrialización de Monterrey: una historia económica y social desde la caída del Segundo Imperio hasta el fin de la Revolución (1867–1920).* Monterrey: Librería Tecnológico, 1971.

Wagner, Philip L. "Cultural Landscapes and Regions: Aspects of Communication." In *Man and Cultural Heritage: Papers in Honor of Fred B. Kniffen,* edited by H. J. Walker and W. G. Haag, 133–142, vol. 5 of *Geoscience and Man.* Baton Rouge: Louisiana State University, 1974.

————. "Foreword: Culture and Geography: Thirty Years of Advance." In *Re-Reading Cultural Geography,* edited by Kenneth E. Foote, Peter J. Hugill, Kent Mathewson, and Jonathan M. Smith, 3–8. Austin: University of Texas Press, 1994.

Wagner, Philip L., and Marvin W. Mikesell, eds. *Readings in Cultural Geography.* Chicago: University of Chicago Press, 1962.

Wall Street Journal. "Border Midwives Bring Baby Boom to South Texas." October 16, 1991. A1, A12.

Ward, Peter M. *Colonias and Public Policy in Texas and Mexico: Urbanization by Stealth.* Austin: University of Texas Press, 1999.

Webb County Heritage Foundation. "Walking Tour of Historic Laredo." Pamphlet, n.d.

Weber, David J. *The Mexican Frontier, 1821–1846: The American Southwest under Mexico.* Albuquerque: University of New Mexico Press, 1982.

————. *The Spanish Frontier in North America.* New Haven: Yale University Press, 1992.

Weddle, Robert S. *Changing Tides: Twilight and Dawn in the Spanish Sea, 1763–1803.* College Station: Texas A&M University Press, 1995.

————. *The French Thorn: Rival Explorers in the Spanish Sea, 1682–1762.* College Station: Texas A&M University Press, 1991.

————. *San Juan Bautista: Gateway to Spanish Texas.* Austin: University of Texas Press, 1968.

————. *Spanish Sea: The Gulf of Mexico in North American Discovery, 1500–1685.* College Station: Texas A&M University Press, 1985.

Weintraub, Sidney, and Gilberto Cardenas. *The Use of Public Services by Undocumented Aliens in Texas: A Study of State Costs and Revenues.* Lyndon B. Johnson School of Public Affairs Policy Research Project 60. Austin: University of Texas, 1984.

Weisman, Alan. *La Frontera: The United States Border with Mexico*. Photographs by Jay Dusard. San Diego: Harcourt Brace Jovanovich, 1986. Reprint, Tucson: University of Arizona Press, 1991.

Weissmann, A. J., M. Martello, J. Hanania, M. Shamieh, C. Said, R. Harrison, and B. F. McCullough. *Overview of the Texas-Mexico Border: Assessment of Traffic Flow Patterns*. Research Report 1976–3. Austin: Center for Transportation Research, University of Texas, 1994.

Weniger, Del. *The Explorers' Texas: The Lands and Waters*. Austin: Eakin Press, 1984.

Weslaco, City of. *City of Weslaco Map*. 1965. McAllen Memorial Library, McAllen, Texas.

West, John O. *Mexican-American Folklore: Legends, Songs, Festivals, Proverbs, Crafts, Tales of Saints, of Revolutionaries, and More*. Little Rock, Ark.: August House, 1988.

West, Richard. "San Antonio: The *Barrio*." In *Richard West's Texas*, 53–88. Austin: Texas Monthly Press, 1981.

West, Robert C. "Surface Configuration and Associated Geology of Middle America." In *Natural Environment and Early Cultures*, edited by Robert C. West, 33–83, vol. 1 of *Handbook of Middle American Indians*. Austin: University of Texas Press, 1964.

West, Robert C., and John P. Augelli. *Middle America: Its Lands and Peoples*. 3d ed. Englewood Cliffs, N.J.: Prentice-Hall, 1989.

Whisenhunt, Donald W. *The Five States of Texas: An Immodest Proposal*. Austin: Eakin Press, 1987.

Wilkinson, J. B. *Laredo on the Rio Grande Frontier*. Austin: Jenkins Publishing, 1975.

Williams, Brett. "Why Migrant Women Feed Their Husbands Tamales: Foodways as a Basis for a Revisionist View of Tejano Family Life." In *Ethnic and Regional Foodways in the United States: The Performance of Group Identity*, edited by Linda Keller Brown and Kay Mussell, 113–126. Knoxville: University of Tennessee Press, 1984.

Williams, J. W. *Old Texas Trails*. Edited and compiled by Kenneth F. Neighbours. Austin: Eakin Press, 1979.

Wine, Chester C., ed. *Description of Laredo, Texas, the Great International Gateway of the Two Republics: Laredo Directory of 1889*. Laredo: Central Power and Light Co., 1969.

Woods, Frances Jerome. *Mexican Ethnic Leadership in San Antonio, Texas*. Catholic University of America Studies in Sociology 31. Washington D.C.: Catholic University of America, 1949. Reprint, New York: Arno Press, 1976.

Woodward, Kenneth. "In Old San Antonio, *Mestizaje* Nurtures New American Way." *Smithsonian* 16 (December 1985): 115–127.

Wooldrige, Ruby A., and Robert B. Vezzetti. *Brownsville: A Pictorial History*. Norfolk, Va.: Donning Co., 1982.

Wright, John Kirtland. "*Terrae Incognitae*: The Place of Imagination in Geography." *Annals, Association of American Geographers* 37 (March 1947): 1–15.

Xavier [Holworthy], Sister Mary. *Father Jaillet, Saddlebag Priest of the Nueces*. Austin: Von Boeckmann-Jones, 1948.

Zamora, Emilio. *The World of the Mexican Worker in Texas*. College Station: Texas A&M University Press, 1993.

Zelinsky, Wilbur. "The Changing Character of North American Culture Areas." In *Regional Studies: The Interplay of Land and People*, edited by Glen E. Lich, 113–135. College Station: Texas A&M University Press, 1992.

———. *The Cultural Geography of the United States*. Rev. ed. Englewood Cliffs, N.J.: Prentice-Hall, 1992.

———. "The Roving Palate: North America's Ethnic Restaurant Cuisines." *Geoforum* 16 (1985): 51–72.

Zelman, Donald L. "Alazan–Apache Courts: A New Deal Response to Mexican American Housing Conditions in San Antonio." *Southwestern Historical Quarterly* 87 (October 1983): 123–150.

Figure Sources

2.1 Adapted from Erwin Raisz, *Landforms of the United States*, and Walter Keene Ferguson and Barbara Hartman, *The Geographic Provinces of Texas*.

2.2 John Russell Bartlett, *Personal Narrative of Explorations and Incidents in Texas*; John Louis Berlandier, *Journey to Mexico During the Years 1826 to 1834*; William H. Emory, *Report on the United States and Mexican Boundary*; Paul J. Foik, "Captain Don Domingo Ramón's Diary of His Expedition into Texas in 1716"; V. Havard, "Report on the Flora of Western and Southern Texas"; Jack M. Inglis, *A History of Vegetation on the Rio Grande Plain*; Frederick Law Olmsted, *A Journey through Texas*.

2.3 W. Frank Blair, "The Biotic Provinces of Texas"; William T. Chambers, "Geographic Regions of Texas"; Lauro Cruz, *Developing South Texas*; Thomas R. Hester, *Digging into South Texas Prehistory*; Terry G. Jordan, "Perceptual Regions of Texas"; Terry G. Jordan, with John L. Bean, Jr., and William M. Holmes, *Texas: A Geography*; D. W. Meinig, *Imperial Texas*.

3.1 Peter Gerhard, *The North Frontier of New Spain*; Robert C. West, "Surface Configuration and Associated Geology of Middle America."

3.2 Antonio García Cubas, *Atlas geográfico, estadístico e histórico de la República Mexicana*. Courtesy of the Benson Latin American Collection, University of Texas at Austin.

3.3 *Estado general de las fundaciones hechas por D. José de Escandón en la colonia del Nuevo Santander, costa del Seno Mexicano*; Lawrence Francis Hill, *José de Escandón and the Founding of Nuevo Santander*; Herbert E. Bolton, *Texas in the Middle Eighteenth Century*; Carlos E. Castañeda, *Our Catholic Heritage in Texas, 1519–1936*, v. 3; Robert S. Weddle, *San Juan Bautista: Gateway to Spanish Texas*; Florence Johnson Scott, *Historical Heritage of the Lower Rio Grande*; David M. Vignes, "Nuevo Santander in 1795: A Provincial Inspection by Félix Calleja"; Oakah L. Jones, *Los Paisanos: Spanish Settlers on the Northern Frontier of New Spain*; Peter Gerhard, *The North Frontier of New Spain*; Wolfgang Trautman, "Geographical Aspects of Hispanic Colonization on the Northern Frontier of New Spain;" Jean Y. Fish, *Zapata County Roots Revisited*.

3.4 Frank G. Pierce, *A Brief History of the Lower Rio Grande Valley*; James L. Allhands, *Gringo Builders*; Hobart Huson, *Refugio: A Comprehensive History of Refugio County*; William H. Oberste, *Texas Irish Empresarios and Their Colonies*; A. B. J. Hammet, *The Empresario Don Martin De León*; Jean Y. Fish, *Zapata County Roots Revisited*; Daniel D. Arreola, "Plaza Towns of South Texas."

3.5 V. W. Lehmann, *Forgotten Legions: Sheep in the Rio Grande Plain of Texas*.

3.6 Homer L. Kerr, *Migration into Texas, 1865–1880*; Terry G. Jordan, "A Century and a Half of Ethnic Change in Texas, 1836–1986."

4.1 U.S. Bureau of the Census, *1990 Census of Population and Housing, Texas*; U.S. Bureau of the Census, *1990 Census of Population*.

4.2 U.S. Bureau of the Census, *Thirteenth Census of the United States*; Terry G. Jordan, "A Century and a Half of Ethnic Change in Texas, 1836–1986."

4.3 Postcard from the author's private collection.

4.4 U.S. Bureau of the Census, *Thirteenth Census of the United States* [Agriculture, Reports by States].

4.5 Daniel D. Arreola, "Mexico Origins of South Texas Mexican Americans, 1930."

4.6 U.S. Bureau of the Census, *Fifteenth Census of the United States: 1930*.

4.7 U.S. Bureau of the Census, *1950 U.S. Census of Population*.

4.8 U.S. Bureau of the Census, *Census of Population: 1950, Special Report, Persons of Spanish Surname*.

4.9 U.S. Bureau of the Census, *1990 Census of Population and Housing, Texas*.

4.10 U.S. Bureau of the Census, *1990 Census of Population*.

5.1 Frances W. Isabel, ed. *Hidalgo County Ranch Histories*.

5.2 Joe S. Graham, *El Rancho in South Texas*; Dale Lasater, *Falfurrias*; Agnes G. Grimm, *Llanos Mesteñas*; Virgil N. Lott and Mercurio Martínez, *The Kingdom of Zapata*; Jean Y. Fish, *José Vásquez Borrego and La Hacienda de Nuestra Señora de Dolores*; Jack Jackson, *Los Mesteños: Spanish Ranching in Texas, 1721–1821*; Armando Alonzo, "Change and Continuity in Tejano Ranches in the Trans-Nueces, 1848–1900;" Oblate Map 1918.

5.3 Daniel D. Arreola, "Plaza towns of South Texas."

5.4 Postcard from the author's private collection.

5.5 Daniel D. Arreola, "Plaza Towns of South Texas."

5.6 Postcard from the author's private collection.

5.7 Postcard from the author's private collection.

5.8 Adapted from *City of Weslaco Map*.

5.9 City of Laredo, *Historic Preservation Plan*.

5.10 Postcard from the author's private collection.

6.1 U.S. Bureau of the Census, *1990 Census of Population, General Population Characteristics, Texas*.

6.2 Patsy Jeanne Byfield, *Falcon Dam and the Lost Towns of Zapata*; Eugene George, *Historic Architecture of Texas: The Falcon Reservoir*; Lori Brown McVey, *Guerrero Viejo*.

6.3 Field survey compiled by author, 1997.

6.4 Courtesy Institute of Texan Cultures, *San Antonio Light* Collection.

6.5 Field survey compiled by author, 1997.

6.6 Photograph by author, 1997.

6.7 Adapted from William Clayton Barbee, *A Historical Architectural Investigation of San Ygnacio, Texas*.

6.8 Adapted from Adrián Martínez, *Adrián: An Autobiography*.

6.9 Photograph by author, 1997.

6.10 Adapted from *Roads of Texas*.

6.11 Photograph by author, 1993.

6.12 Field survey compiled by author, 1997.

6.13 Photograph by Louis de Planque, courtesy South Texas Museum, Alice.

6.14 Field survey compiled by author, 1997.

6.15 Sanborn Map Company, *San Diego, Duval County, Texas* [1885].

6.16 Photograph by author, 1993.

6.17 Cotulla, Texas, *Map of the Town of Cotulla, 1881*; Sanborn Map Company, *Cotulla, La Salle County, Texas* [1933]; Southwestern Bell, *Cotulla* [1996]; field survey compiled by author, 1997.

6.18 Field survey compiled by author, 1997.

6.19 Photograph by author, 1997.

7.1 Daniel D. Arreola, "Urban Ethnic Landscape Identity."

7.2 Guadalupe Acosta family. Courtesy Institute of Texan Cultures, San Antonio.

7.3 San Antonio Development Agency, San Antonio, Texas. Courtesy Institute of Texan Cultures, San Antonio.

7.4 No. Z-1218 Institute of Texan Cultures, San Antonio. Courtesy Zintgraff Collection.

7.5 Postcard from the author's private collection.

7.6 Sanborn Map Company, *San Antonio, Bexar County, Texas* [1888]; Sanborn-Perris Map Company, *San Antonio, Bexar County, Texas* [1896].

7.7 Detail from Sanborn Map Company, *San Antonio, Bexar County, Texas* [1904].

7.8 Courtesy Institute of Texan Cultures, and San Antonio Development Agency, San Antonio, Texas.

7.9 Photograph by author, 1997.

7.10 Courtesy Luciano Guajardo Historical Collection, Laredo Public Library.

7.11 Postcard from the author's private collection.

7.12 Courtesy Luciano Guajardo Historical Collection, Laredo Public Library.

7.13 Caudill-Rowlett-Scott, *Area Development Plan Laredo and Webb County, Texas*.

8.1 Gebhardt Mexican Foods. Courtesy Institute of Texan Cultures, San Antonio.

8.2　Photograph by author, 1997.

8.3　Photograph by author, 1997.

8.4　Photograph by author, 1997.

8.5　Field survey compiled by author, 1997.

8.6　Ruth Dodson, "Don Pedrito Jaramillo: The Curandero of Los Olmos"; Dore Gardner, *Niño Fidencio: A Heart Thrown Open*; Blanca M. Gutiérrez, "The Shrine of La Virgen de San Juan del Valle."

8.7　Photograph by author, 1997.

8.8　Photograph by author, 1983.

8.9　Joe S. Graham, *Hispanic-American Material Culture*; Helen Simons and Cathryn A. Hoyt, eds., *Hispanic Texas: A Historical Guide*.

8.10　Postcard from the author's private collection.

8.11　Ramon Hernandez Archives, San Antonio.

8.12　Photograph by author, 1997.

9.1　U.S. Bureau of the Census, *1990 Census of Population*.

9.2　Courtesy of Mario L. Sánchez, artist, and the Texas Historical Commission, Austin.

Index